All the Stops

ALL THE STOPS

The Glorious Pipe Organ

and

Its American Masters

CRAIG R. WHITNEY

PublicAffairs

New York

Published in the United States by PublicAffairs™,
a member of the Perseus Books Group.

Book design by Jane Raese
Text set in 11 point New Baskerville

Library of Congress Cataloging-in-Publication Data
Whitney, Craig R., 1943–
All the stops : the glorious pipe organ and its American masters /
by Craig Whitney.
p. cm.
Includes bibliographical references and index.
Discography: p.
ISBN 1-58648-173-8
1. Organ (Musical instrument)—United States—History.
2. Organ builders—United States. I. Title.
ML561.W55 2003
786.5'19'092273—dc21
2002037025

FIRST EDITION
1 3 5 7 9 10 8 6 4 2

Contents

Acknowledgments

The teacher who gave me my first organ lessons in Westborough, Massachusetts, Richard F. Johnson, encouraged me, about ten years ago, to write a book about the organ, and to make one of the main characters the great organist and showman Virgil Fox. Dick offered access to the archives of his wife, the late Roberta Bailey Johnson, who had been Virgil Fox's manager for many years. She had intended to write a book of her own about her career and other famous organists whose concert tours in the United States she managed—Pierre Cochereau and Karl Richter among them—before illness stilled her pen. Dick Johnson, too, died unexpectedly, in 2001, but their son, Marc Johnson, sifted through the papers and made them available to me. I could not write the book his mother would have written, but the story of her important role in the development of Fox's career is here.

Richard Torrence, Roberta Bailey's successor as Fox's manager, and Marshall Yaeger graciously gave permission to quote extensively from their book, *Virgil Fox (The Dish),* the first published biography of Fox, with extensive personal recollections by them and many others who knew him. They and other members of the Virgil Fox Society also made photographs and archival materials available.

Special thanks go to Stephen Pinel, the librarian of the American Organ Archives of the Organ Historical Society, at the Westminster Choir College of Rider University in Princeton, New Jersey, and to Amy Fitch of the Rockefeller Archive Center in Sleepy Hollow, New York, for helping me with research in these libraries.

Barbara Owen was indispensable in many ways. First, her superb biography, *E. Power Biggs, Concert Organist,* is the definitive work on Biggs. She is also the curator of the E. Power Biggs Collection in the

American Guild of Organists Organ Library at the Boston University School of Theology, and she showed me how to comb through it for at least a few tidbits that she did not use in her book. Finally, she did not blanch when asked to make criticisms of an early draft of part of the manuscript, and she responded with pointed and helpful suggestions.

I could never have written my book without two other people and their books. They are Dorothy Holden, author of *The Life and Work of Ernest M. Skinner,* and Dr. Charles Callahan, who has assembled two invaluable collections of correspondence, *The American Classic Organ: A History in Letters* and *Aeolian-Skinner Remembered: A History in Letters.* Thanks to these works, great organbuilders of the past like Skinner, G. Donald Harrison, and their friends can still speak up for themselves. Additionally, I am grateful to J. Michael Harrison and Mary Harrison of Cambridge, Massachusetts, for their help. Mr. Harrison shared with me his recollections and his correspondence with his father, and Mary Harrison kindly gave an account of G. Donald Harrison's associations with the Biggses.

Joseph A. Vitacco III knows more about how pipe organs work than I ever will, and his devotion to the work of Ernest M. Skinner—"Mr. Skinner" to Joe—has led to a series of lavishly documented CDs by JAV Recordings of Skinner and Aeolian-Skinner organs, shown off by stellar performers. For his enthusiasm, for his knowledge, and for the digital scans of the family photographs of Skinner reproduced in this book, I thank him, and I thank Stan Howe for granting permission to reproduce the pictures and some of the Skinner correspondence in his possession. Edward Millington Stout III and Richard Taylor in San Francisco took me on a fascinating organ crawl through one of Skinner's creations, at the California Palace of the Legion of Honor in San Francisco, as it was being played by John Fenstermaker, and Joseph F. Dzeda and Nicholas Thompson-Allen in New Haven guided me through another, the instrument in Woolsey Hall at Yale while Thomas Murray put the organ through its paces.

I am deeply indebted to Tom Murray as well for the keen interest he has taken in the manuscript and for his willingness to offer many constructive suggestions and to point out things that needed correction or clarification. Mary Monroe, too, took the trouble to make suggestions that were both wise and helpful, and I am particularly grateful for her encouragement and support.

Jonathan Ambrosino, one of this country's leading pipe organ historians, applied analytical acuity and unmatched expertise to the task of helping me try to avoid writing anything stupider than absolutely necessary. If he failed, that is not his fault. He pressed me repeatedly to think harder, to go deeper, and to question the accepted wisdom on many issues, and he shared unstintingly his knowledge of organbuilding and its history.

Frederick Swann and Ray Biswanger graciously reviewed chapters of the manuscript and made suggestions for improvements. My thanks also to the distinguished organists quoted in the last chapter and to the organbuilders who gave me their comments, especially Jack M. Bethards of Schoenstein & Co. Organ Builders, and Steven A. Dieck of C. B. Fisk, Inc. Dieck and Virginia Lee Fisk shared their memories of Charles Fisk and their ideas about the work of the company since Fisk's death.

None of this, of course, is meant to imply that anyone quoted in the book endorses opinions or judgments that are clearly my own.

Perhaps Peter Osnos and Kate Darnton, my editors at PublicAffairs, now understand better what has driven me to so many organ concerts over the years. I have even spotted Kate herself at the occasional recital. For their support, enthusiasm, and for laboring to make the finished book look so beautiful, my great gratitude to the entire staff of PublicAffairs.

But most of all—thanks to Heidi Whitney for putting up with it all.

Introduction

I have endured bad jokes and embarrassment about my interest in pipe organs ever since I was a teenager growing up in what was then the small town of Westborough, in central Massachusetts. A girlfriend who knew I was studying the organ once greeted me at the door back then with "Hi, Craig, how's your organ?" That was so long ago that when she realized what she had said, she clapped her hand over her mouth and blushed deep crimson.

Later, as a foreign correspondent for *The New York Times* for three decades, I often wrote about interesting organs that I came across around the world. My colleagues in the home office humored me by printing the stories, but also made light fun of my hobby by making off-color jokes about them. Usually the articles ran only after being "overheld" for days or weeks, until there was a lull in the news and space could be found for the pieces to run. So "Whitney's organ," the name usually given to these organ stories, was often postponed, squeezed out, cut, shortened, and otherwise painfully maltreated. An article in the early 1970s about the restoration of a famous organ in the Philippines with pipes made of bamboo, almost unplayable when I had visited it there in the late 1960s, brought me a message of congratulations: "Glad to hear Whitney's organ fully restored and termite-free." The ribbing shows that, for most Americans nowadays, an interest in the pipe organ is an eccentricity, and the organ itself a curiosity.

Yet hearing a great performance on a great pipe organ is one of the most exciting experiences music has to offer. The organ is one of the most ancient of instruments, and the most majestic not only in sound but also in appearance. No other instrument can produce such a great variety of tones. No two organs sound exactly alike, because hardly any two organs are alike. The organ is not a standard-ized instrument; organs are custom-built and designed for the cus-tomer, each to fill a unique space and musical need. Even a small pipe organ can have several hundred pipes behind the few that are visible in the façade, ranging from the size of a pencil to the size of a tree trunk. A large organ can have more than 10,000 pipes, some as tall as a sailboat's mast. The musical power of a large pipe organ in a resonant space is truly awe-inspiring. But even a small, well-voiced organ is unmatched in its ability to bring out the lines of contrapuntal music clearly and harmoniously.

The first small pipe organ may have appeared in Alexandria in the third century B.C.—a "hydraulis," which used a water pump to maintain air under pressure in a windchest beneath a row or rows of pipes like oversized whistles. The Romans later used organs like these in amphitheaters, circuses, and gladiator contests. Nero ap-parently played a mean hydraulis.

After the fall of the Roman Empire, organs were built with bel-lows, and they spread far and wide as curiosities capable of making impressive sound effects, mostly on secular occasions. Gradually, to-ward the end of the first millennium, European artisans started making larger fixed instruments and using them in churches, at first perhaps just to get people's attention with loud blasts of music. By the fourteenth century, organs were standard fixtures in late-Gothic churches, and in the sixteenth century they started becom-ing complex, with more and more pipes organized into separate sections or "divisions," each having its own case and its own key-board, and, notably in Germany and Holland, a separate pedal key-board. By the eighteenth century, pipe organs could produce a tremendous variety of sound, some of it imitative of other instru-ments now extinct except as organ stops: the bombarde, the krummhorn, and the shawm, for example. "The organ is in my eyes and ears the king of all instruments," Mozart wrote when he was cathedral organist in Salzburg, in 1777.

By then, pipe organs built with great mechanical precision and sophisticated engineering existed all over Europe. In the Iberian peninsula, in Italy, in France, in Germany and Austria, and in Britain, they stood at the summit of technological achievement, among the most complex creations of their age, with the exact movements of timepieces, the majestic lines of sailing ships, and the beauty of fine cabinet work. The rich woodwork cases that held the pipes and focused their sound were often ornately crafted, with gilded pipes, fanciful statues of heraldic animals, whole hierarchies of angels sounding fanfares. The English words "case" or "façade" hardly do justice to them; the French "buffet d'orgue" or the German "prospekt" give a better idea of their beauty and majesty.

Johann Sebastian Bach had access to pipe organs built by such master builders as Arp Schnitger and Gottfried Silbermann, instruments capable of playing music of the greatest sonority and sophistication. Bach made the most of them, writing a body of music that even today stands as the greatest in the organ literature. Fifty years ago, the great conductor Leopold Stokowski tried to capture the thrill and the drama of some of these Bach organ works by transcribing them for the Philadelphia Orchestra—the *Toccata and Fugue in D minor* (BWV 565), for example, and the great *Passacaglia and Fugue in C minor* (BWV 582)—twenty-one variations on a theme of fifteen notes, stated simply in the bass, working up gradually to a climax like a cathedral vault, and then becoming a fugue woven about the original theme. The *Passacaglia* is awe-inspiring in its majesty and solemnity, proclaiming the power and the order of the universe as Bach, a profoundly Christian believer, understood it, a musical statement as impressive in its domain as Newton's *Principia* or Einstein's theory of relativity in physics. The popularity of Stokowski's transcription eventually exasperated one of the most famous American organists of the time, E. Power Biggs. "Some people even believe that the organ, after a history of some two thousand years, has finally become transmuted into the Philadelphia Orchestra," he wrote in 1949. "I've even had people ask me whose arrangement of the Bach *Passacaglia* I play on the organ!"

A half century ago in America, Biggs and organists like him walked in company with the giants of the music world. Virgil Fox,

Charles-Marie Courboin, Catharine Crozier—all these names were well known to concertgoers and conductors, and organ music was immensely popular. American organs could rival orchestras in tonal range and expressive capability, as a result of the work of American organbuilders whom all these artists, and many of their listeners, knew well: such great artists in their own right as Ernest M. Skinner and G. Donald Harrison.

It had not always been true that American organs were modeled on an orchestral ideal, and in the late twentieth century, partly because of Harrison's work, it did not remain so. In the American colonies, the Puritans of New England at first rejected pipe organs as the devil's work. But even before the Revolution, Congregationalists and, later, Unitarians relented, and by the mid–nineteenth century organs built by American craftsmen inspired by English and German models had become as central to musical life in New England as they were in the Middle West or the South. Influenced by trends in Europe, American builders also began synthesizing European developments and then finally using electricity to free organs from the limitations of mechanical engineering and make them easier to play. Remote control replaced mechanical action; pipes were enclosed in hidden chambers far from the keyboards and façades became optional and vestigial, while more and more the organ tried to imitate the orchestra in versatile ways. Until about 1930, most Americans, including organists and organbuilders, thought this was progress, another manifestation of the American destiny to take the best other cultures had to offer and then improve on it.

This book first takes readers back to the late nineteenth and early twentieth centuries to see how central pipe organs once were to American musical life. Then it explores how thinking changed about what the organ should be, musically, leading both performers and builders down divergent paths in the mid–twentieth century. The story unfolds through the clashing ideas and conflicting personalities of some of the colorful characters who dominated the American organ world at the time, both players and builders, and by the interactions between them. The central themes in the conclusion are how the importance of the organ receded in the popular mind in the past twenty-five years and what the chances are now for the instrument to make a comeback.

I have written this book for both organ enthusiasts and people who enjoy good music but don't necessarily know much about the organ. Surprisingly, there aren't many such books. There are volumes about the organ and its history, but most are full of technical detail that only experts can understand. Organbuilders and organists write mostly for each other, but few try to win converts to the organ. So here is a book about instruments I grew up with, about the people who built and played them and inspired my lifelong passion, offered in the hope that the enthusiasm will be infectious.

Like most organists, I came to the organ through the piano. When I was about thirteen, I was getting terminally tired of daily piano practice when one day my teacher told me that the organist of the Unitarian Church, Annie E. Fales, then nearly ninety, was looking for a successor. She was beginning to have trouble with the real work it took to make enough noise to lead the congregation in hymns. Was I interested in taking over from her?

I went over to the white-steepled church to take a look. The church was no cathedral, and the little organ, whose builder was identified by a small chipped ivory nameplate as George H. Ryder of Boston, was a simple affair with two ivory keyboards of sixty-one notes and a pedalboard—a keyboard played with the feet—of thirty notes. Ryder had built it in 1895, and it looked quaintly old-fashioned, with Victorian stenciling painted on the single row of display pipes that loomed up eight feet over the keyboards, and florid script on rows of stopknobs on either side of the keyboards. Behind the façade there were 500 more pipes of various shapes and sizes, made of wood or metal.

This machine was much more interesting than the upright piano we had at home. It could make much louder sounds, as well as soft ones, and the notes kept sounding steadily as long as keys were pressed down, rather than dying away, as they did on the piano. The keyboards could be coupled together, so that playing on the lower one would partially depress keys on the upper one too, as if by ghost fingers, to make the pipes controlled by both keyboards play together. Crawling into the pipe chamber behind the keyboards, I could see that wooden slats called "trackers" directly connected the keys and the pedals to the valves that let air under pressure into the pipes to make them speak.

The organ could produce an amazing variety of sounds, depending on what "stops"—controlled by those knobs on either side of the keyboards—were pulled out. Pulling a stop knob moved a perforated wooden slat underneath the pipes of that particular stop so that the slat would no longer "stop" air from blowing into the pipes when notes were played. The stop knobs had names—oboe, melodia flute, diapason, this last being the typical sound that most people probably have in mind when they think of a pipe organ—and the pipes of each stop were arranged in orderly rows, one pipe for each of the sixty-one notes on the keyboard, the longest pipes speaking the lowest notes and the shortest ones—the size of pennywhistles—speaking the highest notes, since an organ pipe, unlike an orchestral wind instrument, can sound only one pitch. "Pulling out all the stops" even on this little organ and playing a big chord produced the combined sounds of as many as a hundred pipes, in a rich and powerful *fortissimo*.

The stops played by the upper keyboard were enclosed in a box with shutters that opened like louvers when I depressed a metal pedal that moved like an accelerator in a car. Playing music on this keyboard with the shutters closed and then flooring the pedal opened the shutters and let the music "swell"; letting up on the gas reduced the volume. As on bigger organs, this enclosed keyboard and its pipes were called the "swell" division.

Here was an instrument on which it was possible to play three lines of music simultaneously, each with a sound of its own—an oboe melody on the swell, a flute accompaniment on the main or "great" division, a bass line on the pedals. Keyboard stops could also be coupled to the pedals, so that a melody could be played with the feet. Ryder's modest instrument, despite having only two keyboards instead of four or five, had the same basic structure and characteristics of all pipe organs, and in the resonant sanctuary, it produced a quite respectable sound.

But I had to practice on an electronic organ, the Hammond that Richard F. Johnson, the organist of the Congregational Church across the street, had brought in as a temporary replacement for his church's old pipe organ, which had been built by one of New England's best-known builders, the Estey Organ Co. of Brattleboro, Vermont. The Hammond had no pipes at all, producing imitations of organ tones with oscillators and speakers instead.

This temporary replacement became permanent, precisely the kind of outcome American pipe organ builders had foreseen in the 1930s when Laurens Hammond, owner of the Hammond Clock Company, started advertising that his new electronic organ sounded just as good as a pipe organ. A group of American organbuilders sued Hammond for false advertising and got the Federal Trade Commission to order him to stop making the claim in 1938. But the commission's order did not stop Hammond and other companies, such as Allen, Baldwin, Conn, and Rodgers, from selling tens of thousands of electronic organs over subsequent decades. In fact, they sold so many of them—to churches, restaurants, sports stadiums, and nightclubs, where the Hammond B-3 came into its own as a jazz instrument—that many Americans today probably have no idea how a real pipe organ actually sounds. Gladys Gooding, who played the organ and sang for the Brooklyn Dodgers in Ebbets Field, was probably a more familiar name, in New York and elsewhere in the 1950s, than the pipe organist Virgil Fox.

Still, when the renowned Mr. Fox came from New York City to Westborough to play none other than a Hammond in the Congregational Church one winter evening in the 1960s, my little hometown buzzed with excitement.

On the night of the concert, however, the New England weather produced a blizzard, a Nor'easter that dumped a foot of snow. Most people who attended the recital had to trudge through the drifts on foot, but even so, about half the 300 or so seats in the sanctuary pews were filled when Virgil Fox swept in, as I recall wearing a scarlet-lined cape over a white-tie outfit. Fox, a trim man about five-ten in height who wore rimless glasses, radiated energy and enthusiasm. He strode onto the raised platform where the pastor usually sat and began, as he always did, with a little talk, delivered in a distinctive tenor voice with a Midwestern accent that chewed and spat out the r's that were customarily ignored around Boston. It was a pep talk for the music he was determined we would learn to love, and he wanted us to love Bach most of all.

"Johann Sebastian Bach would be delighted that you came here to hear him tonight," he said, and the engineers, orchard owners, dairy farmers, storekeepers, and entrepreneurs gathered in the church, many of whom didn't know they cared about Bach and certainly weren't devotees of organ music, suddenly felt flattered, privileged to be there. "Every fugue has a tune, and here is this one," he announced, stepping over to the little two-manual Hammond and playing the theme of the jaunty G major *Fugue à la Gigue* (BWV 577), encouraging us to clap to the rhythm if we felt like it. We did. Fox's playing was enthusiastic and passionate, and it reached everybody in the audience. When at the end of the concert Fox swept out in that cape, we had experienced not only Bach but also French composers some of us had never heard before—Maurice Duruflé, Louis Vierne, Charles-Marie Widor—and we all felt uplifted, inspired, and exhilarated.

What few in the audience realized was how controversial all of this—the cape, the showy Bach interpretations, the lecture—had become in the organ world of the 1950s. Virgil Fox was a polarizing figure, and at the opposite pole was his leading rival, E. Power Biggs. Their vividly contrasting artistic personalities would come to symbolize the radically different approaches to the instrument that also divided the leading organbuilders of the day.

With the example of Virgil Fox fresh in my mind, I kept doggedly at my organ studies. I learned that articulation and phrasing, as on the piano, were the secrets to effective music-making. But touch played a different role, since it didn't matter how hard a note on the organ was struck—what determined tone and volume was registration, the art of learning how to combine stops artistically to match the music. Learning how to play with the feet was the other major challenge, and mastering pedal technique required thinking about music almost three-dimensionally. Eventually, I got the hang of it, acquiring a pair of thin-soled, narrow, pointed brown shoes to help my size-11 feet be nimble with the pedal notes. (Years later, after we married, my wife threw the shoes out, fearing I might actually consider wearing them on the street.)

It was not until I went to Worcester for an audition with Henry L. Hokans, the organist of All Saints Episcopal Church, that I understood what a "real" organ could do. After Hokans heard me play on the small pipe organ in the choir room and agreed to take me as a student, at $7.50 per half hour, he took me into the main sanctuary and sat me down at the four-keyboard console of the church's organ, built between 1933 and 1949 by G. Donald Harrison, whose name was inscribed on a plate above the keyboards that said the organ had been produced by the Aeolian-Skinner Organ Company of Boston. Then he started playing Sigfrid Karg-Elert's postromantic chorale-fantasy, "Now Thank We All Our God." The organ pealed forth with an awesome sound like no other instrument I had ever heard. It had brilliant, piercing trumpet sounds, and a deep, roaring bass produced by pipes of the bombarde stop—named after an ancestor of the bassoon—that were, I learned, up to thirty-two feet long. It was nothing like the Hammond I practiced on, nothing like the little Ryder organ I played on Sundays. I was amazed, thrilled, and hooked for life.

I began looking for records with organ music, and found them on Columbia Masterworks, which almost monthly seemed to be offering recordings by E. Power Biggs on the organ that he and Harrison had designed for Boston's Symphony Hall. My first organ record was in the Biggs "Bach's Royal Instrument" series. His clipped, cool Bach and its rhythmic strictness were quite different from Fox's passionate romanticism, and perfectly suited to the transparently clear, full-bodied sound of the Symphony Hall organ.

The climax of the recording was the *Passacaglia and Fugue in C minor*, whose conclusion, with the deep bass pedal notes making a sound like a B-29, set the needle in my primitive record-player to jumping in the grooves so hard that it eventually all but erased the music and blew out the little speaker in the tabletop radio my father had rigged to the turntable. This hadn't happened with any of my other records, even the one with Eugene Ormandy conducting the Philadelphia Orchestra in the shattering climax of Ravel's *Bolero.*

A year or two later, my grandfather, a schoolteacher in Boston, took me to Symphony Hall (or I dragged him) to see Biggs perform. Trim at 170 pounds and a shade under six feet in height, the great organist strode briskly out onto the stage in tails, looking every bit the formal musician—and far more serious and sober than Virgil Fox. His graying hair was slicked back, but his twinkling eyes betrayed the sense of humor that marked his entire personality and his playing style. He bowed and then slid jauntily onto the bench of the movable console, which had been brought out to center stage so that he could play in view of the audience, as he and Harrison had intended when they designed the organ that way in the late 1940s. He gave such a lively, rhythmical performance of Bach's *Fantasy and Fugue in G minor* (BWV 542) that I thought he might even be enjoying himself, until I thought I saw him spit at the keyboards at one point after he pushed a combination button. Perhaps he had pushed the wrong one.

But there may have been more to his displeasure. By that time, Biggs had decided that eclectic American Classic organs like the one in Symphony Hall, played by electropneumatic remote-control action and incorporating imitative orchestral sounds, were no musical match for the clear-speaking mechanical-action organs that Bach had written his music for. Biggs was by now a champion for the cause of returning pipe-organ design to principles that had been valid for centuries before the discovery of electricity.

Others went far beyond Biggs, believing that not only baroque instruments but also baroque performance practice were essential to making the music of Bach and composers before him come alive.

The "authentic performance" movement—full of "purists," as Fox, who stood on the other side of the spectrum, dismissively called them—had an influence on all kinds of classical music, and certainly it had positive effects on the organ world in America. But it also had profoundly destructive consequences. I don't know many pianists who refuse to play Mozart or Beethoven on a Steinway because it isn't a *pianoforte,* but I have heard of organists in the 1960s and 1970s who would not play Bach on a modern electropneumatic, eclectic organ, let alone an electronic imitation, because it wasn't a baroque tracker-action instrument and therefore not in their eyes authentically an organ. Eclecticism fell out of fashion. When the "purists" insisted that concertgoers would be better off "eating their spinach" and listening to ancient music on reproductions of baroque organs instead of indulging in the romantic "mashed potatoes" that so many people actually liked, much of the general public agreed. Organ music was spinach, all right, and to hell with it.

By the time I finished college, I had studied with teachers on both sides of this musical divide, including Melville Smith, an expert on French baroque music, and an enthusiast of eighteenth-century organs in Alsace that few Americans had ever heard at that time. On a junior year in Paris in 1963–1964, I heard Olivier Messiaen, the great French composer, play the organ at his church, La Trinité; heard the virtuoso Marcel Dupré play at Saint-Sulpice; and was warmly welcomed to the organ loft at Sainte-Clotilde, where César Franck had composed his organ works, by one of his successors, Jean Langlais.

I did not progress far enough in my music studies to be forced to take sides in the organ wars. Traveling around the world later on assignment for *The New York Times,* I mostly kept clear of them, but I took my hobby with me. I played up with the bats in the balcony in the Saigon Cathedral during the Vietnam War on a small French-built organ from the 1890s. Later, I retraced some of Biggs's steps in Germany and Holland and was amazed by the pure tones and clarity of the baroque organs I visited there. When East Germany was still a

Communist country, I played on organs built by Gottfried Silbermann, Bach's contemporary, in Dresden and Freiberg in Saxony, and felt the same thrill Biggs had experienced, playing keys Bach might have played and imagining that I was hearing the very sounds Bach had heard. Like Biggs, I was inspired by the Gothic beauty of the Thomaskirche in Leipzig, where Bach had been Kantor.

When I was stationed in Moscow in the 1970s, I was heartened to see Russians, whose Orthodox liturgical tradition had not used the organ, flocking in droves to hear East German–built organs in concert halls from Siberia to Moscow. Garry Grodberg, one of the Russian concert organists, even had groupies. I never drew such a following, as a journalist or as an organist, but in New York City in the 1980s, I filled a need for a substitute organist in my parish church, Grace Church in Brooklyn Heights, and later, in France, I practiced regularly at the American Cathedral when I was stationed in Paris from 1995 to 2000 as a correspondent of *The New York Times*. Shamelessly, I took advantage of my position to get permission to play in places most organists could only dream about. In Paris, one of them was Saint-Sulpice, where one of the greatest French romantic organs stands, an instrument of 100 stops still much as it was when Aristide Cavaillé-Coll built it between 1857 and 1862. When the sounds of the triple-fortissimo A major chord at the end of Franck's *Choral No. 3* died out, echoing around the church for several seconds, I felt a hint of the sort of awe that radio astronomers must feel when they detect echoes of the original "big bang" still reverberating through the universe. Daniel Roth, the latest successor of Dupré at Saint-Sulpice, asked me if I knew the organ at Woolsey Hall at Yale University, an orchestral instrument enlarged and completed by Ernest M. Skinner in 1929 and was astonished when I said I had never heard it. "But that is the greatest orchestral organ in the United States," Roth said.

That is the sort of statement that is highly debatable in American organ circles. But I understood what Roth meant when I finally heard the Yale organ in 2002. Its inspiring orchestral-organ sound, though certainly quite different from anything Bach ever heard, was original, artistically convincing, and, in Yale's resonant hall, quite exciting. I firmly believe that nineteenth or twentieth-century "orchestral" organs are not intrinsically inferior to eighteenth-century "baroque" organs or to modern instruments inspired by baroque design and tonal principles; they have to be met on their own terms. Bach wrote great music for the organs of his time. Franck wrote great music for the "orchestral" organs of his time. Great music has been written for pipe organs of many different periods.

The twentieth-century American struggle for the soul of the organ was as passionate as it was because of the powerful and passionate characters who personified its causes. Biggs and Fox, Skinner and Harrison, and later another influential American organbuilder named Charles B. Fisk—these fascinating men and their sometimes violently contrasting ideas dominated the world of the organ in America over a span of more than fifty years, in a series of collaborations and clashes that were as colorful as their personalities were outsized.

In the spirit of *vive la différence,* I think of this book as a peace offering in the organ wars. It is not a comprehensive history of the organ, or even of the organ in America. There are many other great figures—organbuilders in centers of the craft beyond Boston—in St. Louis, Cleveland, Chicago, San Francisco, and Los Angeles, in Nebraska, Virginia, Oregon, and Tennessee. Performers, too, like Catharine Crozier, Marilyn Mason, Claire Coci, Joan Lippincott, Diane Meredith Belcher, Marilyn Keiser, Marie-Claire Alain, David Craighead, Harold Gleason, Todd Wilson, Arthur Poister, Pierre Cochereau, and Helmut Walcha, to name only a few, have exercised enormous influence but are mentioned here only peripherally or not at all. The human dramas, the personal triumphs and disappointments of the few great artists sketched in these pages stand for those of generations of other American organbuilders and organists. Their achievements in the service of the king of instruments wove an indelible strand into the fabric of American culture, one that deserves to be broadly known and widely appreciated.

All the Stops

Ernest M. Skinner
and the Orchestral Organ
in New England

Ernest M. Skinner, one of the greatest names in early–twentieth century American organbuilding, got his first organ factory job with the Boston builder George Horatio Ryder, who on October 25, 1895, gave the dedicatory recital on the organ I played as a youth in the Unitarian Church in Westborough, Massachusetts.

The church's organ, Ryder's Opus 180, held up well for more than half a century. But by the early 1960s, it was getting stiff and creaky in the joints, and the church decided that it needed to be replaced. Like so many other churches, it picked an electronic substitute offered by the Allen Organ Co. of Macungie, Pennsylvania, after being persuaded by a salesman that it sounded just as good as a pipe organ and wouldn't break down and produce dead notes and troublesome drones. Speakers were mounted behind the tall, gold-painted pipes of the Ryder organ's façade, and some of the 500-odd speaking pipes inside the organ case were removed, wrapped in newspaper, and laid on top of the bellows that had supplied them. The Allen console went where the choir seats had been when the church had a choir, and the oak cover closed over the Ryder keyboards for many decades.

Old pipe organs like this one have all too often just been thrown out and junked. Had the church been more affluent, it might have renovated or redecorated the plain yet dignified sanctuary, removed the pipe organ and replaced the electronic substitute when it, too, began to fade with age. But, though silent, Ryder's Opus 180 survived into the twenty-first century, long enough to be considered historic and worth restoring. Its design is still as sound as Ryder's factory brochures had advertised a hundred years before, and under a layer of dust, the windchests with their pipes and the mechanisms beneath them are probably as sound as they were when he installed them. The bellows leather is cracked and dried, but basically the instrument is intact and whole—a sleeping beauty awaiting only an awakening kiss.

Ryder's Opus 180 was typical of late nineteenth-century American craftsmanship, made with cabinetmakers' skill and mechanical ingenuity more or less as organs had been built in Europe for centuries. But the way it was sold and marketed was typically American, marked by the entrepreneurship and commercial inventiveness that was changing the United States from an agrarian economy into a manufacturing colossus. Ernest Skinner and others in the generation after Ryder's would take the old skills they learned in shops like his, add something new—the technological advance of electricity and electropneumatic action to replace all those clacking slats and levers—and revolutionize the business.

It had taken a long time for pipe organs to take root in New England's rocky Puritan soil. The first instruments to be built in the United States were in Pennsylvania, the work of German immigrants like David Tannenberg, who in the late eighteenth century constructed exquisitely made organs in the style of his native Saxony for the Lutheran and Moravian churches of the German-speaking "Pennsylvania Dutch" country. Farther north, the first organ was an import, an English one-keyboard instrument that Thomas Brattle, the treasurer of Harvard, brought to Cambridge in the first years of the eighteenth century. But when Brattle willed the organ to his church in Cambridge, it was refused as an unwanted adornment to the plain religious practice of Puritan times.

Admirers of organ music in Boston nevertheless persisted against the odds, and by the early nineteenth century William and Ebenezer Goodrich were building organs full time, teaching a cabinetmaker named Thomas Appleton their trade. Some of the organs and the beautiful wooden cases that Appleton produced still survive, including one from 1830, restored and installed in the Metropolitan Museum of Art in New York City.

This New England tradition in which George Ryder had his roots produced genteel, soft-spoken instruments whose tone was inspired by the English organ sounds that Handel had known. Ryder was born in Bridgewater, Massachusetts, in 1838, and grew up in Boston where his father, Thomas Philander Ryder, who had attended Harvard, was a teacher and administrator at the Boston Latin School. But in November 1852, Thomas Ryder died of epilepsy, leaving his wife, Sarah, and their three children in dire straits.

George's elder brother, Thomas Philander Jr., was sent to a school for indigent boys in Boston, which noticed that he had a talent for music and gave him his first piano lessons. "Philando" Ryder, as he was nicknamed, went on to make a name as a minor composer for organ, piano, and chorus and held a prestigious position as organist of Boston's Tremont Temple. One of his most popular pieces, "The Thunder Storm," instructs the organist how to produce a rumble of thunder by holding down low C, C-sharp, and D simultaneously on the keyboard and low C-sharp and D on the pedal. That and other compositions that were easier on the ear, as well as a collection of hymns, were published successfully by White, Smith & Company, which also printed articles about the Ryder brothers and their activities in a magazine called *The Folio.*

George Ryder's mother sent him to Roxbury to work in what was Boston's biggest and best organ-building firm at the time—E. and G. G. Hook. This was the company of the brothers Elias and George Greenleaf Hook, sons of a Salem cabinetmaker, who had started producing instruments in their hometown in 1827. By the time Ryder joined them, theirs had become a big business, turning out dozens of instruments a year, including one with four manuals (keyboards) for Tremont Temple in 1853. Whether at the Hooks' factory or elsewhere, George Ryder also learned how to play the organ, like his brother, and wrote a "Storm at Sea" of his own. His real talent was in building organs rather than playing them. With railroads beginning to knit the United States together, Ryder followed the example set earlier by the Hooks and Henry Erben, a notable builder in New York City, and used catalogs to advertise his wares all over the country.

In 1881, Ryder was offering seventeen different stock instruments, including nine "choral organs" ranging in price from $400 to $1,200, and eight "large sizes" that went for $1,400 to $4,500. "Our terms are based on cash," the "Descriptive Circular" explained, "though we do not object to a reasonable amount of credit when notes with interest can be given for a limited time, signed by the treasurer or trustees of the Church, with good individual endorsement. The time requisite for the construction of an organ is from three to four months. Frequently longer time is desirable, though we sometimes build in less time, to meet a special need." Only the best materials were promised: real ivory on the keyboards, black walnut capped with white holly wood for the pedals, zinc, tin, and lead for the metal pipes, never less than 33 percent tin for clear, bright musical tone.

The bread-and-butter part of the operation was the business in "choral organs" for small congregations with limited means, with 300 to 500 pipes. Some of these instruments were kept ready-made in stock at the factory, much like the furniture increasingly available from mail-order houses like Sears, Roebuck and Montgomery Ward. The Ryder in Westborough was probably one of these, costing $1,000 in 1895. Ryder custom-built larger, more expensive organs that could have thousands of pipes, with many extras—stops that sounded like trumpets and clarinets, mixtures (stops with several pipes of different lengths speaking on each note to amplify basic harmonics), more than just one booming bass stop so the pedal keyboard could play a line of music independently, three keyboards instead of one or two, and mechanical devices that could turn stops on and off and couple keyboards together on command.

In the early 1880s, Ryder moved himself and the business to Reading, north of Boston. There, in 1886, he took on a strong-willed twenty-year-old shop boy—Ernest M. Skinner. Young Skinner, like the man who hired him, had been forced to drop out of school, partly because of illness, partly out of economic necessity. "I was born in the town of Clarion, Pennsylvania, of poor but disconcerted parents," he wrote later. "After this event they moved away as soon as possible." His parents, Washington and Alice Brett Skinner, were troupers—a tenor and a soprano, itinerant singers, and they happened to be in Clarion for a concert when Ernest suddenly arrived in 1866. Not until he was seven did the Skinners settle, in Taunton, Massachusetts, where they started a light opera company whose productions of Gilbert and Sullivan's *H.M.S. Pinafore* and *The Pirates of Penzance* were his first taste of music in live performance.

His introduction to the organ came, in those pre-electricity days, from pumping the bellows of the organ in the Baptist Church in Taunton to supply air pressure for the pipes when the organist, Edward M. French, needed to practice. "I thus became acquainted with the music of Batiste and Lemmens and added to my love of the organ which so moved me that I kept the bellows entirely filled all the time," he wrote. "One day when something went wrong with the bellows I found the hinge of an entire fold had broken loose. I was very proud of having found unaided the cause of the difficulty. I was permitted by Mr. French to arrive early and go inside the instrument and study its mechanism to my heart's content." Later, Skinner tried to build an organ at home. "It was to be a self-playing organ operated by a drum with pins in the surface to strike the notes," he recalled, but he had not yet succeeded when he left school to start work with Ryder, who was a friend of his father's.

At the Ryder factory, he started by sweeping the shop floor, but as he worked his way around the place he saw a professional organ-building operation in action. An organbuilder's shop is really several businesses in one. At one end of the floor, lumber for the chests, cabinets, and wooden pipes is stacked and aged, and cabinetmakers build frames and carve and treat the decorative casework. At the other end, the pipe department casts pipes out of alloyed metal and forms and solders them into the exact shapes and sizes that determine pitch and quality of sound. In separate rooms, voicers line up the pipes of separate stops in a rank on a windchest and pry, hone, and bevel the "mouths" of the pipes until they "speak" properly and the pipes of each rank produce a clear, tonally consistent sound. Most shops also have a high-ceilinged erecting room where the instruments are fully assembled, so that chests, pipes, keyboards, and all the complicated playing mechanism can be tested before being taken apart and shipped to the customer. On location, the builder and crew reassemble the organ and even revoice stops if necessary to suit the acoustics of the site. An organbuilder has to be an architect, a master cabinetmaker, and a musician all in one, the one person in the shop whose vision can produce a coherent work of art out of the chaos of thousands of pipes and pieces.

Ryder never professed great artistic ambition for himself—"I am content to do the best possible work after the most approved plans, in a modest, unassuming manner," he said—but Skinner had drive and brash self-confidence. He had skill with his hands and a good ear, and he quickly learned how to do the work of voicing himself. He also had an extraordinary gift for mechanical invention. He was able to devise a machine for Ryder that cut in half the time it took to wind the threads that tie the connecting knobs to the ends of wooden trackers, the slats that link the keys to the pipes to make them sound.

Throughout his life, Skinner was a strong-willed man, the type New Englanders called "an independent cuss," stubborn and self-taught. After only four years in Reading, he tangled with Ryder's longtime partner, John D. Brennan, who was, in Skinner's words (and spelling), "an Irish foreman who not only knew nothing but was an illtempered idiot whos manner soon drove me out of the place."

When Skinner started out with George Ryder, most American organbuilders were using traditional methods, and with wooden trackers, the organist's feet and hands did all the work, with no assistance from batteries, electric switches, or electropneumatic leather pouches and magnets. But as Skinner came into the business, organ technology was beginning to change. In England, builders like Henry Willis and William Hill were building large organs with stops imitative of instruments in the modern orchestra. Similar changes in taste and advances in technology had led German organbuilders in the romantic direction too, and they had begun producing larger organs with thicker, louder tones than those that had inspired Bach's writing for the instrument. And in Boston, builders like George S. Hutchings, for whom Ryder went to work for a while after his own business turned slow again in the 1890s, and the Hook brothers (whose firm became known in 1872 as E. & G. G. Hook & Hastings after Francis H. Hastings joined the partnership, and later, after Hastings took it over, as Hook & Hastings) were beginning to experiment with electricity to make it possible for players to operate far larger instruments than most could manage with purely mechanical action. Progressive New York builders like Hilborne and Frank Roosevelt, first cousins of Theodore, were doing the same. Part of an organ the Roosevelt Organ Works built for the Centennial Exposition in Philadelphia in 1876, with three keyboards, even had all-electric key action, with the power supplied by batteries.

Other builders were experimenting with different technologies. John H. Odell, who with his brother Caleb had founded the J. H. & C. S. Odell firm in New York City in 1859, obtained a patent in 1872 for a tubular pneumatic action that used air pressure to make the keys easier to play. In the mid–nineteenth century European builders had also invented devices using the wind pressure of the organ bellows to help the organist's fingers when several keyboards were coupled together. Charles Spackman Barker, an English inventor and organbuilder, had patented one of these, the Barker lever, and in France Cavaillé-Coll had used it on large instruments whose dynamic range and expressivity imitated the romantic orchestra's.

Skinner probably learned about Barker levers while still with Ryder, who had used them in at least one instance. Skinner later made further advances as tuner and later factory superintendent for Hutchings, with whom he spent almost twelve years, except a brief interlude with the firm of Jesse Woodberry, which was also in Boston. Woodberry, Skinner wrote in a 1922 reminiscence, "met my expressed desire to travel as an outside man with a promise to send me with an organ going south. Later I was somewhat crestfallen to learn that said organ was going to South Boston which was as far south as I ever got."

Back with Hutchings, Skinner put his inventive and mechanical engineering skills to work perfecting pneumatic and electrical methods of transmitting the organist's fingertip commands to the pipes with less human effort than mechanical trackers. The importance of this advance was that it made even the largest organ as easy to play as a piano. The 1897 Hutchings organ whose installation Skinner oversaw in the Mission Church in Boston's Roxbury Crossing had entirely electric action mechanisms for both the keys and the more than sixty stops. (Skinner even boasted later that it was things like this that made it possible for the weaker sex to play the organ.) The electricity had to be supplied at first by cumbersome wet-cell batteries as big and heavy as the ones in automobiles. The instrument at the Mission Church also had the novelty of a movable console whose side panels folded up like batwings.

Hutchings also built large parlor organs for wealthy clients who had homes big enough to fit them in—no small requirement, given that the smallest organs required a space about ten feet high and ten feet deep. One of these well-off patrons was Montgomery Sears, a Boston Brahmin whose residence organ Skinner regulated and tuned so well that Sears offered to send him abroad "to learn what I could of the foreign builders."

"He asked me how much money I wanted for the trip," Skinner recalled, "and by pulling a string with the captain of a liner whom I knew I thought I could get round and back for $250.00." Skinner went to Liverpool on a cattle steamer in 1898. There he went straight to St. George's Hall, where he was much taken with the or-

Ernest M. Skinner as a young man

gan installed by Henry Willis and his son Henry Willis II, with powerful stops that produced sounds suggestive of tubas and trumpets. "When I heard it I was wild with enthusiasm," he wrote of the tuba stop in St. George's Hall. "It was so incredibly fine and superior to anything I had ever heard." He had also been drawn to England by the controversial reputation of another inventive genius, Robert Hope-Jones, who was using electricity to transform the very nature of pipe organs.

Skinner was more impressed with the sound than with the technical qualities of the British organs he saw. And he displayed no enthusiasm at all for the great seventeenth- and eighteenth-century Dutch organs he heard on a brief trip across the Channel. "I found the touch of the organs abominable and the ensemble was an aggregation of strident mixtures," he recalled later. The baroque left him cold, but the nineteenth-century romantic instruments he heard in France made an altogether more favorable impression on him. In Paris, he visited Saint-Sulpice and Notre Dame, where he heard Louis Vierne improvising organ responses to the Gregorian chant sung by the choir at the other end of the cathedral. "I have never heard anything so lofty in conception before or since," Skinner wrote.

Neither Skinner nor anyone else would have any trouble recognizing a Cavaillé-Coll organ as being French; its romantic sounds sprang from the tradition of French eighteenth-century classical church instruments that had choruses of powerful reed stops to reinforce and echo the verses of plainchant melodies chanted by priests in the Mass. After the French Revolution, organists played more and more secular music on these organs—symphonies in place of the Sanctus. English organs accompanied choirs of men and boys in Anglican church services, choral music that, in the Victorian age, grew to almost symphonic proportions. British organists and organbuilders also took their instrument outside the church, into town halls across the country where larger organs like the one Skinner was so taken with at St. George's Hall and municipal organists entertained crowds on weekends by playing transcriptions of orchestral music and playing with orchestras in large choral works.

With those English and European sounds resonating in his head, Skinner rode back to America on another cattle boat, but with no intention of slavishly imitating the instruments he had heard on the other side of the Atlantic. His organs did not have to be French, or English, or German—he could pick and choose what he liked from all these separate traditions and use his American ear to create a uniquely American blend.

Skinner wanted to duplicate for Hutchings some of what he had seen and heard in England, though at first he had trouble convincing his employer to let him do the voicing himself. Hutchings wanted Skinner to work on the mechanical side more than the tonal side of the business, for which Skinner had already made several important improvements. Skinner perfected electropneumatic

motors that made it easier for players to open and close the louvered shutters on the "swell" chambers that enclosed pipes, for
crescendo and decrescendo effects. By 1893, he had also developed
a "pitman" windchest that used electropneumatic action for opening and closing the air valves under the organ pipes to make them
play. The name, though he may not have originated it, reflected
Skinner's love of corny wordplay. "Pitman" was not the name of
some engineer or physical principle, but a playful description of the
crucial mechanism deep in the intricate depths of the windchest—a
man-in-the-pit, so to speak, to let air into the pipe on signal from
the organist playing the keys. "There is no Mr. Pitman connected
with it—the man happens to be, instead, Mr. Ernest M. Skinner,"
the *American Organist* explained, years later, giving Skinner even
more credit than he was due.

As he entered his thirties, Skinner had acquired the self-confidence of maturity. He cut an attractive figure as a young man,
vaguely resembling Charlie Chaplin, with his dark hair, mustache,
and solid build. He met Mabel Hastings, a secretary (no relation of
the Hastings organbuilding family) on a blind date in Boston, and
married her in 1896 after a two-year courtship, in the front parlor
of her father's house in Bethel, Maine, on the edge of the White
Mountains. "The name of the minister who married us there was
the Reverend Mr. Beam and just after he pronounced us man and
wife, he started to kiss the bride but I took him by the shoulders and
turned him around and informed him that I was of the opinion that
kiss No. one belonged to me," Skinner recounted in a letter many
years later. A daughter, Eugenia, was born three years later, and a
son, Richmond, in 1898 (a third child, Ruth, was born in 1906).
Fascinated with technology in his chosen business, he was taken
with automobiles when they appeared on the scene, bringing a red
Winton touring car home one evening in 1907 and rousting his
children out of bed for a ride.

The business may have required him to spend a lot of his time in
churches, but he had no toleration for false solemnity or sanctimo-
niousness and was fond of quoting ditties like this one:

Ernest M. Skinner and Mabel Hastings Skinner (center)
at the Hastings homestead in Bethel, Maine

A young theologian named Fiddle
Declined to accept his degree.
He said, "It's all right to be Fiddle
But not to be Fiddle D.D."

He also delighted, perhaps because he regarded his own aged mother as a sort of religious fanatic, in telling a joke about a bum who supposedly appeared in the back yard of a well-off New England matron begging for a bite to eat. The lady of the house came out with a piece of bread, announcing that she was giving it not for the beggar's sake, nor for her own, but for the Lord's sake, and was cut short by the rejoinder, "Then for Christ's sake, would you please put some butter on it."

Skinner, like other American builders of the time, also experimented with automatic mechanisms that let organs play music by

themselves from perforated paper rolls, and reproduce performances by good players just as player pianos could. By 1901, Skinner
had taken out a patent on a refinement in an automatic piano-play-
ing mechanism that allowed for accents on notes that should be
played louder for emphasis, and with the money he made from the
device, he worked on similar improvements for pipe organs. He was
superintendent of the installation of many important Hutchings instruments, including one in the new Symphony Hall in Boston, with
a pedal trombone stop modeled on those he had heard on Willis
organs in England. And when Edwin Votey merged his firm with
Hutchings the same year, Skinner became vice president of the new
Hutchings-Votey Organ Company. But running somebody else's
business was not what he was cut out to do—he wanted to design,
build, and voice his own organs, and so in 1902, with a partner and
$4,300 largely from royalties on his piano accenting device, he
started Ernest M. Skinner & Co., taking on Charles A. Ryder, son of
his first employer, as his New York representative "in order to take
care of their constantly increasing business in the metropolis."

Business did flourish over the next couple of years, as Skinner
took on other partners, incorporating under a new name with practically every one. By 1904, E. M. Skinner & Co., as the company was
then called, was boasting of "a splendid trade, which extends into
many states," and Skinner had invented a new organ stop, called
"erzähler," with quiet tones that reinforced organ sound at the fundamental and octave harmonic. The way the pipe burbled struck
Skinner as engagingly garrulous, and the German name he gave it
means "storyteller."

The following year, newly incorporated as the Ernest M. Skinner
Organ Company, he took on Robert Hope-Jones, who had emigrated to America, as a salesman and vice president. The association
came to an end only fifteen months later, after Hope-Jones installed
a vulgar-sounding horn stop of his own design in a church in Elmira,
New York, that, as Skinner had predicted, rejected it. Skinner could
hardly believe what Hope-Jones did then. "Mr. Hope-Jones claimed
that the stop was mine, and was put in under his protest."

That was the end of Hope-Jones's association with Skinner, but he formed a firm of his own in Elmira, and later sold out to the Rudolph Wurlitzer Organ Company of nearby North Tonawanda, New York. Hope-Jones's attitude was that anything that could get more people to listen to the organ was good. Wurlitzer found Hope-Jones's thinking entirely congenial. (The diaphone, another Hope-Jones invention, was enthusiastically adopted by the U.S. Coast Guard, which modified it and used it as a foghorn.)

Skinner, however, was after subtlety and smoothness. What he was trying to do, better than anyone before him, was to make the organ into an instrument of orchestral beauty, with tones ranging all the way from warm and shimmering to proud and majestic, and solo voices just as versatile, pure and plaintive as any orchestra's.

Hearing an oboe solo at one concert, Skinner went right to his factory in South Boston and gathered various pipes and voicing tools. Then, into the night, he experimented on changing res-onator shapes and other components until he had a pipe that sounded like the oboe he had heard. He called his new stop the or-chestral oboe, and installed it in organs in Brooklyn and Manhattan in 1906 and 1907. He devised a version of the Willis tuba mirabilis, a deep-throated solo stop with the force and volume of the equiva-lents that he had heard on Willis organs in England, and included one in the organ he installed in the Cathedral of St. John the Divine in New York City in 1910 and 1911. And, perhaps inspired by the thirty-two-foot bombarde stop in the Saint-Sulpice organ in Paris, the equivalent of the combination of double-bass, tuba, and trom-bone in an orchestra, he designed a bombarde—but with wooden instead of metal resonators, some pipes indeed as long as thirty-two feet and as capacious as small elevator shafts. They gave the lowest notes a powerful yet warm resonance that could undergird the best that a full orchestra could produce. Dr. Karl Muck, the conductor at Symphony Hall in Boston, had a single such pipe put in the Hutch-ings organ whose installation Skinner had overseen years earlier, just for the lowest note in the deep C major chord in the opening of Richard Strauss's *Also Sprach Zarathustra.* One of Skinner's admirers told his biographer, Dorothy J. Holden, that when Skinner had heard that big bombarde roar out during the performance, he couldn't help himself, jumping out of his seat on the center aisle and exclaiming "Thar she blows!"

Skinner invented several stops that became his trademarks. His flute celeste consisted of two ranks of spitzflute pipes slightly out of tune with each other so as to produce a shimmering beat, the direct result, in Skinner's words, "of hearing the muted strings in the slow movement of the orchestral accompaniment of the B-flat minor piano concerto of Tchaikovsky, which seemed to me to be the most heavenly sound I had ever heard." Taken with the sound of the English horn solo in a performance of the Prelude to Act III of *Parsifal,* he invented a pipe that could passably imitate that instrument, succeeding by his own lights and patenting his English horn design in 1912. This was a modified oboe stop, its sound produced as in all "reed" stops by a vibrating reed in the base of the pipe, amplified by a metal resonator whose top flared out like a cone. Later, in Skinner's final design for the English horn, the top of the cone ended in a bell shape that made the stop sound, to Skinner's ears at least, exactly like the instrument it was designed to imitate.

Skinner organs could roar like elephants or warble as sweetly as nightingales. Soon they were in demand around the country and becoming known around the world, not only for their tonal design but also for the sophistication and playing ease of their consoles, with handsome ivory keyboards that made players feel as if they were performing on a piano, and concave, radiating pedalboards (not flat and straight like the ones Bach knew) that later became standard equipment for all American builders. Skinner organs now had a coast-to-coast reputation, and there was even a Skinner organ in a church in Tokyo, Japan.

Secure as his reputation as an artist might have been, as a businessman Skinner was inept. The elders of Fifth Avenue Presbyterian Church in New York City, up the street from St. Thomas and eager to acquire a Skinner organ as magnificent as the instrument that he had built for that church, were nonetheless wary of one thing. "One careful trustee checked the experience of others and found that Mr. Skinner had occasionally been unable to deliver his organs on time because of limited personnel to handle the large number of contracts he was given, and his having money tied up in the building of a new factory," the church's historian wrote. Indeed, Skinner, who moved operations to a new shop in Dorchester, Massachusetts, in 1914, was late delivering the organ, though the church apparently never invoked a $20-a-day penalty clause written into the contract.

"Ernest Skinner was always the organ builder first and the business man last," his nephew Ned Hastings wrote to Dorothy Holden. "In fact he was the worst business man I know anything about. . . . Apparently the chief problem lay in the fact that Ernest, in the interests of building the best organ possible, usually wound up spending more money on an organ than the contract had stipulated," a business weakness he shared with Cavaillé-Coll, who like Skinner often went ahead at his own expense and installed stops that were extremely expensive to build even if the buyers were unwilling to pay for them.

As a result of his own business practices and of the difficulties caused by American participation in World War I, when strategic materials like tin and other pipe metals became unavailable, Skinner found himself in serious financial difficulty. A wealthy businessman who had bought residence organs for both his home in Akron, Ohio, and his yacht (not from Skinner but from the Aeolian Company of New York City, the leader in the residence field) came to Skinner's rescue. This was Arthur H. Marks, head of the Goodyear Rubber Company, who had become acquainted with Skinner in 1916 and, after the war ended, decided not to go back to the tire business but to pursue his interest in pipe organs full time. Marks looked into Skinner's business, did a financial analysis, and agreed to reorganize it if Skinner would let him run the company. Skinner, whose cash flow was hand to mouth, with money from down payments on new contracts going to finish off work on existing ones, agreed.

Now Skinner was rescued from mundane financial worries. The reorganized Skinner Organ Company had Marks as president and treasurer, with Skinner relegated to one of two positions as vice president—the other was William E. Zeuch, a distinguished organist from Chicago.

The early 1920s were boom years for Skinner Organ Company, with twenty-nine instruments built or contracted for and under construction in 1920. There were fifty-one in 1921, and ninety-two in 1923. Like any expanding business, this one was intent on maximizing shareholder value. The firm hired salesmen and acquired a New York studio to display its artistic and technological achievements, incorporated in a three-keyboard organ with a player attachment. A publicity brochure appeared periodically, and was called, with Skinner's typical fondness for puns, *Stop, Open and Reed.* Organ music played on the studio organ was featured on regular broadcasts that began in 1923 over WEAF Radio, a station owned by the American Telephone and Telegraph Company. The sound quality on home radio sets left much to be desired, though. "The Flutes come through fine and so do such voices as the Clarinet, Oboe, Piccolo and Strings. The Diapason, however, can only be used in a limited way, bass notes are not yet being made audible through the present receiving sets. Some of the lower notes will not come through at all. Selections carrying a large number of chords 'full of notes' so load the radio that it 'blasts;' that is, the music breaks into mere noise. Thus the technique of Radio Broadcasting is a study by itself," Skinner Organ acknowledged. "We are aware that many lovers of organ music regard the results so far obtained as of negative value. We feel, however, that we are making thousands of friends for the organ and that the organists will benefit by this later." Later, the series moved to another New York radio station.

Skinner and Aeolian, like other builders, were also eager to tap into the theater organ market. The ornate movie palaces that were being built all over America had, at first, orchestra pits for live musicians to play music while the audience settled in, and to accompany the action on screen with mood music. But orchestras couldn't improvise music to go with changing scenes—they had to play from sheet music, and they couldn't smoothly modulate between keys. An organist on an instrument fitted out with the right sound effects could do all that and improvise besides, especially with the novelties that Hope-Jones and Wurlitzer put into their theater organs. So, by the early 1920s, the big movie palaces let the organist take over from the orchestra once the film started rolling.

Cinema organs, the British organist Reginald Foort boasted, could reproduce a baby crying or a brass band, and imitate everything from smashing glass to the sound of a steam locomotive's starting up and roaring off into the distance. Wurlitzer ran away with this market, turning out an organ a day by 1926.

Ernest M. Skinner didn't turn up his nose at the silent-movie market. "Moving pictures reflect everything of life and are limited in scope only by the imagination of the producer," he wrote in 1925. "The organ should be able to reflect every shade of human emotion: love, anger, hate, sorrow, surprise, humor, ugliness, the sinister, and national idioms, to say nothing of dogs, chickens, horses, convulsions of nature, etc., dramatic qualities, fine shades of meaning, the military clang, etc. . . ." But the result in too many theater organs, to his ears, was "a noisy, coarse tone of very limited variety and a superabundance of so-called traps i.e. drums, sleigh bells, xylophones and other vaudeville specialties." Wurlitzer loaded its theater organs with these things, and with heavy-breathing stops of Hope-Jones's invention like the "tibia clausa," a wooden flute stop with a thick, hooting tone that took well to the tremolo effect that Wurlitzers used to simulate the vibrato of solo voices and violins.

Skinner resisted putting pipes like those in his theater organs, but not always. The list of stops in one of his finest surviving instruments, the one in the California Palace of the Legion of Honor in San Francisco, includes a "tibia plena" and a full complement of "traps," including bass drum, castanets, crash cymbal, gong, snare drum, and tambourine. The Legion of Honor instrument was not a theater organ but was designed to be played at ceremonial occasions, the pipes heard but not seen in rooms concealed in the palace's ceiling vaults, behind faux-masonry cloth screens, with stops befitting the purpose of the hall, such as the "military trumpet" originally in the orchestral solo division. Skinner's handsome mahogany console stood alone in the hall in front of the hidden pipe chambers, which could be opened to the Legion's outside courtyard.

In the hands of a masterful organist, the sounds of this great old organ could mimic the brass trombones and strings of an orchestra in a work like Sir Edward Elgar's *Pomp and Circumstance,* right down to crashing bass drums and cymbals. The orchestral sound blended, the pipes invisible, in a "tone chute" feeding out to the audience, making the organ sound, as Skinner wanted, velvety smooth and as expressive as an orchestra's—not bold and chuffily assertive like the baroque organs he had so disliked in Europe.

Where Wurlitzer built thousands of theater organs, Skinner built only twelve, installing two of the largest in the Capitol Theatre in Boston and the Colony Theater in New York City in the early 1920s. And those had just as many "traps" as Wurlitzer's. The Capitol Theatre organ's specifications, for example, included snare drums, bass drum, Chinese block, tambourine, cymbal, tympani, auto horn, bird song, orchestral bells, and xylophone—things that a skillful organist could use to provide accompaniment for the action on the screen. "The organ in the Capitol Theatre is designed to be a substitute for the orchestra in the truest sense," Skinner wrote. "It has all of the representative color present in the orchestra; strings of all qualities and strength of tone that will continue the orchestral strings so exactly that one cannot tell when the transition is made. The French Horn, English Horn, Clarinet, 'Cello, Oboe are all exactly duplicated. . . . The organ is fully capable of furnishing a musical atmosphere for every mood shown on the screen whether it be sentimental, angry, sad, militant or merely scenic; in short its resources are as ample as those of the finest symphony orchestra."

Skinner put hundreds, even thousands, more pipes than Wurlitzer in instruments made for the movies. Wurlitzer's organs were built as "unit orchestras," a system Hope-Jones had devised to get many different "stops" out of a single rank of pipes, at different pitches. "Mighty Wurlitzers" were sometimes just blowhards, with far fewer ranks of pipes than the number of stops they boasted. Skinner, too, often made single ranks of pipes do double duty on keyboard and pedal, but not nearly to the extent that Hope-Jones did.

In theaters, concert halls, auditoriums, and churches all over America, organs were at the height of popularity. Great theater organ performers like Jesse Crawford were household names, and Crawford's "Valencia" became the first popular recording to sell over a million copies. In 1927 alone, sixty-three American organ-building companies, employing 2,770 artisans, turned out 2,451 instruments.

Ernest M. Skinner, who had started as a shop boy, was doing better for himself than he would have imagined in his wildest dreams. He had a summer cottage complete with speedboat on Lake Winnepesaukee, in New Hampshire. He had an automobile that he used instead of the train on business trips. He even drove the car to the West Coast in December 1926 with his wife and his daughter Ruth. They took time to stop off at the Grand Canyon and ride mules to the river thousands of feet below—"If the average American knew what there was to see in his own country he would look it over once in a while instead of going *exclusively* to some other country," Skinner wrote later, perhaps inadvertently revealing the rarefied social strata to which his business success had led him.

By this time, Skinner Organ Company needed 200 employees to keep up with the orders coming in. For American organs and organists, it was a golden age. In the roaring twenties, pipe organs were a roaring business, and few could see any reason why the good times should not just roll on forever.

Monster Organs,
Mammoth Audiences

Bigger, better, and louder was the motto as the United States began to transform itself from an agrarian to an industrial colossus in the decades before World War I ratified America as a global power. Marveling themselves at the change, Americans flocked to giant expositions, the world's fairs of the day, to swell with pride at the latest advances in American technological sophistication and manufacturing skill, and large pipe organs were always among the most complicated and sophisticated of the achievements on display. Attractions at all the exhibitions, organs drew audiences of thousands of people, astounding as such numbers would seem for most organ recitals today.

With the novelty of a giant wheel built by George Washington Gale Ferris, at the World's Columbian Exposition in Chicago in 1893, organbuilders had to outdo themselves. There were three organs at the exposition, including a large one by Farrand & Votey, a company in Detroit that had inherited much of the Roosevelt brothers' know-how and staff after their company closed its doors. The most famous French organist of the time, Alexandre Guilmant, made his first trip to America to play the big instrument. Guilmant was used to such occasions, having performed a series of recitals on the large organ that Cavaillé-Coll had installed in the Trocadéro Palace in Paris for the Exposition Universelle of 1878, the first organ built for a concert hall in France. Guilmant's programs were challenging ones, with music of Bach and seventeenth- and eighteenth-century French composers and on-the-spot improvisations by himself. These improvisations were not just the usual noodling that church organists did to fill in at times, as for instance when the choir had finished the communion anthem but the parishioners were still at the altar rail. Guilmant could compose musically coherent pieces on the spot, using melodies submitted to him at the performance, with contrapuntal and harmonic development, from pianissimo to fortissimo, through various keys, and back again.

Guilmant's programs dazzled listeners in Chicago and, on the tour that followed, in New York City and Brooklyn, where he played at the New York Avenue Church and harmoniously incorporated a cipher—a note that got stuck and would not stop playing—into his improvisation.

Guilmant returned for another tour five years later, and again in 1904, for a series of recitals on another enormous new exhibition organ, with 138 stops and about 10,000 pipes, built for the Louisiana Purchase Exposition in St. Louis by Murray M. Harris of Los Angeles. Making the organ had been a huge challenge for Harris. He selected a design by a British organ theorist and architect, George Ashdown Audsley, whose ideas for making organs into imitations of orchestras were much in vogue at the time. This would be the grandest plan of all, for "the largest organ in the world," as Audsley described it in a booklet published in advance of its installation. He envisioned an instrument with pipes imitating the sounds of violins and cellos in chambers with louvered doors that the organist could open and close with foot pedals to make the volume swell and recede just like an orchestra's string section. Other pipes would sound like flutes, clarinets, horns, trumpets, trombones, and tubas. Audsley foresaw registration aids and devices to assist expressive playing—double touch on the keyboard, so that the organist could play along on one step of stops and then, with additional finger pressure, bring on more stops and louder tone; combination pistons to change stops in midperformance, couplers to connect separate keyboards and make keyboard stops playable on the pedals—all in greater profusion and sophistication than on any previous organ, Audsley boasted, making the instrument "capable of producing musical effects never before heard outside the Grand Orchestra." The pipes, of wood and metal, would range in length from thirty-two feet for the low bass notes that would shake listeners to their very bones, to a few inches for the highest notes of the piccolo, all arranged on a frame of Oregon pine that towered as high as a three-story house.

Nothing so huge had ever been undertaken by any American builder before. Harris's superintendent was a man who had begun his organ-building career with George H. Ryder's firm in Boston in 1874—William Boone Fleming, a fastidious but feisty New Brunswicker whose first trade had been carpentry. He believed, like Ryder and the other New Englanders with whom he had worked, in using five screws where most people thought four would do. Accused of designing some parts of the organ without making them accessible for repairs, Fleming's reply was, "Damn it, I build it so it doesn't need repair."

Fleming was thoroughly familiar with the new techniques, electrical devices, and playing aids pioneered by the Roosevelts, for whom he had also worked, and Fleming had perfected and patented his own electropneumatic action, but the company needed an infusion of new capital to undertake the project. Harris had built a new factory three stories high to assemble the huge instrument and expanded the staff to 125 employees; however, the new building cost $105,000, nearly $40,000 more than projected. In 1903, stockholders threw Harris out and replaced him with Fleming, who now found himself supervising and directing a reorganized enterprise dubbed the Los Angeles Art Organ Company.

The finished organ was to have a player console of Fleming's design, with an automatic mechanism using perforated-paper rolls that, as on a player piano, would run through and make the huge organ play music automatically. But this feature immediately brought on a suit by a formidable competitor—the Aeolian Company of New York City, whose tight hold on the lucrative market for residence organs Harris had hoped to break. Aeolian was exhibiting a player organ at the St. Louis exposition, one much smaller than the one Harris was building, and did not want its thunder stolen. In fact, Aeolian held the patent on a key part of the player-roll mechanism that Fleming had constructed, and refused to release it.

Because of an Aeolian injunction, the "largest organ in the world" was allowed to play itself on only one occasion in St. Louis. But it was finally finished at the factory and, with its 130 miles of electric wire, 13,000 magnets, and 250,000 pounds of pipes and chests, it was loaded into thirteen freight cars and pulled to St. Louis by a steam locomotive at the end of February 1904.

Legal bills and cost overruns on the organ, which had some pipes made in Germany because no American builder had the wherewithal to construct them, created more difficulties, and in St. Louis, the Festival Hall, a 4,000-seat pavilion designed by the great architect Cass Gilbert with a dome the size of St. Peter's, was not yet ready for use.

The exposition opened at the end of April, before the organ was completed—small wonder, given its size and complexity and the limited time available for installing it. It was playable, but still not fully assembled, in September, when Guilmant, by now as famous in America as he was in Europe, arrived to begin his recitals. They were billed as a cultural high point of the exposition—high enough for the organizers to raise the admission price from the usual 10 cents to 25 cents a ticket, in anticipation of revenues of $1,000 per sold-out concert—and they were a smashing success. Guilmant performed forty recitals on the St. Louis organ without ever playing the same composition twice, but he almost brought down the house literally at the seventh concert, when part of the ceiling broke loose and crashed to the floor. "The tremendous vibration from the monster organ at the Fair should have been taken into consideration by the builders of Festival Hall," a reviewer wrote. "A more serious accident, with loss of life, might easily have happened. The walls and ceilings now are being strengthened with girders."

As a tourist attraction, the organ held its own, even against the Ferris Wheel, which came to St. Louis from Chicago. "Few of the 13,000,000 people who paid 50 cents to enter the Exposition grounds, and 6,000,000 more who had complimentary tickets, had ever seen anything other than a church organ of two manuals and 12 to 16 stops," Frederick R. Webber, an organ historian who had visited the fair as a boy, wrote years later. "To them the enormous organ was just another sight to be included in their rounds."

Artistically, as the musicologist Wayne Leupold has observed, Guilmant's recitals in St. Louis and twenty-four others that led up to a final program of his own compositions at Symphony Hall in Boston on November 24, 1904, opened American ears to a new, higher standard of performance and musical taste. Thus the St. Louis organ became an artistic landmark in the history of the organ in America. But as a business venture, it was a disaster for the Los Angeles Art Organ Company, which went bankrupt after the cancellation of its contract to keep the organ running after the exposition closed. "Four or five men must be constantly employed to keep it in repair," officials told the *Los Angeles Examiner;* "only an organist of extraordinary skill can play it, thereby requiring an organist's salary of from $3,500 to $5,000 a year." So the huge instrument was disassembled and loaded onto railroad cars again and taken to a warehouse.

A trip to another fair with an exhibition organ, the Pan-American Exposition in Buffalo in 1901, literally proved fatal for one listener—President William McKinley. The celebration of industry and culture in Buffalo included one of the largest pipe organs built in the country up to that time, installed in a "Temple of Music" by Emmons Howard & Son of Westfield, Massachusetts, where McKinley held a reception on the afternoon of September 6. The official organist of the exposition, William J. Gomph, was demonstrating the instrument for the president and 2,200 people who had come to meet him when an assassin struck. "Organist Gomph had reached the highest notes in one of Bach's masterpieces on the great pipe organ," the *Buffalo Courier* reported, "and as he stopped at the height to let the strains reverberate through the auditorium," at precisely 4:07 P.M., "two shots rang out." The president's assassin, Leon Czolgosz, a young anarchist of Polish origin from Cleveland, Ohio, had sneaked up on McKinley in the crowd with a revolver under a handkerchief wrapped around his hand. Czolgosz was seized on the spot and nearly lynched.

The Courier's story, like most newspaper articles about organs, was not musically accurate. According to one of Gomph's organ students, M. Searle Wright, his teacher had been playing a piece of transcribed orchestral music by Wagner often used by organists of the time—"To an Evening Star," from *Tannhäuser*—when McKinley was shot as he made his way through the crowd to the podium where he was to speak. Seeing the president lying on the ground, the organist stopped playing, grabbed a sheet of music, and ran over to begin fanning him. McKinley opened one eye and said only, "Kindly desist, young man." But the president died in Buffalo of an intestinal infection eight days later. Czolgosz was convicted of murder and put to death by another modern technological invention that was just beginning to come into use—the electric chair.

Two famous British concert organists came to California to open two more exposition organs in San Diego and San Francisco in 1914 and 1915, both built by the Austin Organ Co. of Hartford, Connecticut, whose founders, John and Basil Austin, were also English immigrants.

Humphrey J. Stewart dedicated the Organ Pavilion at the Panama-California Exposition in Balboa Park in San Diego on New Year's Eve in 1914. The organ, the gift of John D. and Adolph B. Spreckels, sugar and shipping magnates who had immigrated to California from Germany, had obvious symbolic importance, with the world war raging across the Atlantic and the United States staying safely out of the fray. With four keyboards and more than sixty stops, it was installed in a reinforced-concrete building open to the outdoors, and—before the days of freeways and airports—could allegedly be heard ten miles distant. Stewart, who became municipal organist, stayed after the exposition left, and, subsidized until 1929 by John Spreckels and his estate, gave almost daily recitals on the organ from 1915 to 1932.

The Panama-Pacific International Exposition in San Francisco in 1915 was a major event, but so was the announcement before it opened that Edwin H. Lemare, the most famous British concert organist of his day, would be one of the exposition's official organists and would design the organ console, news that the National Association of Organists took as something of an insult to American patriotic pride. With 113 stops, this was the largest organ that Austin had built up to that time, and Lemare, who had been forced to cancel nearly all his engagements in England after the war began, was happy to have the work.

The organ was opened on February 20, only hours after Austin's agents, Felix Schoenstein & Sons, completed the job after racing against a $100-a-day penalty for delay. It was not Lemare, though, but another Englishman, Wallace Sabin, a San Francisco organist, who gave the first recital. He played a transcription of the Hallelujah Chorus from Handel's *Messiah*. But of the 406 noon recitals that followed before the Panama-Pacific exposition closed on December 4, Lemare played 121. Best known for his orchestral transcriptions of everything from Beethoven to Wagnerian opera, Lemare was largely responsible for drawing most of the 307,897 people who paid to come and hear these concerts. As Lemare later recalled, the program note read as follows: "Mr. Lemare will be glad to improvise on a theme submitted by the audience. Themes should not exceed three bars, should be written plainly, and handed to an attendant during the intermission." Sitting at the organ bench looking over the submissions one day, Lemare found a card on which was written, "The only three bars that I know are the ones at the St. Francis Hotel, the Palace Hotel and the Bohemian Club—so do your darndest."

After the exposition closed, the organ began a second life as the San Francisco municipal organ, and Lemare—with the munificent salary of $10,000—was named municipal organist and given the job of supervising its reconstruction after a move to what was later to become the Civic Auditorium, a much larger hall that required strengthening the volume and the tonal character of the instrument. Lemare peremptorily ordered a slew of changes. "The Tuba Magna is one of the most unsatisfactory stops in the Organ, and is in no way worthy of its name; send new tuba from factory," he commanded, for example. When he finally played a rededication recital on Easter Sunday in 1917, 10,392 people paid a dime apiece to hear him.

Even at only 10 cents a ticket, this seems extraordinary today, when many Americans probably think of the organ as only the pipeless electronic instrument that plays "da-da-da-dump-de-da" every so often out of sight at baseball stadiums. Why would colossal, and colossally expensive, contraptions of wooden beams and panels, knobs, chests, valves, pipes, and wind have such great appeal?

One reason is that music in those days was not instantly accessible, in full fidelity, anywhere, as it is today, whether in a department store elevator, a car, or a living room. Radio was only in its infancy. High-fidelity FM broadcasting lay in the future. Microphones could capture musical sounds, but not well. As for recordings, Victrolas were cumbersome, primitive machines that had to be wound up by hand, and hard-shellac records produced a tinny sound. Music was just beginning to be something the middle classes could listen to in their homes at leisure. It had always been something to dress up and go out for. To hear a full orchestra play symphonic music was a rare privilege for most Americans a century ago, but the cultural elites who could afford it also believed they had a duty beyond themselves.

Just as Andrew Carnegie had provided millions of dollars to start public libraries across the land to educate and uplift the millions, the business and cultural leaders of America's great cities, from San Francisco to New York, Boston, Chicago, Cleveland, Cincinnati, Pittsburgh, and places in between, began building concert halls and municipal auditoriums and equipping them with orchestral pipe organs. A small part of the reason was that there was music in which both organ and orchestra figured, from Bach's *Saint Matthew Passion* to Saint-Saëns's *Organ Symphony*. But another part was the difficulty of assembling the hundred, and sometimes hundreds, of musicians it took to bring off an orchestral concert. On an organ that could passably imitate an orchestra, orchestral music could be made by a single musician, at an affordable price—a dime a customer in San Francisco in 1917. Ten thousand people came again to hear Lemare when he returned to the Civic Auditorium in 1927, giving him a five-minute standing ovation. Lemare's wife, a former student of his, sharply corrected an organ journal that printed an account of the recital reporting the size of the audience as 1,000. "One must even forgive a *printer* for the omission of an aught, as it is very seldom one hears of an organ recital audience of 10,000 people," Lemare himself wrote in his memoirs.

"Music is a religion," Carnegie had said, and he had a $15,800 pipe organ installed in his Manhattan mansion at Fifth Avenue and Ninetieth Street, and engaged an organist, Walter C. Gale, to awaken him to its strains every morning he was in residence. But he also created the Carnegie Organ Fund, which gave millions of dollars in matching grants between 1873 and the 1920s to help American schools, churches, and concert halls acquire organs—more than 8,800 of them, from one coast to the other.

So one "monster organ" followed another in municipal auditoriums and other public spaces across the land. Austin built one in 1910 for the auditorium-armory in Atlanta, where an audience of 7,000 came to hear Lemare play the first concert on May 31. Two years later, Portland, Maine, acquired an Austin instrument with sixty-nine ranks of pipes for the municipal auditorium of the City Hall, given by Cyrus H.K. Curtis, the magazine magnate and a native son of Portland. He named the organ for Hermann Kotzschmar, a German-born conductor and organist who had brought European musical sophistication to Portland at the end of the nineteenth century (and, incidentally, brought Curtis his two middle names). Portland appointed a municipal organist, Will MacFarlane, whose "America the Beautiful March" had given "O Say Can You See" a run for its money in a contest for the National Anthem; Lemare succeeded MacFarlane after he left in 1921.

There was fierce competition for the prestige that came with the

municipal organ business, each company asserting its unique quali-
fications. Austin advertised, "Orchestral organs as built by the
Austin Organ Company startlingly imitate the strings, flutes, reeds
and brass of the symphony orchestra, even harps, chimes, celestas,
drums, cymbals and other percussions if desired."

Ernest Skinner built his first large civic organ for the municipal
auditorium in Portland, Oregon, in 1916, and another one four
years later for the auditorium in St. Paul, Minnesota, where Chan-
dler Goldthwaite drew 8,000 people to the first of four concerts.
The overall attendance was more than 30,000, and 3,000 people
were turned away. The four programs consisted mostly of transcriptions of orchestral music by Wagner, Handel, Sibelius, and Dvorak.
The chairman of the St. Paul committee that selected Skinner later
attested, in a *Stop, Open and Reed* brochure, that experts thought "we
have one of the best, if not finest, instruments in the United States."

The municipal auditorium in Cleveland filled to almost double
its capacity of 13,000 in 1922 for the debut of a big new Skinner instrument that cost $100,000. "Edwin Arthur Kraft, at 3 P.M. on Sep-
tember 10th, opened the giant Skinner Organ and brought the
audience of 20,000 Cleveland Citizens to their feet with the first
measures of the Star Spangled Banner," the Skinner Company
proudly reported in *Stop, Open and Reed.* "Despite the oppressive
heat the crowd which had been collecting since noon soon ex-
ceeded the capacity of the mammoth hall and long before the time
set for the inaugural recital all seats were filled and more than
5,000 men, women and children were crowding the corridors of
the colossal structure. The police which were out in large numbers
were at first able to hold the crowd into a semblance of order, but
soon gave up in despair as the eager mob swept all before it," J.
Harold MacDowell, the Cleveland city architect, attested.

A riot to get into an organ recital? Skinner publicity was never
understated. But neither MacDowell nor Skinner said a word about
the unfavorable placement of the organ, whose 10,000 pipes were
in chambers behind the right wing of the stage. Undaunted, Skinner advertised the organ with an unattributed admiring quotation

describing it as "The Finest Musical Instrument ever built by man." There, again, the opening concert included very little music written for organ. Instead, the vast crowd heard things like the grand march from *Aïda,* Handel's *Largo,* Rimsky-Korsakoff's *Song of India,* and Wagner's *Ride of the Valkyries.*

Three years later, in Chattanooga, Tennessee, Austin edged out Skinner, W. W. Kimball, Wurlitzer, and other companies for a contract for an instrument for the Soldiers and Sailors Memorial Auditorium. More than 4,000 people came to hear Lemare play *The Star-Spangled Banner,* Bach, and four transcriptions of orchestral pieces. Lemare had landed in Chattanooga after frictions with the new city manager of Portland and was named Chattanooga's municipal organist with a salary underwritten by Adolph S. Ochs, the Chattanooga newspaper publisher who later bought *The New York Times.* Between 1925 and 1929, Ochs made possible a total of 128 recitals by Lemare on the new organ. In Spokane, Washington, the $26,000 cost of the Austin organ in the Lewis and Clark High School was raised partly by students, faculty, and alumni, with sales, gifts, and projects of various kinds, much to the amazement of Louis Vierne, who played there in 1927. "They were seen sweeping sidewalks, washing windows, running errands, driving trucks, etc., and turning over their earnings to a fund," he reported to his French readers—things unheard of on the Continent.

What Vierne had seen in Spokane, like the national competition to build concert-hall organs, was an example of the striving of the American middle class for cultural refinement, exemplified in churches, town halls, and municipal auditoriums. In middle-class homes, pianos filled the same need, on a more intimate scale. Upright pianos made by scores of American firms—Chickering, Mason and Hamlin, Kimball, Baldwin, even Sears, Roebuck and Montgomery Ward—graced living rooms across the land. Usually it was women who were expected to learn to play them and to elevate the level of the home.

Families that could afford them also bought small reed organs, table-top instruments that sounded and worked like miniature organs (or overgrown harmonicas) and that were being mass-produced by 247 different companies by the 1870s. A decade later, some had been developed into more sophisticated devices, the size of upright pianos, that could play music automatically with perforated paper rolls. William Barnes Tremaine, a New York piano maker, began marketing "the Aeolian," the most successful of these new inventions, in 1883. "On the Aeolian, any one, without regard to any knowledge of music they may or may not have, can, after a week's practice, play any piece of music ever composed," his advertising boasted, and in 1887 he had sold so many of these machines that he changed the name of the firm to The Aeolian Organ & Music Company.

But such paltry devices as pianos and reed organs that could be found in practically every home would not do for the new class of moguls and captains of industry that was proliferating in the pre-income-tax era of American capitalism. They, too, wanted to demonstrate their cultural sophistication with music, and Aeolian discovered just the thing for them, in 1895, by finding a way to combine the player mechanism with a $10,000 pipe organ made by Farrand & Votey of Detroit for "Belcourt," the palace Oliver Hazard Perry Belmont had built for himself in Newport, Rhode Island. Now he could entertain his new wife, Alva Smith Vanderbilt, and their friends with organ arrangements of orchestral works in the vaulted French Gothic ballroom of their summer "cottage." All this without ever lifting a finger himself, or even hiring an organist!

Aeolian began affixing its builder's plate on player pipe organs for "the private dwellings of the wealthier classes." Cyrus Curtis had one built for his mansion in Wyncote, Pennsylvania, in 1896; Frank W. Woolworth acquired one in New York in 1899, and Andrew Carnegie got his the following year. Joseph Pulitzer and Louis Comfort Tiffany ordered Opus 924 and 925, respectively. By the beginning of the twentieth century, Aeolian was the world leader in the field. Famous organists vied to record performances on increasingly sophisticated player rolls, which could then unwind to reproduce these recitals for their privileged owners. Victor Herbert wrote

Symphonic Fantasy for the Aeolian pipe organ, and Camille Saint-Saëns wrote *Fantaisie pour Orgue Aeolian* with eleven sections "un-playable by the fingers and feet" of an average organist.

Charles Schwab, the first president of U.S. Steel, had a harp stop included in the organ Aeolian installed in his ninety-room mansion on Riverside Drive between Seventy-second and Seventy-third streets in Manhattan in 1904, adding drums, cymbals, castanets, and tambourine jingles in 1905. Hundreds more pipes were added in 1906 and 1919 under the direction of Schwab's house organist, Archer Gibson, who was paid a $10,000 annual salary.

Gibson also did consulting work for John D. Rockefeller Jr., who ordered a three-keyboard Aeolian organ with an automatic player mechanism in 1907 for Kykuit, the estate he had built for his father at Pocantico Hills in Sleepy Hollow, New York, near Tarrytown. The organ cost $26,250, and additions and a second console in 1911 cost another $6,850. Though the automatic player didn't always work, Frank Taft, Aeolian's vice president and a noted organist, convinced Rockefeller to part with another $15,500 for an Aeolian in his city mansion at 10 West 54th Street in 1912. Inspecting, play-ing, and troubleshooting these two instruments was a good source of income for Archer Gibson, who nevertheless warned Rockefeller that the Aeolian was a business about money as well as art. "Nothing but the customer's purse is being kept in view. . . . Whether Taft sells eggs or organs makes no difference to him or the company," Gibson wrote at one point.

"To his many enjoyments, the very wealthy man of New York and its suburbs now adds what only a prince of affairs could possess," an article in the magazine section of *The New York Times* marveled in 1911, reporting that there were 200 to 300 great homes with pipe organs in the metropolitan New York region. The article's focus was on money—the $40,000 or even $100,000 (a colossal sum in 1911) that a music-loving magnate had to pay for one of these organs, and the $1,000 or $2,000 a year that he paid his "private organist" for "music at his own fireside that the Midases of any other day than this would have longed for in vain."

THE AEOLIAN COMPANY
Aeolian Hall, New York
PIPE-ORGAN DEPARTMENT

John W. Keins, Manager   Frank Taft, Art Director

MANUFACTURERS OF
*Aeolian Pipe-Organs
for Salons, Music Rooms, Foyer
and Reception Halls in Private Residences*

LONDON
135 NEW BOND STREET
PARIS
32 AVENUE DE L'OPERA
BERLIN
UNTER DEN LINDEN 71
WORKS
AEOLIAN, NEW JERSEY
CABLE ADDRESS
SYRENO

CORRESPONDENCE
SHOULD BE ADDRESSED TO THE
PIPE-ORGAN DEPARTMENT

362 FIFTH AVENUE March 7th, 1907.

*Specification for an Aeolian Pipe-Organ
prepared for*

The Residence of Mr. John D. Rockefeller,

Pocantico Hills,

New York.

(THREE MANUALES AND PEDALS)

MANUALE I (Great)

Expressive.

1.	Principale Grande,	8 ft.,	61	Pipes.
	(organ-tone)			
2.	Viola Pomposa,	8 "	61	"
3.	Viola,	8 "	61	"
4.	Viola d'Amore,	8 "	61	"
	(string-tone)			
5.	Flauto Primo,	8 "	61	"
6.	Flauto Ottava,	4 "	61	"
	(flute-tone)			
7.	Clarinetto,	8 "	61	"
	(reed-tone)			
8.	Tromba,	8 "	61	"
	(brass-tone)			

"Such an instrument has become an almost necessary equipment of the great American mansion," the newspaper went on. "New York and its surrounding country colonies have at least 200 of them, and possibly nearer 300 in the great homes of riches and fashion." Those who could afford them put organs into basements, bathrooms, clothes closets, butler's bedrooms, and hallways, from coast to coast. Henry Clay Frick wanted organ music to accompany meals in his mansion on Fifth Avenue and had a $40,000 Aeolian installed in 1913 at the top of the staircase landing opposite the dining room. The master of the house sat on a Renaissance throne to listen, and, as Samuel N. Behrman observed, "Surely, Frick must have felt, as he sat there, that only time separated him from Lorenzo and the other Medicis."

But the organ pipes were so bottled up behind the walls that Frick called the builders back in to make them louder. Pipes spoke, or tried to, through elevator shafts, stained glass windows, book-cases, picture frames, and fireplaces. Organs were even installed on yachts. Horace E. Dodge, who had an Aeolian at home in Detroit, paid $19,140 to have one installed in "The Delphine," with two key-boards, sixteen ranks of pipes, harp, and chimes. After the yacht burned and sank at the Ninety-fifth Street pier in New York City in 1926, Dodge had it raised and refitted with an organ of the same size, this time complete with player mechanism.

By this time, Aeolian had a worldwide reputation. Its residence organs could be heard in England, Germany, France, and South America. There was an Aeolian Hall in London and a Salle Aeolian in Paris; the Aeolian Hall in New York City, the company's world-wide headquarters, was the city's premier concert venue, in a seven-teen-story building at 29 West Forty-second Street that was filled with showrooms for organs, pianos, and other instruments. The largest Aeolian organ survives: it was built for the conservatory at "Longwood," the garden estate of Pierre S. DuPont in Kennett Square, Pennsylvania, in 1929. An enormous instrument with four keyboards and 146 ranks of pipes, it cost the huge sum (in 1929 dollars) of $124,450.

Other companies tried to compete with Aeolian in the residence-organ market. Austin and M. P. Möller, a company that had been founded by a Danish immigrant in Hagerstown, Maryland, both developed and marketed their own player mechanisms. E. M. Skinner sold scores of house organs, including two bought by the breakfast-cereal magnate W. K. Kellogg, in Gull Lake, Michigan, and in Pomona, California, and printed advertisements for these instruments with testimonials from satisfied customers in *Stop, Open and Reed*. "Some member of the family starts a roll while you are dressing in the morning and you begin the day right," began the pitch in a Skinner advertisement in 1922. "After dinner your guests want to hear the organ, and you play the Quartet from Rigoletto, something from Butterfly, Fritz Kreisler's Caprice Viennois, the Meditation from Thaïs, The Ride of the Valkyries, Old Folks at Home and the End of a Perfect Day. Then some one suggests a dance and you put on a modern fox trot played with accent, rhythm and dash. Perhaps there is a musician among your guests. He will find to his surprise that the Skinner Organ is not only a self player but also a perfectly appointed recital organ with all the finest mechanical equipment for effective hand playing."

The pipes could go unobtrusively into the basement and speak through a grille on the parlor floor, or stand out in the open, as the customer wanted. Skinner player rolls had separate volume control for six separate parts in melody and accompaniment, culminating in a system called the "orchestrator," the most complex any company of the time offered. "You have seen many times the conductor of an orchestra signalling the solo instrument for louder tone with his right hand and with the left subduing the violins," a lavishly printed Skinner Residence Organ brochure explained in 1927. "That is what we accomplish with our rolls through double expression." It was, as the organ expert and historian Jonathan Ambrosino noted almost a century later, "a binary computer assembled from organ parts and operated by wind pressure," and Skinner filed for a patent on it in 1916. But only five or six orchestrators were built, two of them for Skinner demonstrator organs. Still, Skinner boasted that his instruments were more refined than those offered by competitors. Skinner organs for home and movie theater could produce a light tremolo, for example, that was not at all like heavy theater-organ tone—the sound we think of when we hear the thick vibrato of a Hammond electronic organ playing jazz. That sound was more characteristic of the "mighty Wurlitzers" and their "tibia clausa" stops that Skinner said he so despised. "The Skinner Tremolo is substantially a true vocal vibrato, adding a beautiful quality to all the voices," the Residence Organ brochure assured prospective buyers.

And the price of all these pipes in the parlor? Just "the cost of a high grade automobile."

Long before Muzak, American retail entrepreneurs had also discovered that music could be used to entertain, divert, and even seduce customers into parting with their money for merchandise. John Wanamaker, whose Grand Depot department store in Philadelphia was the city's largest, also had a sizable store on lower Broadway in New York City whose merchandise included pianos. Wanamaker ordered five residence-size organs for resale for the piano store between 1904 and 1907. His son Lewis Rodman Wanamaker, a Princeton-educated aesthete, could play the organ, and perhaps it was Rodman who in 1904 persuaded his father to order a four-keyboard Austin organ for a concert hall seating 1,500 people in the New York store. It was a theater-style organ with forty-two stops, including snare drum, cymbals, triangles, and kettle drums, and its own staff organist and director of music, George Alexander Russell, who had studied with Widor in Paris. Wanamaker's idea was to use the organ to make the auditorium one of the city's most prestigious concert venues.

Four years later, John Wanamaker ordered two more Austin organs for the showroom auditoriums of the huge new store he was building at Market and Chestnut Streets in Philadelphia. He then put on concerts to attract customers who might be interested in buying one of the 500 pianos kept in stock. Pianos had previously been marketed as cars still are, with a Byzantine mix of base prices and bartering, but Wanamaker's moved them with a new and welcome tactic: fixed prices, with full guarantees and money-back refunds.

Then in 1909, John Wanamaker acquired—for a fraction of its original cost—the "world's largest organ," the one that Guilmant had made famous at the Louisiana Purchase Exhibition in St. Louis, for the new store's magnificent central interior space, the Grand Court.

William B. Fleming, who had signed on with Wanamaker to take on the job of relocating and reconstructing the organ, teamed up with George W. Till, a craftsman on the Wanamaker player-piano payroll who had learned the organbuilding trade in New York City. Once more the pipes and thousands of parts were loaded onto freight cars. The train steamed east that August, the cars festooned with muslin banners: "St. Louis World's Fair Organ/John Wanamaker, Philadelphia."

Once it got there, no effort or expense was too great to get the organ into playable condition. Reassembly in the department store took nearly two full years. In the meantime, the Wanamakers commissioned the designer of the store, the Chicago urban architect Daniel Hudson Burnham, to create a multiturreted, gilded façade for the pipes on the second level of the Grand Court. But the organ delivered an unexpected surprise: The thousands of pipes, now spread out in chambers on the second-, third-, and seventh-floor balconies, at opposite ends of the vast hall in the center of the store, did not adequately fill the space with their sound. Wanamaker's organ technicians did what they could to increase the volume, beefing up the wind pressure, but more pipes would clearly be needed to do justice to the hall.

Ten thousand people came for the dedication—the rededication, really—of what was already being called "The Reigning Monarch of All Instruments" on June 22, 1911, the time (9 A.M.) and date chosen to coincide with the coronation of George V in Westminster Abbey in London. Six months later, the organ pealed forth again, with the "Triumphal March" from *Aïda* and the "Coronation March" from Meyerbeer's opera *Le Prophète,* as President

William Howard Taft presided over the official dedication of the new store.

But Wanamaker's monarch had potential rivals. Bigger organs were being planned in Hamburg, and even in Denver. To preserve the Grand Court's preeminence, and to produce more volume, Wanamaker added 4,000 more pipes by 1914, and another 3,000 in 1917. All these new pipes required a new console so that performers could draw stops, play different sounds on different keyboards and pedalboards, and control the fade and swell of volume with separate foot pedals that, like accelerators, opened and closed the louvered shutters at the front of the pipe chambers. Wanamaker's, under Fleming and Till, built the required new five-keyboard console right on the store property.

The enlargement called for a new rededication, a concert combining the resources of the organ and the Philadelphia Orchestra in an after-hours "Musicians' Assembly" that was held on the evening of March 27, 1919. Rain was coming down in sheets, but people flooded the store—12,000 people, by Wanamaker's count. Tickets had been given out free for the asking, and no doubt the place was packed, every seat taken on the Tennessee-marble main floor of the Grand Court and the six balconies surrounding the atrium.

The conductor was Leopold Stokowski, who took up position beneath the massive gold-leafed pipes of the organ façade and opened the program with *The Star-Spangled Banner*. Then the orchestra fell silent as the store's associate organist, Charles-Marie Courboin, began the stately bass pedal theme of the first piece of the evening, J. S. Bach's *Passacaglia and Fugue in C minor*. Courboin, a Belgian virtuoso who had emigrated to the United States, had a flamboyant lifestyle and an ego that were a match for Stokowski's. Now here they were together in the Grand Court, the "Rachmaninoff of the organ" under the direction of one of the greatest showmen ever to mount a podium.

Stokowski knew Bach's organ masterpiece well, for he was also an organist. He had studied at the Royal College of Organists in London, and when he had first come to the United States it had been to

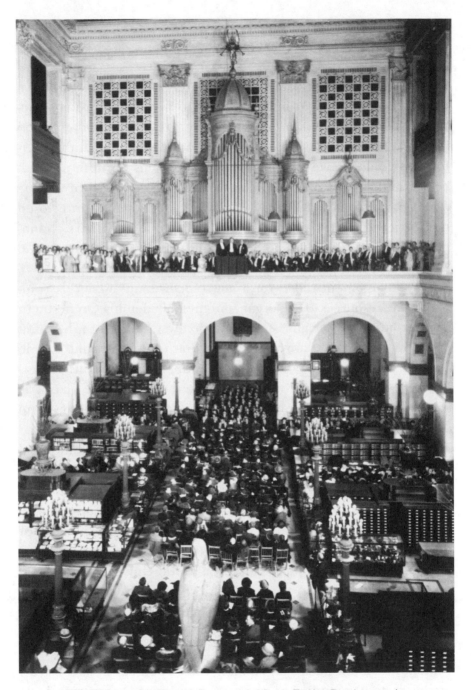

*The Wanamaker Grand Court with Marco Enrico Bossi, organist,
and the Philadelphia Orchestra in a concert on February 4, 1925*

take a job as organist of St. Bartholomew's Church in New York City in 1905. His blue eyes and shock of long blond hair charmed most of the women in that patrician congregation but worried many of the men, including the church's rector, Leighton Parks, whose daughter Ellen briefly fell under the musician's spell. At the 5 P.M. Sunday organ recitals Stokowski established at St. Bartholomew's, programs ranged far beyond sacred music, including transcriptions for organ of whole movements from Tchaikovsky's Fourth and Sixth (*Pathétique*) Symphonies, the overtures to Wagner's *Parsifal* and *Lohengrin,* and the *Ride of the Valkyries,* in addition to Bach. At the end of one of these reveries, "Prince Charming," as some jealous fellow church musicians in New York called him in those early days, would throw his hair back and gaze up at the gilded dome of the church, displaying his aquiline profile for his listeners to admire.

The confines of a church organ loft had become too constricting for a musician who had the ambition to be seen out in the great world, and Stokowski resigned in 1908 to make himself into an orchestral conductor. He was soon hired as one by Cincinnati and then by Philadelphia, whose orchestra he made into one of the greatest in the world. But the musical fascination of Bach's great works for organ remained. Perhaps, as he listened to Courboin play the *Passacaglia* at Wanamaker's in 1919, he was already thinking of the transcription of the piece for orchestra that he would write and that his orchestra would first perform three years later.

Charles-Marie Courboin had come to America the year before Stokowski, in 1904, from Antwerp, and had also started off in New York, as a church organist in Oswego and Syracuse. He, too, cultivated a romantic image, and in the 1920s distributed a press kit that even laid claim to the sort of erotic magnetism that Liszt and Chopin had exemplified at the piano. "He is first and foremost musician," his publicity material announced, "but he combines with that the roles of aviator, motorist, speed-boat pilot, mechanic and fond father. One's first impression of Mr. Courboin is of great virility. He is a tall man, broad-shouldered and slim-hipped. His face, vivid and animated in conversation, in repose is that of the vision-seer, the dreamer, the idealist." This was no self-effacing church organist, but a man's man who aimed literally to be racy, taking flying lessons and driving a Stutz Bearcat and a Lincoln.

Courboin and Stokowski brought electricity to the Wanamaker's event, and at the end the 100 instruments of the Philadelphia Orchestra and the 17,000 pipes of the organ combined to produce what the store's musical director called "a perfect Niagara of sound" in the orchestral arrangement by Widor of his *Sixth Organ Symphony.* "No indoor event of exclusively musical interest was ever attended here by so many persons," the periodical *Musical America* wrote of the event. "It was difficult to determine which was the most impressive, the multitude in this magnificent environment or the billows of opulent sound."

The organ was getting plenty of use. Just in the year following the Stokowski concert of 1919, Courboin played twenty-seven recitals after store-closing hours, and they were attended by an estimated 150,000 people, an impressive number even though the tickets were all free. For Wanamaker's, the organ produced big business as well as big sound. Associating the Wanamaker name with prestige and taste, John and Rodman Wanamaker firmly believed, tens of thousands of those recital audiences would come back to spend money in their store—though they would never say so publicly, of course.

"If anyone asks you if we built this organ for advertising purposes," John Wanamaker, a pious Presbyterian who liked it to be known that he spent the Sabbath teaching Sunday School, said, "tell him I would rather tear the organ down than allow such a thought a place in my mind." But it did not escape Wanamaker that soothing music played on the pipe organs he installed in his stores put people in a mood to buy the things he had for sale. "I can't scarcely make you understand that this big House grew out of a song, and the song of a little Mason and Hamlin Organ," Wanamaker told a convention of organists in 1921, explaining why he had allowed organ pipes to take up so much of the floor space in his big Philadelphia store. "There came out of that little organ so much pleasure to people, that we soon found a larger organ. From that we came to sell church organs, and the pleasure that the people had, not only people that came as purchasers to the store, but the influence it had upon our own people to hear music in the mornings—I think it stopped many little misunderstandings between them. I think it sent people that walked along, who took the store for its convenience to get to another street—it changed the spirit of their minds. . . ."

Nor had Rodman Wanamaker neglected the New York store at Broadway and Ninth Street. When the Austin organ in the auditorium there was damaged by fire, he saved what he could and incorporated it into a new instrument built under Till and Fleming between 1919 and 1921 in the organ shop in the attic of the Philadelphia store.

During business hours, the organists who performed daily concert interludes in the stores were instructed to keep the music soft, perhaps because loud noises would keep the cash registers from jingling. "You must entertain without distracting," Mary E. Vogt, who held the organist job in the Philadelphia store for decades, explained. "If the music is very loud or flamboyant, it will annoy people who after all have come into the store to shop." There were more after-hours musicians' assemblies in February and December 1922, and in a post-Christmas concert that year, Stokowski conducted the orchestra in one of the first performances of his own transcription of the Bach *Passacaglia*.

The giant concerts with organ and orchestra continued through the 1920s, with astounding attendance figures—15,200 people turned up for a "Concert a Cappella" on April 28, 1926, with Stokowski, the violinist Efrem Zimbalist, and Courboin at the organ, which joined the orchestra in a rendition of Tchaikovsky's *1812 Overture*. The concluding number was another Stokowski transcription, of Bach's *Toccata and Fugue in D minor* for organ—a work he conducted fourteen years later in Walt Disney's full-length animated cartoon feature *Fantasia*.

Rodman Wanamaker intended to make Wanamaker's, in both

New York and Philadelphia, premier concert venues, and he sent Alexander Russell to Paris in 1921 to find a brilliant organist to inaugurate the new 117-stop instrument in the New York store. Dr. Russell's old teacher, Widor, recommended his understudy, Marcel Dupré, who gave a private opening recital on November 21 to an invited audience that included the press and the leading virtuosi of the American organ world at the time—Lynnwood Farnam, Clarence Dickinson, T. Tertius Noble, and Courboin among them. The high point of the recital was Dupré's improvisation of a four-movement organ symphony on themes these organists submitted to him on the spot. "A musical miracle," the critic Henry Finck reported on the front page of the *New York Evening Post.*

Two weeks later, Dupré repeated the feat in the Grand Court in Philadelphia, improvising on plainchant melodies and hymns that included *Adeste Fideles* (*O Come, All Ye Faithful*) and, inspired by the sounds of the great organ, deciding "in a flash" to make it a musical depiction of the life of Jesus: "The world awaiting the Savior," "Nativity," "Crucifixion," and "Resurrection." Told what the organist was intending to play, the audience rose to its feet. Dupré improvised, "feeling as I had never felt before." The result, after he set down notes on paper, was what became one of the most moving pieces in modern organ literature, the *Symphonie-Passion,* a sophisticated yet enormously affecting piece of program music that conjures up visions of the Gospel narrative, reaching a dramatic high point with a dissonant chord at the moment of Christ's death on the cross that is then followed by a triumphant toccata on the resurrection theme, the plainchant melody of *Adoro Te Devote,* Aquinas's hymn to the presence of Christ in the Eucharist, "Thee we adore, O hidden Savior, thee, Who in thy Sacrament art pleased to be." All from the inspiration of a cathedral of commerce where the organ, in Ernest Skinner's words, sounded "like a million dollars."

"The organization of these concerts was remarkable," Dupré wrote later in his memoirs. "After the store closed an 'army' of workers arrived. The counters and display cases disappeared, seats were set up everywhere, and a printed program was placed upon each chair. (The concerts were by invitation only; however, all an individual had to do to receive one was to send his name, address, and telephone number to the store. Each family was allowed two seats.) Sometimes there were as many as several thousand listeners."

Dupré returned for a transcontinental U.S. tour in 1922 and played ninety-four concerts, topping the feat in 1923 with 220. Dupré's audience numbers seem staggering today, when organ recitals sometimes draw no more than a few dozen listeners. A 1929 concert tour brought 10,000 people to the Chicago Stadium, 8,000 people to a program with the San Francisco Symphony, 2,000 people to a recital in St. Louis. Dupré did fifty recitals in six weeks, including three to packed houses at the Wanamaker Auditorium in New York.

Louis Vierne, the titular organist of Notre Dame, took issue with Dupré's use of the title "Organist at Notre Dame" on his first American trip—and Dupré did little to disabuse his American audiences of the mistaken notion that *he* actually held that prestigious post. Their relationship never recovered from this blow, but Vierne also drew large audiences on his three-month tour in the United States and Canada in 1927. "As in England, in America the organ is king," he wrote that summer in the French review *Le Courrier Musical*. He told his friend and biographer, Bernard Gavoty, that he had given fifty organ recitals and had been heard by 70,000 people, including 5,800 at the Wanamaker store in Philadelphia—not an unreasonable claim, judging from contemporary newspaper accounts.

By 1924, Rodman Wanamaker had doubled the original size of the instrument in his father's Philadelphia store, but he was not finished. Marcel Dupré had played in the Grand Court again that year and heard Courboin, Stokowski, and the Philadelphia Orchestra conclude the program with a performance of Wagner's *Ride of the Valkyries*. The following day, Rodman Wanamaker asked Dupré and Courboin to travel to New York to see him in his office there. "I have decided to enlarge the organ in my Philadelphia store," he told the two organists. "Work together to draw up a plan for the instrument. Use everything you have ever dreamed about. . . . The organ presently occupies two floors; you have six left!" And what about the budget? Dupré asked. "No limit" was the answer.

In the next few years, with guidance from these and other organists and experts, the organ expanded yet again, acquiring a huge, ancillary "string" section with 6,340 more pipes, stop after stop of narrow metal tubes voiced to sound like violins, violas, and cellos in combinations that could swell, shimmer, and sing like the string section of an orchestra. The massed effect of its eighty-eight ranks of pipes added a dimension to the organ that made it sound like nothing else on earth. These and other additions eventually gave the Grand Court organ a total of 28,482 pipes. Work finally stopped around 1930, with pipes spread out like tree nurseries in room-sized chambers on five different levels and two sides of the Grand Court—rooms that could otherwise have been used for retail display. All of this was controlled by a giant new console built to William B. Fleming's exacting standards, a colossus with six keyboards and a pedalboard, in its own niche up among the fashions on the second selling floor. The console alone was big enough to walk around in, E. Power Biggs said when he saw it; Fleming's associate, George W. Till, asked him where he planned to install the toilet.

Courboin reportedly used to duck inside to take a swig from a hip flask before his concerts, which by 1925 and 1926 had made his popularity the equal of Lemare's. In October 1926, driving his Lincoln home from a service at his church in Scranton, Courboin crashed into a trolley and suffered injuries that forced him to cancel all his concert engagements for the rest of the year. Courboin recovered and resumed cross-country tours that made him well enough known by the 1930s to have a "Courboin cocktail" named after him, and in the 1940s he was heard weekly on NBC radio broadcasts; in 1943 he became organist of St. Patrick's Cathedral in New York City, where he died in 1973.

Big as it was, the Wanamaker organ might have become even bigger if Rodman Wanamaker had not died in March 1928. His father was also dead by then, and his successors would spend the store's

Marcel Dupré at the console of the Wanamaker organ in 1948

money on other things. (The organ in the Grand Court survived after Wanamaker's was sold first to Carter Hawley Hale Stores, then to Woodward & Lothrop, and later to Lord & Taylor, which has maintained it with help from the Friends of the Wanamaker Organ. The organ in the New York auditorium was unceremoniously sold at auction for $1,200 and dismantled in 1955.)

Wanamaker's decision not to proceed with further enlargement opened the way in 1929 for another organ enthusiast, state senator Emerson L. Richards of New Jersey, to design and have built an even bigger pipe organ, the largest and loudest instrument in the world, in the gigantic Atlantic City Convention Hall, at a projected expense to the citizens of Atlantic City of $349,630.

Senator Richards, an organist and serious student of organbuilding who earned a comfortable living as a lawyer, knew what he was doing. He had traveled frequently to Europe to gather technical data on historical instruments there, and he was in frequent correspondence with both Henry Willis III in England and with a former associate of Willis's who had come to America to work with Ernest Skinner: G. Donald Harrison.

Senator Richards convinced the Atlantic City authorities that a huge organ would cost them less over the long run than an orchestra. The monster that he designed was originally planned to have more than 43,000 pipes. Scaled back somewhat after the stock market crash, the organ as built has somewhere between 29,092 and 33,893 pipes of tin, zinc, lead, wood, and brass (there is no exact count)—seven to eight times as many as the biggest "Mighty Wurlitzer" ever built, the Radio City Music Hall organ in New York City, its exact contemporary. "The most fantastically glorious sound I ever heard," the English theater organist Reginald Foort declared of it. To play the Atlantic City colossus required a battery of turbines that roared like a jet airliner and were said to be so hungry for electricity that a call to the local power station had to be made before they could all be turned on. The tonal resources of the organ started with the delicate and clear sounds of a small "unenclosed choir" baroque-inspired division meant to reproduce the clear sounds of the eighteenth-century classics Richards had heard in North Germany and Holland, and ranged all the way to a massive and deafening sonic-boom full organ that would have amazed (or perhaps horrified) Bach and Handel. The console had seven keyboards; the longest pipe, speaking at the lowest C in the pedal, was 64 feet 9 inches long, and the heaviest pipe, standing thirty-two feet high and made entirely of metal, weighed more than a ton. Blasting out over the climax were stentorian "tuba maxima" and "trumpet mirabilis" stops fed by compressed air at five times the highest pressure of most other organs—so high that some of the pipes had to be strapped down.

To hear the behemoth, 41,000 people filled the hall in May 1932, when the builder, the Midmer-Losh Organ Company of Merrick, Long Island, got it as finished as it ever would be—just how finished became the subject of protracted legal wrangling between the city, which was near bankruptcy as the Great Depression took hold, Senator Richards, and the company, which later did go bankrupt.

The senator had succeeded in one thing: building an organ bigger than Wanamaker's. The department store might have frustrated him if it had gone ahead with plans to fit out its instrument with yet another division of pipes in a "Stentor" section, as Courboin wanted, with tuba and fanfare pipes working on high compression and capable of producing blasts as powerful as air horns. Henry Willis III in England was asked for ideas on designing it, but would do the work, he said, only if that part of the organ stood tonally separate from the rest as a "Willis" section. Harrison, for Skinner Organ Co. in Boston, also submitted a draft specification for the Stentor division, but the store let the project die.

The world was changing, and musical tastes were changing. In 1929, the pipe organ, in its orchestral, theater, and residential incarnations, stood near the center of a major part of American musical life. But with the great stock market crash and the depression that followed, everything was different. Gigantic municipal organ projects like Atlantic City's were no longer possible, and soon seemed undesirable. (Although the organ, much damaged by wind and water over the years, is only partially playable, it still exists, and its supporters hope to raise more than $10 million for a restoration after the $100 million renovation of the convention hall, now called Boardwalk Hall.) The market for residence organs collapsed, not to revive until electronic home organs became popular decades later. Pipe organs in homes were no longer affordable, not only because of the advent of high income taxes that made even millionaires think twice about buying ersatz orchestras for their homes, but also because improving radio and phonograph technology made it unnecessary to buy an imitation orchestra when an approximation of the real thing could be heard on the radio and on records. As for theater organs, they were doomed from the moment *The Jazz Singer,* the first of the "talkies," appeared in 1927. By 1931, movies had sound tracks with orchestras playing music that was written for films. Leopold Stokowski and the Philadelphia Orchestra didn't have to play in the Wanamaker store anymore; they could play sound tracks for Walt Disney, to a much bigger and broader audience. The only place the organ remained indispensable was the church. In this context, in the 1930s, G. Donald Harrison made an indelible mark on the history of the pipe organ in America—not at Wanamaker's expense, as it turned out, but, in an entirely different meaning of the word, at Ernest M. Skinner's.

G. Donald Harrison and
Aeolian-Skinner:
The American Classic Organ

Ernest M. Skinner's financial alliance in 1919 with the rubber industry millionaire Arthur H. Marks had left him free to pursue the art instead of the business of organbuilding. Through the Roaring Twenties, Skinner was at the top of his game, and, coast to coast, it seemed that every church and concert hall worthy of the name wanted a Skinner organ. But his sometimes lackadaisical attitude toward the practicalities of the business annoyed his new principal partner. Skinner came back from one business trip with measurements for a new job marked with numbers that seemed too low to his chief drafting engineer, A. Perry Martin, who said, "Well, Mr. Skinner, this can't be feet." Skinner's response was, "Oh God, no! Those are the lengths of my umbrella and—I lost the damned umbrella!"

When Skinner's son, Richmond, graduated from California Institute of Technology in 1923 and Skinner proposed hiring him as his assistant, Marks agreed, suggesting a salary of $35 a week. Young Skinner wrote his father in reply that he was about to get married, and all his classmates were getting starting salaries of $50 a week, which would be more like it for a young man about to get married, as he was. Ernest Skinner took the letter and showed it to Marks, who was incensed. Later, out of Skinner's earshot, Marks remarked,

"I've had enough of the Skinners," and decided "that man will never work for us."

Richmond Skinner went off to work on a dam construction project in Maryland. Marks apparently thought Richmond's father could learn a thing or two from a return visit to the Willis firm in England, and in early March 1924 Skinner and Marks sailed from New York City on the steamship Olympic. They spent a week with the head of the Willis company, Henry Willis III, grandson of "Father" Henry Willis, the founder, whom Skinner had met on his first trip in 1898.

Willis organs in the early twentieth century had a characteristic ensemble sound that was partly due to the use of mixtures—stops with three, four, five, or even more ranks of pipes, one per rank for every one of the notes on the keyboard—to reinforce the natural harmonics of other stops to create a clearer, richer sound. Skinner visited and heard Willis and other organs in Liverpool, Bristol, York, Leeds, and London, where Willis's assistant G. Donald Harrison—his "able lieutenant," in Skinner's words—took him to see the large organ the company was building in Westminster Cathedral. Skinner told Willis later that the chorus mixture in that instrument gave him "a real thrill," and alone justified his trip to England.

On March 22, Skinner continued on to France to visit Joseph Bonnet, the titular organist of Saint-Eustache, and Louis Vierne, organist of Notre Dame, and filmed home movies of both Charles-Marie Widor and Marcel Dupré at Saint-Sulpice. The French organs, in spacious acoustics, produced some sublime sounds, Skinner wrote later in *Stop, Open and Reed,* but imagine what a fine Skinner organ might sound like in one of these resonating cathedrals—and how much easier it would be for an organist to play compared with the inconceivably awkward nineteenth-century French consoles.

Skinner returned to Boston in April. Over the next few years, he corresponded frequently with Henry Willis III, who was interested in Skinner's electropneumatic key action and in some of his patented orchestral stops, the French horn first among them. From their letters, it is clear that Willis thought Skinner had more to learn from Willis trumpets, trombones, and mixtures than Willis had to learn from Skinner's flute celestes and erzählers. What Willis wanted from Skinner was technology—the switches and magnets and other products of American ingenuity that made Skinner consoles such models of practical design.

Skinner had learned a great deal from his second European trip, for the organs he built afterward produced music with a new clarity and sense of ensemble that came in large measure from the new Willis-type stops he began putting in his instruments, starting with one he built for Jefferson Avenue Presbyterian Church in Detroit in 1926. There were others, equally memorable, built for Trinity Church and for Temple Emanu-El, both in San Francisco (the Temple organ had a Shofar stop); Trinity Church in Boston's Copley Square; the Toledo Museum of Art, and even the Holy Trinity Episcopal Cathedral in Havana, ordered in 1926. "The most serious problem to overcome is to find an organ that is proof against wood lice, called in Cuba 'Comejen' which ultimately gets into all soft woods and eats them away," the church leadership wrote to Skinner, asking him to use nothing but Cuban cedar and mahogany—too hard for the bugs to bite into—which the church would supply. Skinner provided a small organ for $7,950.

In America, young musicians such as Aaron Copland, Elliott Carter, Walter Piston, and Virgil Thomson had returned from studies in Europe with new theories about harmony and composition from Nadia Boulanger, the most influential music teacher of the early twentieth century and herself a fine organist. Copland met Melville Smith, a young organist from Cleveland, in Boulanger's salon and learned about the organ's range and limitations from the two of them. When Boulanger learned in early 1924 that the great Russian conductor Serge Koussevitzky, then in Paris, was going to lead the Boston Symphony Orchestra the next year, she took Copland along to visit, and Koussevitzky, impressed with the composition young Copland played for him, commissioned a symphony for organ: "*You* vill write an organ concerto, Mademoiselle Boulanger vill *play* it and *I* vill conduct!"

The symphony, Copland's first, had its premiere on January 11, 1925, but in New York, not in Boston, with the New York Symphony Orchestra under the baton of Walter Damrosch—with Nadia Boulanger at the console of the Aeolian organ in Aeolian Hall. The 1,352-seat auditorium, where George Gershwin's *Rhapsody in Blue* had had its premiere the year before, had the largest pipe organ of any concert hall in the city, with seventy-six ranks of pipes.

Copland was thrilled to hear his own work for the first time. It was an astounding achievement—a four-movement symphony that started off calmly enough, with an organ motif that was almost a riff on the children's song *Au Clair de la Lune,* taken up and complicated by the orchestra, eventually to rollicking rhythms with a jazz accent and clashing dissonances. After it was over, Damrosch told the audience, famously, "Ladies and gentlemen, I am sure you will agree that if a gifted young man can write a symphony like this at twenty-three—within five years he will be ready to commit murder!"

Later, Copland arranged the work for orchestra alone as *Symphony No. 1*. It established him as one of the great modern American classical composers. But when Boulanger did play the organ symphony in Boston, with Koussevitzky, on the old organ that Ernest Skinner had installed for George S. Hutchings in Symphony Hall, things did not go smoothly. One of the organ notes ciphered, sticking "on" with a loud and jarring honk that forced the orchestra to stop so that technicians could make repairs.

Melville Smith and other American organists had also come back to the United States wondering why antique European organs sounded so much brighter, clearer, and more articulate than newer instruments at home. The young organists were also influenced by the organ reform movement in Germany, which aimed to strip romantic encrustations from the clean and classical baroque organ-building ideals.

Ernest Skinner and his associates were not deaf to such complaints, nor to the advice they were getting from people like Willis, who came to the United States and Canada in 1924, visited the Skinner, Hook & Hastings, and Austin factories, and heard organs from Montreal to Philadelphia, including the Wanamaker instrument.

"Tonally, I must confess, I was disappointed on the whole with the effect of organs in the States," Willis wrote in an article for *Stop, Open and Reed* in 1925. "The pernicious teachings of Hope-Jones would seem to have had a deplorable effect upon tone production which is only now being overcome, the result being instruments representing a mere collection of stops without any true ensemble. Specifications also seem to be drawn up in too many cases without due regard to the fact that an organ should be an organ first, last and all the time—not a heterogeneous collection of solo voices, however charming." Willis aimed some of his criticism directly at Skinner, who had tried to brighten up his latest instruments with more powerful mixtures and treble stops than he had used in the past, but otherwise thought he was on the right track.

"To be quite candid," Willis wrote to Skinner in May 1925, "you don't get a *true* ensemble and won't until you adopt the necessary design, forms of construction, and voicing that are necessary to obtain this result. To merely add proper mixtures is not sufficient though a step in the right direction. I have got a lot from you mechanically and I want you to *get* all I can give you tonally."

But Willis's attitude changed after a second visit to the United States later that year. In May 1926, Willis wrote privately to George L. Catlin, a businessman whom Marks had brought in as Skinner Organ Company's treasurer: "Skinner is hopeless and, I am afraid, will not progress. It is the same old trouble, 'You can't teach an old dog new tricks.' What you need is somebody to take Skinner's place when he is away and be in charge of the artistic side of production in Boston. I wrote to Bill [the other vice president of the firm, the organist William Zeuch] and said that my chap Harrison would 'fill the bill'—what about it?"

G. (George) Donald Harrison had quiet presence, "six feet tall and a little over, about the correct weight, slightly sandy and somewhat curly hair, . . . mild-mannered and soft-spoken, with much of

G. Donald Harrison, Skinner Organ Company's assistant general manager, around 1929

the English manner left in his speaking," as *The American Organist* later described him. "In a crowd it will be the others who do the talking. He's an English gentleman, not an American go-getter." But in his quiet way, he helped start a revolution in the American organbuilding world, a rejection of excess in favor of cleaner lines that was in the spirit of what Frank Lloyd Wright was doing in architecture and Ernest Hemingway in literature at the same time.

"Don" Harrison, thirty-seven years old at the time of Willis's letter, was born in Huddersfield, in Yorkshire, on April 29, 1889. He had grown up with English organs, learning how to play well enough to become assistant organist in the chapel at his boarding school, Dulwich College near London. After graduating, he tried unsuccessfully to get a job with the T. C. Lewis organbuilding firm, where he was discouraged with the warning "There is no money in it." So Harrison went to work as a patent agent with his father and also took an apprenticeship to learn mechanical engineering, which he described to Skinner as "my second love." But he kept up his music studies, taking lessons with Arthur Pearson, the city organist of Huddersfield, who presided over a four-keyboard nineteenth-century organ that "Father" Willis had built in the Town Hall.

Harrison met Henry Willis III just before World War I, when both men were called into military service; Harrison went to the Royal Air Force and served for three years in its Sixth Brigade. After the war, he joined the Willis company as an assistant to the director, learning voicing methods and studying notable organs around England with Willis and with J. Stuart Archer, a well-known organist with whom E. Power Biggs later studied in London.

The Harrison family spent part of the summer in the French fishing village of Saint-Valéry-en-Caux, where Marcel Dupré also summered, and Harrison became well acquainted with the famous French organist there. By the late 1920s, Harrison had visited France often enough to be thoroughly familiar with the characteristics of Cavaillé-Coll organs. He had also been named a director of the Willis firm. Harrison was married to Dora Lang, the daughter of a prominent London musician, and, with her and their two sons, Michael and Stephen, to support, he was looking for a way to ensure financial security for his family. But he also knew that his star in the Willis family business would probably stop rising as soon as Henry Willis III sired a Henry Willis IV—which indeed Willis had done by the time he wrote the letter to Catlin, for Henry Willis IV was born on January 19, 1927.

That spring, Arthur Hudson Marks went to England, interviewed Harrison, and offered him a job in Boston. Catlin sent a formal proposal to Willis in June, after Harrison had come for a short look at the factory. "We of course could not pay any fancy salary without also making trouble," Catlin wrote, "but his future would be dependent pretty much on himself and, from all accounts, his ability would have a tendency to make him more and more valuable as time goes on."

Harrison sailed again for the United States on July 5, 1927. "Harrison will help you guide Skinner's feet which stray from the straight and narrow path," Willis wrote Zeuch, apparently seeing an opportunity to spread his own ideas about organbuilding and enhance his company's reputation, through Harrison, in the new and vast market of the United States. Willis was confident, as Harrison later put it, that Harrison would "influence the Skinner people to build imitations of the Willis organ." If Skinner was aware of these threats to his position and on his artistry, he gave no outward sign of it. He wrote a glowing portrait of his new associate, then assistant general manager of the firm, printed as an open letter to *The Diapason* early in 1928 and later reproduced by *Stop, Open and Reed.*

"Mr. Harrison is destined to be a great figure in the art of organ building in America," Skinner wrote. "He is a modern by temperament and inclination. His musical taste is of the highest order. . . . My confidence in his judgment stands at 100 per cent, which is somewhat better than I rate my own, to be perfectly frank about it."

Harrison returned the compliment, praising the mechanical perfection of devices like the pitman chest and commenting on the "wonderful orchestral imitative stops" and the "exquisite and colorful soft work" found in Skinner organs.

"On the other hand, admitting this wealth of orchestral color it seems strange to find in the traditional voices which are peculiar to the organ, a paucity of color not only in the individual stops but by the omission of upperwork," he observed, referring to the comparative absence in American organs of high-pitched treble pipes that lent clarity and definition to the separate voices in contrapuntal music. "Only recently I was reading a criticism of an organ recital in which it was lamented that the inner parts in the tenor of a certain composition were inaudible or obscure. It was intimated that this was a fundamental defect in the organ. It may be so in many modern instruments, but need not be so, and certainly was not so when Bach wrote his great works."

Already in this essay, published in early 1929, G. Donald Harrison made clear that he had a different kind of organ sound in his head than the blended orchestral tone that people associated with Skinner. People would soon begin to notice that the Harrison sound was brighter, clearer, more assertive, better capable of articulating the inner voices of contrapuntal works like Bach's fugues. Harrison's aim, he wrote, was organs with a coherent tonal and harmonic ensemble composed of pipes "so voiced, scaled and regulated that when combined together they produce one single tone of

Ernest Skinner in the experimental voicing room of his factory in
Dorchester, Massachusetts

great clarity, brilliance and transparency the various units fit together something like the pieces of a jig-saw puzzle and present a
perfectly blended picture to the listener."

The organs Skinner built before he met Harrison on his second
trip to England could often sound muddled in contrapuntal music
and, though grand and majestic, their overall tone was dark. Under
Harrison's influence, Skinner continued adding mixtures to some
of his tonal designs to lend them a somewhat brighter character
without changing the basic concept.

Harrison was careful at first about expressing criticism of Skinner's work. "The ideal instrument seems to be a combination of the
properly designed, produced and finished classical organ with the
new, beautiful and subtle tones which have been produced in this
country," Harrison wrote in the 1929 essay. "The Skinner Company
believes in it and intends to follow this policy already begun and
placed on a firm foundation."

The collaboration had started off well enough. Harrison and Skinner worked together on a large instrument for the University of Michigan in 1928, Skinner remarking on the success of "some fine reproductions of the best English and French reeds and mixtures, which (to say the least) have not suffered under the American technique," and by the Skinner Company's count, 5,000 people came to hear the dedication concert that May 15. Together, Harrison and Skinner designed and built two other notable instruments that year, one in Princeton University's Gothic chapel and the other in Rockefeller Memorial Chapel at the University of Chicago.

The Princeton organ was regarded as the first one in which Harrison's distinctive musical voice could be heard. Perhaps Harrison remembered how the Willis firm used chartered trains to lure London organists and critics to hear its new organs in other cities, for the Skinner Organ Company chartered private railroad cars from New York City and Philadelphia and brought in an audience to hear the Princeton instrument on October 13, at the hands of a gaggle of famous organists, including Ralph Downes, Courboin, Lynnwood Farnam, and the Italian virtuoso Fernando Germani. In November, Marcel Dupré played a recital on it, sending a handwritten note of praise on the 20th, not to Harrison but to Skinner, who often solicited such testimonials to use as advertisements for the company. "My dear Mr. Skinner," Dupré wrote from the Royal York Hotel in Toronto, "it is a great pleasure for me to congratulate you for your magnificent organ at the Princeton University Chapel. I experienced the highest artistic joy playing a recital on it."

Skinner felt the need to reassure Harrison—"I want to say right here that I hold your contribution to the quality of that great instrument to be such that my opinion of you as an artist, publicly and privately expressed, is more than justified," he wrote his associate on the 23rd, but he kept (indeed, he may have solicited) another personal note from Dupré that December praising "that recent masterpiece of yours, the Princeton organ."

Perhaps Skinner was only now beginning to realize the full implications of what he had done in 1919 when he had accepted Arthur

Marks as company president. He had lost all control over the business that bore his name, and competitors were beginning to use his reduced influence against him. When the huge new Riverside Church in New York City bypassed Skinner Organ Company to give Hook & Hastings a $64,275 contract in 1926, Skinner wrote to the church's main financial backer, John D. Rockefeller Jr., a letter that gives a hint of his feelings:

"I am told by someone connected with the office of the architects of your new church building that the Skinner Company were considered with respect to the new organ, but were passed by on the strength of the impression that has gone out that I am personally no longer actively connected with the Skinner Company and that the work 'is not what it used to be'; that the business has been commercialized," he wrote. "If any such report as this had any weight with you, I wish to say that there is no foundation for these stories. I never was more actively connected with the technical end of the Skinner product than I am at the present moment. I wish further to say that the quality of our work was never so good as it is in present. . . . These stories have undoubtedly cost the Skinner Company a million dollars worth of business in the last five years and were started and broadcast by the most unethical set of salesmen on the face of the earth."

It wasn't the business that was the problem. Business kept coming in, even in 1929, with sixty-three organs completed and new orders still coming in after the stock market crash. But tension was beginning to build between Skinner and Harrison as their visions diverged. They worked together on a major rebuild of the organ in Woolsey Hall at Yale University in 1928 and 1929. The resulting organ incorporated some of the work of the two previous builders—Hutchings, Skinner's previous employer who had built the first organ in the hall in 1902, and J. W. Steere and Sons, who enlarged it in 1915. (The Steere factory in Westfield, Massachusetts had been taken over by the Skinner Company in 1920 after a fire.)

Skinner and Harrison added 7,580 pipes to the 2,899 by Hutchings and the 2,138 by Steere in the Yale organ, but revoiced some and changed the overall tonal balance. The result was an instrument with more than 12,000 pipes that was regarded as a great orchestral organ, a *Skinner* masterpiece. But Skinner was not amused when Prof. Harry Jepson, in charge of overseeing the progress of the work for the university, suggested that it would go faster and more smoothly if he would "stay away and let Mr. Harrison finish the organ."

There was more trouble when organists started to ask Harrison to "improve" some of Skinner's earlier organs, like the one he had built in Harvard's Appleton Chapel in 1912. The Harvard authorities wanted to brighten up the sound and bring it up to date with the new man's new ideas, but Skinner fought them. "If that Great Diapason No. 1 is changed," he wrote Prof. Archibald Davison, who was overseeing the work at Harvard, "it will be over my dead body." What might have seemed heavy and overpowering to Davison was "warm" to Skinner's ears, and besides, he thought, organs should be able to play something besides contrapuntal music. "Youngsters," he lamented, "read up on these points and get the old world idea of an ensemble, also that of a contrapuntal specialist, and have nothing in common with the ear that loves a beautiful tone on account of its beauty. After all is said and done, I have put what you call a friendly characteristic in the organ which has given to it something of the warmth and temperamental qualities of other instruments. I have never agreed with the idea that the organ should be cold and unsympathetic. . . ." Harvard was unsatisfied with Skinner's performance on the contract and withheld $3,000 from the final payment in 1931. Marks asked Harrison to "straighten things out," but a year later Harvard did that by deciding to demolish the building and construct a new Memorial Church in Harvard Yard, and with it, a large new organ—but one designed by Harrison. (The old E. M. Skinner instrument was removed before the chapel was torn down and was eventually sold to Allin Congregational Church in Dedham, Massachusetts.)

Skinner, growing increasingly frustrated, began thinking of leaving the company and starting anew in partnership with his son,

Richmond. When an organ company in Methuen, Massachusetts, came up for sale in 1929, Skinner thought he had found the deliverance he was hoping for.

The organ factory in Methuen was attached to one of the most glorious follies in the American organ world, a cruciform English-baroque auditorium as big as a Christopher Wren church. Edward F. Searles, an interior decorator who had married the widow of Mark Hopkins in San Francisco and then inherited her millions upon her death only four years later, had constructed this auditorium in Methuen, calling it Serlo Hall after himself, to house a huge and famous organ that he had acquired. It was built by E. F. Walcker & Cie. of Ludwigsburg, Germany, between 1857 and 1862 to be the musical centerpiece of the old Boston Music Hall, and brought over during the Civil War on the Dutch brig *Presto,* in a rather largo voyage lengthened by the need to evade Confederate vessels. Installation in Boston began in the spring of 1863, with the organ encased in American black walnut, with sculpted muscular Hercules figures groaning to hold up the great burnished-tin pipes of the façade. It was an imposing and overwhelming sight, and it produced a mighty sound, with Boston's finest German-trained musicians, including the leading American composer of the day, John Knowles Paine, of Harvard, performing at the dedication.

But time and tastes changed. The new Boston Symphony Orchestra, founded in 1881, tried to take center stage in the Music Hall but found itself playing second fiddle to the organ. So, in 1884, the organ was expelled and put into storage. There it remained after the new Boston Symphony Hall opened on Huntington Avenue in 1900, until Searles bought the organ at auction and built the hall in Methuen to enshrine it in all its solo glory.

Now it was Skinner's turn to make this instrument his own. He sold most of his shares in the Skinner Organ Company and bought concert hall, Walcker organ, and Methuen Organ Company lock, stock, and barrel, asking his son to join him as partner in a new business. He did not tell Richmond that the Essex Savings Bank held title to the concert hall as security for a $50,000 mortgage.

Mabel Skinner, who knew how fragile the family finances were, was appalled at what her husband had done, and feared even worse. "Richmond, your father cannot afford at this time to leave the Skinner Organ Company. Please don't let him," she told her son.

As Skinner later wrote to his client the cornflakes king W. K. Kellogg in Battle Creek, Michigan, the action had the desired shock effect on his partners. "When Marks found this out there was a great reversal of behavior," Skinner wrote. "Much repentence [*sic*] was expressed and I was told that if I would remain where I was their attitude would be satisfactory and that if I left the stock of the company would not be worth over $5.00 a share. I was, therefore, talked out of my plans to leave and signed a contract with them for five years more." At this time, in January 1931, Skinner stock was selling at $36. According to Richmond Skinner, Marks drew up a new five-year contract and paid Skinner $5,000 a year, basically so that the company could keep using the Skinner name even if in fact Skinner now had little to do with it. "He was not forbidden to enter the doors, but he didn't have to. He could do whatever he wanted," his son told Skinner's biographer, Dorothy Holden, years later. Skinner had to agree that Methuen Organ Company would not compete with Skinner in the building of new organs but would confine its work to rebuilding old ones.

But, with a mortgage on a new house in the tony Chestnut Hill neighborhood of suburban Boston and with Serlo Hall to keep up in Methuen, Skinner was in bad financial shape. Skinner Organ Company, despite Marks's success in persuading Skinner not to withdraw, was also beginning to stagger as the Great Depression took hold. In 1931, the company installed only twenty-seven new organs, with work proceeding on important projects like a large and majestic instrument at Girard College in Philadelphia. But for the American organbuilding industry as a whole, not just for Skinner, boom was turning to bust. The wealthy were feeling the crunch and cut down on donations; church budgets shrank. The residence-organ market, which the Aeolian Company had all but monopolized in America, simply evaporated. Pipe organs in homes were suddenly an unthinkable luxury even for millionaires. And "talkies" had killed the theater-organ market. Skinner Organ Co.'s net earnings after expenses, more than $271,000 in 1928, shrank to $10,670 in 1931. Arthur Hudson Marks had joked, seven years earlier, "I came to the conclusion that organ building was not inviting as an occupation for profit." But now it was no joke. Something had to be done.

Given the difficulties, Marks engineered a merger of Skinner Organ Company and the pipe organ division of Aeolian in January 1932, when the Aeolian-Skinner Organ Company, Inc., was born. "We wish to state emphatically that this is not a step in the direction of big business, trusts or monopolies," Marks and Skinner said in a joint letter to *The Diapason* magazine that month. "On the contrary, we are firm in the opinion, which we have often expressed in your columns, that the field for the highest quality is limited; that artistic merit and big business do not get on well together." Both companies maintained their showrooms, complete with demonstration organs, in New York City—Skinner's studio at 677 Fifth Avenue and Aeolian's up the avenue at 689, where it had moved from West Forty-second Street in 1927. Despite appearances, the transaction was less a merger of equals than a takeover of Aeolian by the more powerful Skinner company, which owned 60 percent of Aeolian-Skinner stock and whose factory in Dorchester, Massachusetts, became Aeolian-Skinner's headquarters.

For Marks, the main point of the acquisition may well have been the Aeolian player mechanism, against which Skinner's had never made real commercial headway. Besides Aeolian's "Duo-Art" mechanism and the earlier, less technologically advanced versions of it, Aeolian-Skinner probably coveted an even greater treasure—the hundreds of player rolls that had been recorded by famous artists. Prominent organists such as Courboin, Joseph Bonnet, Dupré, Archer Gibson, and Vierne left behind recorded performances of their own works and popular music by others. Their virtuoso displays of talent, often lavished on mediocre transcriptions of popular orchestral music, were instantly reproducible on any residence organ that had the right player equipment, and there were also rolls of original music written for the Aeolian organ by popular composers, including Victor Herbert and Camille Saint-Saëns.

But in 1932 it was already clear that both the player mechanism and the library of recordings made for it were inexorably on their way to obsolescence. The high income taxes that the New Deal introduced to alleviate the misery of millions as a result of the depression ended millionaires' excesses. Besides, ordinary people could listen to Victor Herbert on Victrolas by now, and the sound quality of these record players was getting better all the time.

In churches and concert halls, Aeolian-Skinner soon became the preeminent name in American organbuilding, producing instruments with an assertively clear tonal architecture that, once heard, was hard to forget. Harrison's aim was to produce organs with a "clarified ensemble" that, even with many stops playing at once, contrasted with the thick and muddy effect so often characteristic of earlier American organs, including Skinner's. If what made a Skinner organ stand out was the beauty of its individual solo orchestral stops, the trademark Harrison sound began with this idea of ensemble.

One organbuilding shop could thus turn out instruments that sounded very different from one another—such is the alchemy of the organbuilder's art. Skinner had his ideas of how pipes should be shaped and what sort of metals and woods they should be made from, how high the wind pressure should be for a trumpet stop or for a principal chorus. Harrison had other ideas—experimenting with lower wind pressures and different metal alloys for milder tone, changing the "scaling" of principal and mixture stops, the relationship between the length and cross-section of the pipes, to reinforce harmonic development in a way that would improve the clarity of the melodic line. On what stops an organ must have, and how they should be distributed in the various divisions, Harrison also differed with Skinner, though of course on all these questions each organ was different, and in every case the customer also had a voice; organists had their own firm notions of how they wanted their instruments to sound.

Harrison had something new to say in the music world of the 1930s, and more and more organists were asking Harrison, not Skinner, to be in charge of designing and finishing Aeolian-Skinner installations. Harrison had also experimented in an organ he installed at Trinity College Chapel in Hartford, Connecticut, in 1931, and the following year, at the Church of Saint Mary the Virgin, a cathedral-sized resonant space on West Forty-sixth Street in Manhattan, where he strove for "a return to the principles of the classic organ, the organ of the Thomas-Kirche and the older French and German builders." While the Saint Mary the Virgin organ, far from complete when the organist Palmer Christian played the first recital on it in January 1933, certainly sounded quite unlike the German baroque organ Bach had at his disposal at the Thomaskirche in Leipzig, an organ that had disappeared long before Donald Harrison was even born, it was also very different from any organ Ernest Skinner had ever designed, with high-pitched pipes and mixtures intended to lend clarity and tonal pungency to the ensemble.

The Saint Mary the Virgin organ—much modified and expanded by Harrison ten years later, and again long after his death—sounded very different from all the others in New York City at the time, and the first eight recitals drew capacity audiences in the vast and reverberant space of the neo-Gothic church. But Skinner hated the way it sounded—"shrill" and harsh to his ears, which he blocked with his fingers at one recital. In a letter to Marks, he criticized some of the reed stops that made Harrison's work so distinctive, the sharp, incisive trumpets and French-inspired bombardes that, instead of the wooden resonators that Skinner favored for their mellow tones, used metal ones. "They were bad musically, and they were causing criticism," Skinner complained.

Skinner insisted that his style had earned the respect of some of the greatest musicians of the day. Vierne had dedicated his *Claire de Lune* to Skinner in 1927, and in 1932 Sigfrid Karg-Elert, Max Reger's successor as professor of composition at the Leipzig Conservatory, had stayed with the Skinners on a trip to the United States, much to Mabel Skinner's annoyance when she found that their distinguished visitor had been smoking in bed and simply tossing the butts onto the new rug she had installed in the guest room in his honor.

But Marks had bet his company's future on Harrison's work. "I am particularly sorry that you persist in the patently erroneous idea that no one but yourself ever has contributed or ever can contribute to the success of the Company," he wrote to Skinner, also criticizing him for excessive travel expenses, for example by running up hotel bills in New York City when he could have used the accommodations in the company showroom.

Skinner was outraged. On May 31, 1932, he protested to Marks, "Why can't Harrison sell Skinner organs? The public think they are going to get Skinner organs when they come to us, and the Skinner quality. What do you want to knock it down for? . . . I think it is an outrage that another man is invited into this organization after all the years I have worked somewhere and put on a par with me and allowed to thrust his ideas into the thing in spite of my wishes, when my wishes are based wholly on preserving the name for the quality that I produced." He resented being put in the position, Skinner wrote again on June 3, of being "a stool pigeon, a cat's paw, a figurehead to attract business, which position I decline to accept." And on June 6, in yet another letter, he told Marks, "You don't want harmony—you promote discord. You are responsible for all the trouble I ever had with Harrison. We got along perfectly before you put him up to going over my head."

That November, more discreetly but still openly, Skinner began making his disagreements with Harrison public. He wrote, in *The Diapason*, "I do not see the point in making a fetish of ensemble and setting it against solo or orchestral voices. It is another vogue of the moment, making the usual mistake of glorifying the past to the disparagement of the present. When we say modern orchestral voices must be thrown out and a return made to the time when transcriptions were taboo because the organ was cold and unresponsive, we undo everything that has been done to give the organ an increased vocabulary, warmth, and make it a really responsive instrument." As to whether "modern" organs could do justice to Bach, of course they could, in Skinner's view; he also thought the old master would have written different music if he had had the resources of the twentieth-century organ, and it was unenlightened to think it necessary to return to the pre-electricity past to play Bach correctly. "P.S.—Bach had no telephone," he added.

Skinner had never liked the North German and Dutch instruments he had heard, in dank, unheated churches when they were probably wildly out of tune. His attitude toward the organ was thoroughly American, with the brash confidence that came from being self taught. Electrification, console design, the smooth voicing of Skinner's organs—all these were advances that in his view left the musty past, Europe and the baroque, in the dust of history. *Stop, Open and Reed* had been proudly subtitled "A periodical presentation of pipe organ progress." "The organ as I first heard it, and as I occasionally see surviving examples, was a shrill, cold affair, inexpressive to the last degree—hardly a musical instrument," Skinner wrote in *The Diapason* in August 1933; "the organ of today is devotional, churchly, vital and filled with tonal charm."

But by then Skinner was spitting against the wind. In June 1933, on business in California, he found that the contract Aeolian-Skinner had signed for a new organ in Grace Cathedral in San Francisco specified that Harrison personally was to supervise construction and installation. After Skinner apparently tried to get that stipulation removed, Marks, infuriated, ordered him back east.

Things had deteriorated to such a point by mid-1933 that on July 14 Marks wrote an extraordinary directive to Skinner, now sixty-seven years old, in the tone a scolding father might use towards a reprobate youth:

"Unless otherwise directed, in writing, from time to time by George Catlin or myself, you are to remain in Boston or at your summer camp in New Hampshire, or if desired by you and agreed to by Mr. Catlin or myself, elsewhere," Marks wrote. "You are to come to the factory or elsewhere, for consultation or other service when—but only when—directed by Mr. Catlin or myself. You are to travel in the service of the Company when directed by Mr. Catlin and myself and not otherwise." He concluded with threats to hold Skinner responsible for damages suffered by the company if he talked with competitors, which Skinner was forbidden to do under pain of losing his salary. Crowning Skinner's downfall, Marks then appointed Harrison to be technical director and chief of the Aeolian-Skinner staff.

"I have done everything in my power to keep E. M. on the pedestal and to avoid humiliating him," Marks explained a few days later. "It has not been possible to get him to realize that he went over the top a few years ago and has been slipping since that time. . . . He himself chose to try and hold the limelight and apparently felt that he could oust Harrison. . . . The fact is that Harrison has arrived and is today in the limelight as a result of his achievements. Neither E. M. nor the Company can keep E. M. in the center of the stage."

Skinner was effectively frozen out of the company that bore his name, associated with it now in name only. But it was not only at Aeolian-Skinner that tastes were changing. To the romantic-orchestral organ that Skinner had built in the Cleveland Museum of Art in 1922, the young Cleveland organbuilder Walter Holtkamp added in 1933 something new and revolutionary—a small rückpositiv division designed along German classical lines. Though technically the term applied only to that part of a baroque organ that was detached from the rest and behind the organist's back, typically in the gallery of a church, Holtkamp's imitation was freestanding, playable via electropneumatic connections to the organ console, but its clear-speaking high-pitched stops were intended to produce a brighter tonality than the rest of Skinner's organ had. The addition produced much comment among organists and other builders, and it was seen as another blow to Skinner's now old-hat notion that an organ should try to imitate an orchestra. At an organists' convention, Holden's biography relates, Holtkamp saw Skinner standing alone, ignored now that he had gone out of fashion, and thought, "Now, this is a perfect shame! There stands one of the greatest figures in the art of organ-building, and all those sissies are afraid to go up to speak to him, for fear they might lose face among their peers!" As Holtkamp told the story to Robert Baker, an organist friend, he went up to Skinner and said, "Mr. Skinner, I am Walter Holtkamp from Cleveland, and I just want to thank you for all you have meant and done for the art of organ-building through your splendid career." Apparently, "Cleveland" was all that registered on Skinner, who was by then hard of hearing, and rejoined, "Cleveland! Say, you know, I have one of my best organs out there in the Art Museum, and some damn fool has come along and just ruined it."

Skinner, with his patrician features and a mane of white hair, was beginning to resemble David Lloyd George, Britain's beleaguered prime minister during World War I, and in fact was rather proud of the likeness. His face-saving contract with Aeolian-Skinner expired in January 1936, and this time he was ready to try to strike out on his own again. With Richmond Skinner at last as his partner, he started the Ernest M. Skinner & Son Company, and opened the factory doors in Methuen to orders for new organs.

He had independence again now, but money worries forced him to move with his wife into a smaller house in Chestnut Hill. "Do you ever stop to think how much the need to make a living delays advance in art and science?" he wrote a friend. "If I could devote all my time to development of the organ I would make something so much finer than I have ever done that you wouldn't believe it. But no; I have to plug to support myself and half a dozen others. So I only build 'em pretty good."

Skinner still had his admirers, and he enjoyed one last spectacular success, securing a contract for a large organ with 120 stops in the National Cathedral in Washington, D.C., that was dedicated in the fall of 1938. After the opening concert, one reviewer wrote, "Three thousand music-lovers attended the dedication of the great organ at the Washington Cathedral last night. They heard one of the greatest instruments in the world today in so far as its capacities, ordinary and unusual, could be demonstrated in a program of less than an hour's duration, and left with the conviction that they had touched another world of sound and beauty so vast that its possibilities exceed finite imagination."

Even that organ, great as it was, would later be tonally revised and rebuilt by Aeolian-Skinner. And undertaking so great a project had been a strain on Skinner's limited finances. To the sense of victimization by a business cycle that had been especially unkind to an organbuilder who was a better artist than a businessman was added an old man's bitter resentment at having been shoved aside, a predicament that was by now evident even to outsiders.

Skinner, of course, saw no fault in his own stubborn cantankerousness, which had always been both his greatest asset and his worst liability. "My only handicap is insufficient capital which the Aeolian-Skinner Company helped to bring about as far as they could," Skinner wrote in 1941 to W. K. Kellogg, who had bought one of his house organs that year. He was hoping for an infusion of $10,000 to help him and his son make a success of their new business, but in reply, Kellogg sent only sympathy. "It seems too bad that a man of your experience and ability should have been crowded out of the old company," he wrote Skinner.

Aeolian-Skinner was also struggling. Marks's business acumen and Harrison's creative energy had kept the company afloat in the powerfully ebbing economic tide of the 1930s, but the boat was leaking, according to company financial statements that showed a steady drain of $34,000 to more than $50,000 a year even after the closing of plants in New Jersey and western Massachusetts and the consolidation of all operations in Dorchester.

The U.S. entry into World War II brought a halt to American organbuilding. With the outbreak of hostilities, organ companies were put to work producing spare parts for airplanes and manufacturing caskets and wooden wings for gliders. Supplies of tin, an essential ingredient of many organ pipes, were requisitioned by the government, and a 10 percent luxury tax was levied on new organs. Aeolian-Skinner's reserves would enable it to survive while the workmen who had not been drafted were put to work making coffins and wooden cases for artillery shells. But all Ernest M. Skinner & Son could do for the duration was compete for what little business there was in keeping old organs in repair. Bankruptcy forced the company to close on October 1, 1942. Skinner's bankers foreclosed on the mortgage and took over the factory and the organ concert hall in Methuen, and then, on June 17, 1943, the factory burned to the ground; Serlo Hall next door, which had been built with four-foot-thick walls to ensure optimal acoustical conditions for the organ, was unscathed.

In the twilight of his life, Skinner briefly lent his name to the Schantz Organ Company in Orrville, Ohio, driving there in his car at least once, but he had nothing to do at the factory except play chess with the owner, Victor Schantz, across the street. In the 1950s, he fretted over Harrison's rebuilding of some of what he considered his greatest instruments—Hill Auditorium at the University of Michigan; Saint John the Divine, St. Paul's Chapel at Columbia University, and Saint Thomas in New York City. "We in our day throw away magnificent examples from existing organs in our efforts to sterilize—I mean clarify—the organ," he protested in 1941; "I care nothing for the organ apart from what it can do *musically*." Now his organs were being shoved aside, relegated to the scrap heap, as he himself had been. He fought with the few means he had, deprecating Aeolian-Skinner's work at every opportunity. In 1951, when Harrison and Joseph S. Whiteford, the company's vice president, were planning an extensive rebuilding of the organ that Skinner had completed three decades earlier in St. Bartholomew's Church in New York City, Whiteford had to dispel rumors that the plans included removal of a thirty-two-foot stop "to tonally castrate this organ." Whiteford wrote to his friend Searle Wright, "I might say that I feel rather certain that Mr. Skinner is responsible for starting this inasmuch as I saw the note that he wrote on St. Bartholomew's stationery to the new Rector, indicating that it was our intention to remove this stop. In addition to the poor taste displayed in this, it most certainly was inaccurate."

Stricken after the death of his wife, Mabel, in 1951, Skinner stayed for a few years with their daughter Eugenia in Reading, Massachusetts, where they had moved in 1947, and then moved to a cousin's in Dorchester. He pined away, with occasional eruptions of acerbic wit. "You know we have a cat," he wrote to Mabel's nephew Ned Hastings, a church organist in Boston, in 1953, "and I wonder once in a while who will live longest, me or the cat." After his daughter Ruth succeeded in getting his driver's license revoked because of his advanced age, he complained constantly about his immobility. "I wish I could hear your Church service once in a while," he wrote to Hastings in 1955, "but I don't seem to know the way from here without my car as I would probably land at Symphony Hall where Harrison did such fine work," a barbed reference to the Aeolian-Skinner organ that Harrison installed to replace the one Skinner had finished for Hutchings half a century before. Without Mabel and without his work, he was bored. "I stay mostly at home and read and write letters or watch television. I should hate to be without that television as I watch it for hours every day," he confessed.

Around 1958, invited to speak to a chapter of the American Guild of Organists, the loss of wheels still rankled, according to the taped message he sent to the meeting. "Were it not for the fact that because of my 92 years the Commissioner of Motor Vehicles has insisted on taking away my driver's license, I might be with you in person," he told the group. He added, "In spite of the fact that I was born a music lover, I do not care to hear Bach often. I prefer Offenbach." About the same time, Skinner asked Henry Willis III, "As I am sick of sitting around and doing nothing but reading ads in *Musical Opinion* I am writing you to see if you have any need for a flue voicer?"

Ernest Skinner died two years later, on the night of November 26–27, 1960. By that time, his style of organbuilding was held in contempt by most of the builders and organists of the day. "My love of tone and the music of the great composers in their employment of orchestral color made it inevitable that I should do what I could to bring those voices to the organ," he wrote in summing up his own work and the reactions to it, in a book that he could not get published in his lifetime. "I have devoted the best years of my life to improving organ tone and giving it the gamut of color found in the orchestra. Having been successful in reproducing these colors with organ pipes, I have been charged with trying to make an orchestra out of the organ." But, he told himself, "The organ has one gamut of effects and the orchestra another."

In tribute after his passing, *The Diapason* wrote: "Few of Mr. Skinner's masterpieces—and masterpieces of their time and taste they surely were—still remain in their original design. The quality of a striking personal expression which they all had made a complete swing of the pendulum in the other direction natural. A whole generation of organists, though, regretted that Mr. Skinner had to live to watch it happen. But the mid-century was that kind of a time: great men all saw their worlds crumble about them!"

His polished granite gravestone, next to Mabel's in the grass in Woodland Cemetery in Bethel, Maine, says all that needs to be said:

ERNEST MARTIN SKINNER
GREAT AMERICAN ORGAN BUILDER
1866–1960

For years after Skinner's departure from Aeolian-Skinner, under its nameplate Harrison produced signature organs that were respected as the Cadillacs of the American organbuilding field. Harrison became the company's president in 1940, and by the end of the decade, nearly all other organbuilders in the United States were measuring themselves by the standards of tonal quality and workmanship set by Aeolian-Skinner—some trying to match it, others trying to stand out from it or rebel against it.

Harrison continued to draw some of his inspiration from where Skinner had found none—in the sounds of the German baroque organs of the time of Bach. In 1935, Harrison had corresponded with Henry Willis in London about just what it was that made the Saxon eighteenth-century instruments of Gottfried Silbermann so distinctive. Bach had admired them for their silvery tones, but not for their antiquated uneven-temperament tuning system, which made music written in some keys impossible to play. Harrison read Willis's analysis of what produced the powerful, yet clear and transparently articulate Silbermann sound, and set about trying to make his own instruments capable of producing the same clarity.

The Aeolian-Skinner version of what became known as the American Classic organ was born with two instruments that Harrison designed in the mid-1930s: the first, completed in 1935, for the chapel of Groton School in Massachusetts and the second, finished in early 1936, for Boston's Church of the Advent. Both captivated listeners and fascinated organists by their bright, singing tones and by their unusual stoplists. Where Skinner had almost always built powerful English-type trumpet stops into the very foundations of his organs, the "Great" divisions on which the rest of the tonal ensemble rested, Harrison put trumpet batteries of the brilliant French type into the "Swell" division of the organs he built, where rows of pipes were enclosed in shuttered boxes that could be opened and closed. Like Cavaillé-Coll and Willis, like Skinner for that matter, Harrison thought enclosed divisions were essential to give an organ the full dynamic range needed for romantic and postromantic music. What made Harrison's new instruments radically different from the romantic Skinner sound was the distinct harmonic clarity of their unenclosed divisions, often including a German-style "positiv" whose pipes stood out in the open, separate from the rest, to produce clear, light tones like the organs of Bach's day.

Harrison's aim was to build organs that would be musically successful in the American context. He was not about to "go baroque" and give up modern electric and electropneumatic advances to build organs the way they had been made for centuries, nor did he want simply to copy Henry Willis's English ideas. "When I came to America H. W. felt that I would influence the Skinner people to build imitations of the Willis organ," Harrison wrote to one of his sons in England in 1944, but he soon developed his own musical style. "In the first place, England and the United States are two very different places, particularly as the latter is a kind of mixing pot," he wrote. "The country is too young to have any artistic traditions to live up to, and they are at present in the making. I think they are going to develop along the highest lines, and eventually we will have a culture that is second to none in the world." Harrison believed that some of his own work made a contribution to that culture.

Another of Harrison's early successes, the organ at All Saints Episcopal Church in Worcester, Massachusetts, was an instrument that William Self, the church's organist, hoped would produce sounds like those of the great classic and romantic organs he had studied in France. There had been a Skinner organ in the church, but a fire on the morning of January 20, 1932, destroyed the sanctuary. "How fortunate All Saints Worcester was burned down!" Henry Willis wrote Harrison when he heard the news. "You will now be able to do something fine there."

Harrison, along with Zeuch and Self, who had studied with Bonnet in Paris, agreed to a specification that had stops designed along French tonal lines. "All of us were influenced by French organs and by the French school of composition," Self wrote later. "The organ we planned was a tremendous step in the French direction, but we were still in a time of experiment."

Harrison finished the All Saints organ, Aeolian-Skinner's Opus 909, in 1934. It was not yet the French instrument Self was trying for, however, and he and Harrison would keep experimenting for another decade and a half, replacing "trumpets" with "trompettes" and "clairons" at unison, superoctave, and suboctave pitches, removing the swell shutters from the bombarde division, adding stops here and changing the voicing of others there, even shipping the lower twelve metal pipes of the thirty-two-foot bombarde in the pedal back to the Aeolian-Skinner factory to be reworked, at extraordinary expense, all to make the organ sound more French.

The result, when Harrison finally finished most of his modifications in 1948, was a decidedly American instrument of 6,000 pipes that could indeed speak fluent French. But it did so with a bold, English-tinted American accent. Instead of the massive, dark sound of a Cavaillé-Coll, it had a steely brilliance, with such an abundance of treble tone that it could seem almost harsh. Nonetheless, it delighted generations of visiting French organists, from Joseph Bonnet to Marcel Dupré to Pierre Cochereau (before later alterations and additions to the All Saints organ changed its character).

Harrison himself never lost his British accent. Not an extrovert like Ernest Skinner, he was the reserved and taciturn Englishman. "His classic response to many comments was a deep-chested purr, which the speaker could interpret as he wished," his son Michael, who came to Boston to work with him for a while in the late 1940s, recalled. Only his closest friends called him "Don." To the staff, he was as cordial and respectful as only an English gentleman could be, and came to be affectionately called by all of them "The Boss." He had a dry sense of humor, and he earned the respect of the men on the factory floor and on the road when installations were in progress; not a few of them found it hard to keep up with him at the bar after work was done.

But Harrison's heavy drinking, his wandering eye, and his frequent absences from Boston, where social life was no match for what Dora Harrison had been used to in London, had put an intolerable strain on their marriage. In 1931, Dora Harrison left her husband, taking their two boys, Michael and Stephen, to England, where she obtained a divorce. Eventually, she was married again—to Henry Willis III.

Harrison, so often in New York on business, had met Helen Caspari, a wealthy American woman, there, and in 1935 they married. The new Mrs. Harrison had an apartment on Third Avenue in Manhattan, a summer house in Hampton Bays, and another, larger house in Southampton. Harrison decided to make New York his base of operations, commuting to the Aeolian-Skinner factory in Boston on the New Haven Sunday evening night train and returning to Manhattan on the overnight "Owl" Thursday nights. Three years after the marriage, in 1938, with his wife's support, he was naturalized as an American citizen. And after Arthur Hudson Marks died suddenly in 1939, Harrison was able, with his wife's help, to buy a controlling financial interest in Aeolian-Skinner company.

He truly came into his own after the war ended, with a contract that would make his name and Aeolian-Skinner's reputation known to the broader public, nationwide. This, the biggest opus Aeolian-Skinner had yet produced, was the replacement of the famous organ in the Mormon Tabernacle in Salt Lake City. The result, completed in 1948, was an almost new instrument that soon made the American Classic organ sound familiar to radio audiences coast to coast, through the Mormon Church's weekly radio broadcasts of "Music and the Spoken Word," with Alexander Schreiner at the organ and accompanying the Tabernacle Choir.

Among the few remaining original pipes in the Tabernacle organ that Harrison saved were the lower twelve notes of the thirty-two-foot wood open, the pipes that produced the lowest rumbling deep bass notes on the pedals, and the towering pipes of the organ's distinctive façade—looking like metal but made of wood by Joseph Ridges, the English carpenter Brigham Young himself had selected to build the organ in the nineteenth century. "A real chance that one rarely gets," Harrison described the job. "I was able to work out something which more or less carries the ideas on which I have been working to their logical conclusion."

Harrison installed all the orchestral stops that the music of Romantic composers called for, plus the clear and articulate baroque sounds Bach's music needed, including a "positiv" division with more than a thousand pipes voiced on the low wind pressures characteristic of early German instruments.

"We want the trebles to sing," Harrison wrote Schreiner in 1946, explaining that he would not follow the usual American practice of making the pipes in the upper notes of the principal stops significantly narrower, and therefore less full-bodied in tone, than the lower pipes (Cavaillé-Coll had made the treble pipes of his organs proportionately wider than the bass pipes, and put them on higher wind pressures, for the same reason: to avoid a thinning-out of the sound on upper notes).

With over 11,000 pipes, the organ produced a majestic sound that washed over the Tabernacle auditorium even with 6,000 people in the congregation, with a power that took even Harrison's breath away, as he wrote to Whiteford back at the factory in Boston, describing hearing Alexander Schreiner demonstrate the full organ to a visitor: "I took him to my private place in the back gallery over the clock. Alex built up the organ and the organist said, 'My God, I have never heard anything like this. Is that full organ?' I said yes. Hardly were the words out of my mouth when there was a sudden extra surge of sound that lifted us off our seats. . . . I am a cold, clammy Englishman slow to show emotion, but to my surprise shortly after this episode I went over to the hotel to sign a letter I had dictated to the public stenographer. I read the letter through, took out my pen and tried to sign. My hand was trembling so much I couldn't sign my own name for a half an hour. I couldn't compose myself. . . . This organ does something to the nervous system that passes belief. . . . It has proved my theory that the complex sound composed of many elements, all mild but different, builds up a sound of indescribable grandeur. My God it does it."

A decade earlier, Harrison's friend Emerson Richards had said, "He has set up for himself, taken all the ideas that he was heir to as well as some others that he has been talked into, and made something which in a shadowy sort of way may be considered American." But there was nothing shadowy at all about Harrison's status at mid-century. He had become the premier American organbuilder of his time.

The Invention of
E. Power Biggs

Popular organist—surely the term would apply only to a nightclub artist today. But fifty years ago, E. Power Biggs was an organ star, a classical organist who earned a respectable living from concerts and the scores of albums he recorded (often by himself, or with his wife's help) for Columbia Masterworks. In person, E. Power Biggs was not as intimidating as his imposing name sounded. I remember, as a student at Harvard in the early 1960s, working up the courage to ask Biggs for permission to play on the organ he owned in the university's Busch-Reisinger Museum. I finally called him at home, but he put me at ease right away after hearing that I was studying organ with his friend Melville Smith. "Have a go, and a jolly good time," he told me, or something like that.

Biggs's intelligence and jaunty sense of humor were as much evident in his writing—over the years he wrote most of his record jacket notes himself—as in his personal style. A bit more than average in height, with keen features and penetrating dark eyes, he dressed like an English country gentleman, usually with a nattily folded pocket handkerchief. At his concerts he was more formal but radiated energy and enthusiasm, bounding on and off the organ bench. He kept his chin up and he played as he spoke, with a clipped and very proper accent that came from growing up in England.

Edward George Power Biggs was born on March 29, 1906, to Alice Maud Tredgett and Clarence Power Biggs, in Westcliff-on-Sea, east of London. His father, an auctioneer, suffered from tuberculosis, and although the family moved to the Isle of Wight a year after the boy was born in hopes of helping Clarence Biggs recover his health, he died in 1909. Mrs. Biggs was a Christian Scientist who did not believe in medical treatments.

She sent "Jimmy," as he was known to family and close friends, away to boarding school when he reached the age of seven, to Hurstpierpoint College in Sussex. There he began piano lessons, and later, as the First World War was raging, he joined the college's officers training corps, but he left school in 1922 to begin an apprenticeship in a London electrical engineering firm. "A keen cadet who left before developing into a leader," his training corps instructor wrote of him then, but A. H. Coombes, headmaster of Hurstpierpoint, said, "He is especially good at mathematics and science and, in my opinion, should do very well in this direction."

Instead, influenced by studies with J. Stuart Archer, a famous British organist of the time, young Biggs auditioned in 1926 for a scholarship to the Royal Academy of Music and was admitted. He studied organ there with George Dorrington Cunningham, the municipal organist of the City of Birmingham, a well-known concert recitalist, and, in Biggs's recollection, a great teacher. "His own playing projected a wonderful sense of accent, a splendid ongoing rhythm," Biggs wrote, words that could equally apply to himself. Cunningham's verdict on his pupil in his first year: "Made a capital start."

Biggs had found his calling; now he had to make a name. But could "Edward Biggs" ever attract hundreds of listeners to a concert hall? He apparently thought not, so he tried out others: "Edward G.P. Biggs," "Edward Power Biggs," "Power Biggs." But by 1929 he had settled on "E. Power Biggs"—a name as majestic and as catchy as Johann Sebastian Bach.

Unlike most English organists, Biggs had not grown up singing in the local Church of England boys' choir; his Christian Science upbringing had seen to that. His usual haunts as a student in London were apparently not St. Paul's and Westminster Abbey but tennis courts, the Old Vic and its Gilbert and Sullivan operettas, and dates with young ladies who were fellow students. His student concert programs also show little churchly flavor, with performances of Dupré's *Prelude and Fugue in G minor,* a fiendishly difficult work, and the opening *Allegro Vivace* from Widor's *Organ Symphony No. 5,* another virtuoso and entirely secular work. He must have excelled at the required piano studies as well, playing Schubert's *Fantasy in C major (The Wanderer),* Liszt's *Rhapsody No. 6,* and De Falla's *Ritual Fire Dance* at a "Pianoforte and Song" recital in Leighton House in April 1928. Later that year, he played two concertos for organ and orchestra under Sir Henry Wood, and by 1929 he was playing all of the Widor Fifth Symphony as well as Liszt's *Fantasia and Fugue on "Ad nos, ad salutarem undam"*—romantic organ music par excellence, none of it church service music.

Like all aspiring organists, however, Biggs had to pay the rent and eat. He took church positions but did not last long in any of them. One, possibly the first, was at the Third Christian Science Church on Curzon Street, which fired him in 1928. "I wanted to play the organ and I suppose I wasn't interested in the day-by-day routine," he confessed to *The New York Times* half a century later. He took other jobs in London, at St. Columba's Church of Scotland on Pont Street, and at Chiswick Parish Church.

But he seized the chance to escape the cloister and the close confines of England after graduating from the Royal Academy in 1929, by joining a pickup English touring choral group called the Cambrian Concert Company, which was lacking a keyboard player as its members prepared to embark on a six-month tour of the United States. Cunningham, Biggs's teacher, had toured the United States and Canada that spring and on his return had told his students, in Biggs's recollection, that he had found "the Americans wonderful, the country magnificent, and many of the organs terrible."

The Cambrian Concert Company sailed from Liverpool at the end of September. On arrival, Biggs's diary noted enthusiasm for the New York City skyline but disappointment over Times Square: Broadway, he wrote, "is not very broad & doesn't seem to have the dignity of say Regent Street, or Piccadilly. We went down to Times Square station & that looks as if it were built in a hurry & never properly finished," a description that applied equally well seven decades later.

His real business in New York was his own professional prospects. He took to the subways and the trolleys to leave his calling cards with people who could help—a note for Alexander Russell, in charge of the organ in Wanamaker's New York store, a telephone message to T. Tertius Noble, the Yorkshireman who was the organist and choirmaster of St. Thomas Church on Fifth Avenue, and another message for Lynnwood Farnam, the leading American organ virtuoso of the time. "There's a certain dignity and beauty about London which New York lacks entirely," Biggs wrote, "& on the other hand, New York has pep, go, zip, or anything you like which is reflected in the buildings everywhere & which London hasn't."

Before the Cambrian Company left for its first concert, in Bridgeport, Connecticut, Biggs succeeded in meeting all these organists and getting promises of assistance. Over the course of the next eight months, the Cambrians played 190 engagements in twenty-four states, in churches and municipal auditoriums from New York to Oklahoma and Texas and back again, playing and singing wherever they could for whatever they could get, which was apparently less than the tour cost. But Biggs took notes on promising organs for return engagements. At the end of the tour, he went back to Russell and arranged to make his "New York concert debut" in the Wanamaker auditorium on May 14.

After a trip to Boston and Portsmouth, New Hampshire, where he played another recital, Biggs sailed for home in June 1930, but not to stay. Three months later, he was back in New York, looking for a job. T. Tertius Noble referred him to Emmanuel Episcopal Church in Newport, Rhode Island, a socially well-connected parish then looking for an organist-choirmaster.

His first recital, on the church's Welte-Mignon organ, of the early twentieth-century type he later came to despise, was a success, reviewed in the local newspaper as "a happy introduction for this new organist, whose pedal technique is most remarkable, if not quite flawless." The new organist also had grandly ambitious plans for the choir, which presented the first half of Handel's *Messiah* that December and Bach's *St. Matthew Passion,* with Biggs playing the orchestral parts on the organ, the following March.

Yet this was not what Biggs felt to be his true calling. "What can an organist do except get a position in a church? Practically nothing," he wrote to himself in exasperation in early 1931. "A mere handful find positions as city organists and as recital organists. Herein lies the great disability of the organ—it is a mere prostitute to the church—bought for so much to attract people to the orthodox teaching.

"Will residence organs help? Will there be a number of organists who will become known as artists; and who will achieve the popularity in broad musical circles of a Paderewski? I doubt it," the young Biggs concluded, but he was also trying to prove himself wrong. He began scheduling his choir rehearsals at the end of the week, leaving Monday through Wednesday free to hop aboard one of the Fall River Line steamers to New York and negotiate engagements there with Bernard Laberge, whose concert management agency had taken Biggs on. Just as well that he didn't try to drive to the city; he had already run his first car into a ditch.

In mid-February 1932, he left Newport for the broader cultural and career opportunities of Boston, but here, too, he needed a church job to support himself and took the post of organist and choirmaster at Christ Church, Cambridge, across the Cambridge Common from Harvard Yard. The organ was a two-keyboard Hook & Hastings instrument in a room with acoustics that were as dead as a tomb's. But Biggs immediately plunged himself and the choir into a challenging musical program, which led to a full performance of the *Messiah* in the fall. As in Newport, he was at the same time actively pursuing an ambitious agenda as a concert organist, and not just in Boston. He gave another Wanamaker recital in New York in the spring of 1932.

A year later, he was in Chicago for a concert at Northwestern University on March 28. Like his Wanamaker program, it was constructed to appeal to all tastes, even including a Debussy transcription, music that suited the 1933 W. W. Kimball organ it was played on. In short, a selection of crowd-pleasers.

In the fall of 1932, Biggs began supplementing his income by teaching music history and organ at the Longy School of Music in Cambridge, where Melville Smith was on the faculty (and much later was director). Biggs was also working hard to try to get his personal life in order. He had met a young Frenchwoman named Colette Josephine Lionne, an honors piano graduate of the New England Conservatory of Music, in the spring, and married her a little over a year later, in June 1933. There was no letup in the Biggs concert schedule, but the concerts were his, not his wife's—in New York City, for instance, where Biggs played three consecutive Wednesday evening recitals in January 1934 on the new Aeolian-Skinner organ in the echoing expanse of St. Mary the Virgin, and in Canada for a series of concerts that April.

Juggling all this took its toll, and when the rector of Christ Church asked Biggs to read the early Sunday service in addition to his musical duties, Biggs refused. The upshot was reported by Charles Fisk, a nine-year-old member of the church's boy choir, in a note dated January 2, 1935 in the diary his mother had given him for Christmas. "I went to choir practice," Fisk wrote. "Mr. Bigs wasnt there." For (at least) the second time, Biggs had been fired from a church job. The leadership of Christ Church had decided that "Mr. Bigs" was more interested in his professional concert career than he was in being a good church musician, and they were right. "One of the best things that ever happened to me," Biggs said many years later. "Realized you can't train choir, practice boys' choir, etc. etc. & find enough time to develop as a player."

He was now, as he later put it, "pushed out into the cold world," but breaking out of the cloister was clearly what he really wanted to do, and he made the most of his new freedom over the following few months, with a transcontinental tour, arranged by Laberge, that took him to Fort Worth, San Antonio, California, Ontario, and

Montreal. "The organ contains a vast range of orchestral color, [and has] a vast literature for concert use," he told the *Fort Worth Star Telegram* on that tour. "It is certainly good for something besides an accompaniment to hymns or the Wedding March from Lohengrin." On his return, in February, Biggs gave the first performance of a new work by the composer and organist Leo Sowerby, the organ *Symphony in G*, on the new Aeolian-Skinner organ by Harrison in Harvard's Memorial Church. "The brusque rhythms, the smashing dissonances, the abrupt harmonic transitions of the symphony came with clear incisions," a reviewer commented in the *Boston Evening Transcript*. "His own musical temper seems well matched to that of Sowerby's Symphony."

Still, Biggs needed another church job to support himself, and in May he became organist and choir director of the Harvard Congregational Church in Brookline (now called United Parish, on the other side of the Charles River from Harvard University, and not connected to it). Here was another Aeolian-Skinner, the last new church organ built under Ernest Skinner's personal supervision at the Boston factory. In addition, Biggs managed to keep up a heavy concert schedule, touring Toronto, Guelph, Kingston, and Ottawa in the fall of 1935, to good reviews. Another recital on the Harrison organ at Harvard University brought a review by the *Boston Transcript* that touched a chord, judging by Biggs's underlining: "Organ recitals are still essentially church services," the reviewer wrote.

The history of the instrument is intimately associated with the church. The best organs have been, and usually are even today, in churches. Not all the "literature" written for the organ is ecclesiastical, but no matter how secular, it takes on a churchly tinge, because of association.

Especially in our day such considerations have the effect of keeping potential listeners away from recitals of organ music because, they reason, a service is not likely to be entertaining. This is an unfortunate error. *Organ music, well played, can be as engrossing as operatic or symphonic.* The best tunes are not—in spite of the proverb—necessarily assigned to the devil. *Last night's recital by E. Power Biggs, in Appleton Chapel, Harvard University, was an instance in point.*

Biggs's program had been all meat and potatoes—Bach preludes and fugues, the first three *Trio Sonatas,* and the *Passacaglia and Fugue.* Properly played, fine organ music could attract big audiences, and Biggs proved it with more concert tours, to Canada, Washington, D.C., California, and Oregon at the end of the year and at the start of 1936.

That summer, he gave a series of weekly recitals, the first of many over the years, on the big Boston Music Hall organ that E. M. Skinner had opened to the public in Serlo Hall in Methuen—with works by Bach, Handel, Dupré, Elgar, Karg-Elert, and Vierne on the programs. In the fall, he was on the road again, playing Austin's Kotzschmar Memorial Organ in Portland and Harrison's Aeolian-Skinner at All Saints Church in Worcester, where he assured the *Worcester Telegram* that he saw "a bright future for the organ."

⊙⥾⊙

It would be Harrison who brought Biggs's vision of that future sharply into focus over the next decade. How the two men met is not clear, though their paths could have crossed at several junctures. Biggs was in contact with his old teacher in England, J. Stuart Archer, who had known Harrison well while he was still with the Willis firm. And in Boston, Harrison's attempts to restore clarity of ensemble in modern organs had surely struck a chord with Biggs.

Both were certainly aware of stirrings in Europe, where Melville Smith and other Americans had been so impressed with the sounds of baroque organs. Ideas about returning to old organ-building principles had been circulating in what was called the "Organ Movement" in Europe ever since Albert Schweitzer had first articulated them in Germany in 1906, in an essay on organs and organbuilding, and again in 1908 in his great work *J. S. Bach.* Schweitzer's criticisms were directed mainly against German romantic organs using pneumatic key action—not the electropneumatic action that Skinner and later American builders used, but a tubular system using air pressure to link keys and pipe valves, far less responsive than the pre-electric mechanical systems that had been used for centuries. He was also critical of the harsh sound of newer organs. "We have lost the old organ sound that Bach requires," Schweitzer wrote of German organs of the late nineteenth and early twentieth centuries. "Our stops are all too loud or too soft. If all the foundation stops and mixtures are pulled on, and the flutes are added, a sound that after a while becomes practically unbearable results. . . . Our pedal divisions are tubby and thick." Schweitzer complained that pipe wind pressures had been pushed higher and higher to increase the volume of sound at the expense of clarity and articulation.

In 1909, a convention of the International Musicological Society in Vienna drew up regulations for organ building that started a return to the best tonal and mechanical principles of the past. These ideas gained currency among European organists and builders in the 1920s and early 1930s. New organs were once again built with tonally distinctive separate divisions, and many old organs by Silbermann in central Germany and Arp Schnitger in northern Germany and Holland that might have been discarded and replaced by more "advanced" instruments were saved from extinction.

In Cambridge, Massachusetts, in 1935, with Harvard's 300th anniversary looming the following year, Biggs suggested that the university commission a "Bach organ" as part of the university's tercentenary celebration, but Harvard shrugged off the idea. But, Biggs explained later, he mentioned the idea to Harrison, who had been encouraged by Emerson Richards, the New Jersey legislator and organ expert who had assembled the gigantic instrument in Atlantic City, to explore the tonal possibilities of the organs of Bach's time. Harrison went to Holland and Germany with Carl Weinrich, the organist of Princeton University, in the spring of 1936 on a tour of eighteenth-century organs.

What they made of the political, social, and economic turmoil in Germany under the Nazis they did not set down for posterity. Their interest now was in understanding and carrying forth a piece of the rich German cultural heritage that Hitler would do so much to destroy. And when Harrison returned, he set immediately to work on an experimental organ with sounds along German classical lines.

Harrison "had come back with a number of ideas he wanted to put into practice," Biggs recalled years later. "In those years, business was rather slack at the Aeolian-Skinner Company, and Harrison proposed to use some of the free time to plan and build a small organ to be used as a demonstration model, and this was to be put up in a small room at the factory."

Biggs thought that the organ would need better placement to be properly appreciated, and that he knew just the spot for it—the Germanic Museum, across Harvard Yard from his home in Cambridge. The central hall of the museum was a resonant room with full-scale plaster casts, donated by Kaiser Wilhelm II before the United States declared war on him, of the features of some notable medieval German church buildings, including the Cathedral at Freiberg, in Saxony, which Biggs knew by reputation as the location of one of the greatest surviving Silbermann organs. The room was surrounded on three sides by a balcony, deep and wide enough on one side for the Harrison organ, and Biggs lost no time in suggesting the idea to Dr. Charles Kuhn, the museum's curator. "He was very sympathetic, but of course remarked that there was no money available," Biggs said, so he went back to the organbuilder: "I was able to suggest through Donald Harrison and Bill Zeuch, who was Vice-President of Aeolian-Skinner, why not put that organ in the Germanic Museum, at any rate, say for a year, on loan. See how it sounds; it would certainly sound much better than in a small room at the factory."

The "Baroque organ—Experimental," Aeolian-Skinner's Opus 951, was entirely unenclosed—no swellboxes or shutters bottling up the pipes, no shimmering céleste stops imitating the muted strings of an orchestra, no French-style trumpets with the power of orchestral brass. Instead, it had stops that would have been familiar to Bach or Handel, from the German-style sixteen-foot bass

posaune that undergirded the pedal section to the backbone section of the instrument, the Hauptwerke, up to the chirping stops of
the one-foot sifflöte on the positiv. Where the conventional American organ of the 1920s and 1930s sounded deep, thick, and heavy,
this one, with a center of gravity high in the treble registers, was
light and piercingly clear. Though many of the pipes were conventional Aeolian-Skinner stock, and the windchests on which they sat
were the usual electropneumatic ones, the air pressure that made
the pipes speak was even lower than in the eighteenth-century German organs. Harrison's main point may have been simply to show
that the higher pressures then in vogue in American organs were
not necessary to produce good organ tone.

Into the museum balcony the organ went in 1937, the pipes of
the twenty-five stops laid out on three windchests, standing bravely
in the open without any decorative casework or any attempt at visual design; a showroom for the new American Classic idea. Harrison was not interested in becoming a builder of neobaroque
organs, but, he wrote at the time, "The organ has been romanti-
cized, and its fundamental character has been lost." Harrison
wanted to get back to the basics: "Classical organ music, particularly
that of J. S. Bach, is polyphonic in form and, therefore, great clarity
of tone is essential for the proper rendition of these works in order
that the interweaving of the various voices or parts may be heard
distinctly by the listener. It is not surprising, therefore, to find that
clarity and transparency of tone are the most striking characteristics
of the organs of the seventeenth and eighteenth centuries. An attempt has been made to recapture these desirable qualities in the
Germanic Museum instrument."

The opening recitals by Biggs on April 13 and 18, 1937, were a
major musical event. He played identical programs of music by
Handel, Louis-Claude Daquin, who was the court organist at Ver-
sailles during the reign of Louis XIV, and Bach—the *Fantasy and
Fugue in G minor.* The impression the instrument created was as dramatic as he could have hoped for. "The beautiful tone of the instrument, lighter in texture, sweeter and more mellow than that of the

average instrument built according to modern specifications, was yet capable of grandeur," the *Christian Science Monitor* found, and Moses Smith, the *Boston Evening Transcript* critic, was an enthusiastic convert after hearing Biggs play Bach's transcription of the A minor Vivaldi concerto. "It was apparent as soon as he had begun the Allegro," Smith wrote, "that the greater clarity of parts resulting from the structure and materials of the new organ was no mere boast on the part of the designer, G. Donald Harrison. The polyphonic development was far clearer than it is on the typical contemporary instrument." That, Smith observed, was "a tonal anomaly, a bad imitation of an orchestra." Not that the Harrison baroque organ was perfect: "There were times when the voices did not seem to 'blend.'" But on the whole, the general press covered the new organ, and Biggs as its leading exponent, as major cultural news. The *Boston Herald* even wrote an editorial about it, entitled "The New Classical Organ: A Victory for Bach."

Biggs had found his vehicle, an instrument that in his hands, as Richards wrote, "revealed to us a music so new, so arresting, and so alive that we cannot believe it is the same old stodgy, uninteresting and decadent set of notes that have been running through the fingers of our organists since the middle of the last century."

On September 27, Biggs was naturalized as an American citizen. Later that fall, he celebrated with a series of twelve recitals in the Germanic Museum of the complete organ works of Bach, a major feat that had been performed by only one American organist before him, Lynnwood Farnam. The concert posters had a marvelous woodcut in Bauhaus style, drawn by Crawford Livingston, showing the pipes and the organist illuminated by a shaft of light. The tickets, $10 for the series, and not sold for single concerts, were snapped up in advance, leaving Biggs both excited and a bit worried about being pigeonholed. "In between the two halves of the Bach concerts," he wrote in *The American Organist*, "I am to go on tour. I'm very anxious that these Bach recitals shall not label me a 'specialist.' I revel in all organ literature and play Sowerby, Vierne, Widor, Karg-Elert, etc. with as much gusto as J.S.B."

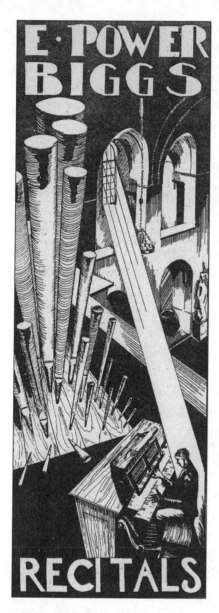

E. Power Biggs's program for twelve recitals of Bach's complete organ works at Harvard, 1937–1938

The Bach recitals were a huge success. "If we were writing this for Variety we would say that Mr. Biggs 'laid them in the aisles,'" Emerson Richards wrote in *The American Organist* in March 1938, though he was not entirely convinced by the new organ. "Personally, I am rather inclined to the idea that the instrument is too limited to properly convey to an American public the possibilities of this type of design. . . . It also lacks those very soft and ethereal effects that add such great charm," Senator Richards wrote; "this organ is not for everybody. . . . Most certainly it plays organ music with a force, clearness, and certainty we have never before heard in America. The organ is only the instrument. The music's the thing."

Biggs finished the Bach series in Cambridge that spring after a transcontinental tour. That summer, he and his wife Colette sailed for Europe for a vacation and visits with family and friends in France and Britain, including J. Stuart Archer, who wrote him: "I have been looking at your programme and press notices again to-day—and feel I should like to have heard you play Bach on that organ. You must tell me how you registered. I wish we could have an instrument like that over here."

On his return to the United States, Biggs made his first commercial recordings on the organ in the museum, a five-record Bach album (78 rpm, of course) for a label called Technichord, and a single disc with the "Cuckoo and Nightingale" movement from Handel's *Organ Concerto No. 10* and a Daquin Noel. "He who finds his audience does not like Bach, will do well to buy these Bach albums and learn why. Here we have Bach as Bach should be, and we can each of us for himself readily compare and find out what he lacks to make Bach as vital and living as on these records," T. Scott Buhrman, editor of *The American Organist,* wrote in early 1939.

Harrison also found the recordings useful, as selling tools for his new American Classic ideas: "I was able to play them to many prospects and gave them some idea of how an organ sounded built to classical lines. It convinced many of them that such an organ need not be all top," Harrison wrote to W. King Covell, "top" meaning high-pitched and screechy.

Biggs persuaded Arthur Fiedler to bring his pickup chamber ensemble, the Fiedler Sinfonietta, to Cambridge to record the Handel *Organ Concerto No. 10.* Soon afterward, Biggs and Technichord had a falling-out over royalties, and Biggs went looking for a new label. Finding Charles O'Connell, director of Victor Red Seal Records, at a recording session with the Boston Symphony in 1939, Biggs invited him to come to Cambridge to hear the new organ. "I had heard of Mr. Biggs, but was not at the time acquainted with his playing," O'-Connell recalled later. "I was candidly more interested in the instrument than I was in Mr. Biggs. I readily accepted his invitation, after which I was more interested in Mr. Biggs than the instrument."

By that time Biggs was doing quite well for himself. Since 1938, he had been playing so often with the Boston Symphony Orchestra, on the old Hutchings organ at Symphony Hall and later at Tanglewood in the orchestra's summer Festivals in the Berkshires, that he was describing himself in his promotional literature as the orchestra's official organist. Biggs helped Harrison obtain a contract for a pipe organ at Tanglewood in 1939 after the music director, the great Serge Koussevitzky, had been disappointed with the thin electronic sound of a Hammond organ that was used in a performance (not by Biggs) of the Saint-Saëns symphony that summer. "Koussevitzky was thoroughly disgusted with the electronic device," Biggs recalled long afterward, "and announced, 'Next year we shall give Beethoven's *Missa Solemnis and for that occasion I must have an organ.'*"

"I do not believe that Dr. Koussevitzky had any technical knowledge or even any particular liking for the organ and its characteristic sounds," Biggs wrote. "But he was certainly accustomed to the splendid organs that complement European concert halls, and to the 'plus' that they afford to an orchestra. Koussevitzky followed his basic principle, which he never hesitated to enunciate. 'It must be the best.'"

So George Judd, the orchestra's manager, asked Biggs in the autumn of 1939 to show Koussevitzky the Germanic Museum organ. "I remember that I called at the Koussevitzky house in Brookline, on a sunny Saturday afternoon, with my Model A Ford Convertible, recently purchased for seventy-five dollars from a Harvard student," Biggs wrote. "I *hope* he enjoyed the ride, but I *know* he enjoyed the organ. For after listening to a little Bach, he came promptly up to the gallery, saying 'Fine—send it up to Tanglewood.'" That, of course, was impossible, but it meant a new contract for Don Harrison and Aeolian-Skinner, which with Biggs as a consultant designed Opus 1002 for the Music Shed at Tanglewood. This small but versatile instrument had more romantic stops than the one in the museum, plus a single thirty-two-foot pipe, on low C, for the Saint-Saëns *Organ Symphony,* the Strauss *Also Sprach Zarathustra* and other works requiring a full-organ rumble underneath the orchestra. The organ, its pipes suspended from the ceiling girders of the music shed, was paid for in part by the Carnegie Foundation, and in the early summer of 1940 Koussevitzky, Harrison, and Biggs climbed up the vertical ladder to inspect the pipes and wind chests "from end to end," Biggs reported. In July 1940 he played it in three solo recitals; on August 15 it was used to accompany the orchestra and a chorus in the Bach *B minor Mass.* Harrison called it "one of the most successful instruments we have made. . . . it is a far finer organ than the Germanic."

Biggs also used his association with the orchestra to encourage composers to write more music for the instrument. "When I came to the United States," he wrote, "I brought from Sir Henry Wood a promise that if I could turn up a large scale concerto for organ and orchestra by an American composer, preferably a new work, Sir Henry would program it at the Queens Hall 'Proms.' Quite brashly, I wrote to Leo Sowerby, the Chicago composer—then at the height of his fame—asking if he would write such a piece. He replied that he would think about it, but made no commitment." Around the end of 1937 or the beginning of 1938, the Boston Symphony played a concert in Chicago, and Koussevitzky, seated next to Sowerby at a luncheon, asked him what he was working on. Hearing what it was, the conductor told the composer, "Fine, *I* will play it, but I must have the *first* performance." When the work was finished, Sowerby asked Koussevitzky to schedule Biggs as the soloist, and his wish was granted. When Biggs turned up at Symphony Hall to rehearse his part and asked for practice time, though, Koussevitzky seemed not to recognize Sowerby's name. "I had the funny feeling that the whole thing was a mirage," Biggs wrote. "Suddenly, at the words 'organ concerto,' Koussevitzky smiled and said 'Oh, So-vair-bee!'" and all was well when Sowerby's *Concerto in C for Organ and Orchestra* received its premiere performance in 1938.

Despite his growing reputation, Biggs still worried about expenses. He held onto his teaching job at the Longy School, at $1,000 a year plus $55 for each private student, despite the constraints lessons placed on his ability to schedule concerts and tours. But in 1939 RCA Victor signed him up as an exclusive artist and kept him until 1947, recording about a dozen discs with him as soloist on the Museum organ, and fourteen others on the Harvard Memorial Church instrument and various bigger organs for larger romantic works, as Biggs worked to fulfill a "five-year plan" he had drawn up for his recording projects. Always on the plan, but never recorded by Biggs, was the Sowerby concerto. Biggs was attentive even at this early stage in his career to every detail of the recording process, down to the jacket design and the program notes. "Church associations" were to be studiously avoided in publicity, Biggs insisted. Pipes, he advised, would "lend themselves to very striking shots" on the albums.

Soon, he came up with a way to put the Harrison organ in the Germanic Museum to use in a new medium—radio, which by the late 1930s had become capable of reproducing organ sounds without the distortion of earlier years. He would realize this ambition through the patronage of the redoubtable Elizabeth Sprague Coolidge, then already in her late seventies and nearly deaf, but a musician to the core and a distinguished pianist in her youth. After her husband, a Boston Brahmin, and her parents all died in the space of fifteen months in 1915 and 1916, she inherited a fortune that she spent the rest of her life giving away to support music programs in the Berkshires and in Washington, D.C. The foundation she established gave the Coolidge Auditorium, complete with pipe organ, to the Library of Congress for performances of chamber music, and she commissioned works for music-starved Washington by composers from Igor Stravinsky to Aaron Copland, then throwing lavish parties for everybody involved in the inaugural performances in her Washington apartment on Sixteenth Street, but she also had a home in Cambridge, and perhaps Biggs had met her there.

At any rate, Biggs had been in close contact with Mrs. Coolidge after playing one of the works she had commissioned—*Fantasy Choral for Harp and Organ*—by one of the greatest harpists of the twentieth century, Marcel Grandjany. At the inaugural performance of the work in Coolidge Auditorium in the spring of 1940, Biggs had accompanied the composer at the console of the hall's E. M. Skinner organ. The following January, Biggs wrote to Mrs. Coolidge and asked for help in bringing the Grandjany work to Cambridge, along with another new piece, which he mentioned almost casually: "I have found an excellent new concerto, for organ and small string orchestra (with kettle drums) by Francis Poulenc, written two years ago, and not yet performed in this country," he reported. Biggs planned to give the Poulenc concerto its American debut with the Fiedler Sinfonietta in the Germanic Museum the following month, he said, but Harvard wanted to allow free admission. "Since tickets may not be sold," Biggs went on, "the possibility of such an affair depends entirely on some generous and interested person who would be willing to underwrite all, or part, of the expenses." For his own performance, he said, he would ask only $200.

Could Mrs. Coolidge have known that the Poulenc concerto had been commissioned by a fellow American, Winnaretta Singer, who married into French nobility and used her sewing-machine fortune, as the Princesse de Polignac, to become a patroness of the arts? The concerto had its first performance in the grand salon of her home in the Sixteenth arrondissement of Paris. From the sheaf of correspondence preserved in the Biggs papers, it is hard to tell what either Biggs or Mrs. Coolidge knew about the genesis of the Poulenc work. Certainly, she was happy to give the Grandjany piece another hearing. "It will give me great pleasure to cooperate with you," Mrs. Coolidge wrote to Biggs, but she knew Grandjany would expect $300, so she sent a check for a total of $600, to cover the two soloists and the Sinfonietta.

The first American performance of Poulenc's concerto took place on February 24, and although his benefactress had been unable to attend, two days later, Biggs wrote "Dear Mrs. Coolidge" in longhand, "We all owe you very many thanks for the enjoyable evening of last Monday!"

A year later, he appealed to her again for help with what he described as "a fairly ambitious project that I have been considering for some time," and had discussed with officials of NBC's Blue Network and the Mutual radio network, both of whom said they would be interested "if I could find an interested sponsor." That was Mrs. Coolidge, whom Biggs now sought to interest in an idea that could help him achieve his goal of breaking out of the box and becoming a nationally known concert artist. "As you know, the organ literature is second only to that of the orchestra and string quartet, and yet it is practically unknown to the public at large," Biggs wrote. "It has seemed to me that the radio offers a perfect medium for bringing such music, played on a good organ, to the public, and that while the orchestral and instrumental repertoire has been well represented on radio programs for some years, the organ literature has been completely neglected. In fact—the organ has been thoroughly abused and discredited in its use on the radio. With the technical progress of broadcasting, as of recording, organ tone can now be transmitted faithfully, and the time seems ideal for a really striking series of organ concerts, covering the finest compositions of the very large repertoire. Such programs would have the originality of presenting a completely new aspect of musical life." Biggs sketched out a plan for six programs, all on the Germanic Museum organ, and said it could easily be expanded to eight. Would Mrs. Coolidge underwrite the project?

Initially, she was hesitant. "Your plan interests me enormously," she replied, but she would prefer the concerts be broadcast from Coolidge Auditorium in Washington. For nearly six months, discussions continued, and Biggs did negotiate with both the Blue Network and with Harold Spivacke of the Library of Congress, who took the idea to Columbia Records and the Columbia Broadcasting System radio network. In September 1942, Biggs was able to report to Mrs. Coolidge: "This fall Columbia has revised its Sunday morning timetable, and out of our negotiations there comes from them an offer of a weekly program from the Germanic Museum in Cambridge. It would be from 9:15 to 9:45, coast to coast. I am of course very interested, for their proposal of 'an extended period' provides a wonderful opportunity to perform the best of the organ literature on the air."

"Would you care to lend the weight of your name and sponsorship to the launching of this series?" he asked, adding that the only cost would be $50 "to the player" for each of the ten proposed concerts, with programs of music from Daquin to Bach, Mendelssohn, Schumann, Guilmant, Sowerby, and a premiere of a sonata for organ by Richard Arnell. Mrs. Coolidge was still unable to understand why the programs wouldn't work just as well from Washington. But she agreed to give the $500 to Harvard.

The first of Biggs's historic series of radio broadcasts went out live from the Germanic Museum over Boston's CBS affiliate, WEEI-AM, at 10 A.M., eastern time, on September 20, 1942, with James Fassett announcing: "This is the first of a series of ten organ recitals given by Harvard University through the generosity of Mrs. Elizabeth Sprague Coolidge. . . . The player, at the invitation of the University, is E. Power Biggs, and this series of concerts will present much of the finest organ literature, and particularly the 'great' Preludes and Fugues of J. S. Bach."

The program included Handel's *Organ Concerto No. 2* in B-flat major, a charming trifle by Daquin, *The Cuckoo,* and Bach's *Toccata and Fugue in D minor.* The sign-off was Biggs's transcription of *Sheep May Safely Graze,* the soprano aria from Bach's secular "Birthday" Cantata No. 208, "Was mir behagt, ist nur die munt're Jagd," written for Bach's patron, Duke Christian zu Sachsen-Weissenfels. This arrangement, published in 1940 by The H. W. Gray Co., Inc., became Biggs's signature piece, appearing on every one of the broadcasts over the next sixteen years.

With the war on and few other distractions available, this series became a smash hit with classical music lovers across the country, starting with Biggs's neighbors at Harvard: "Please transmit to Mrs. Coolidge and Mr. Biggs my deep appreciation for the Sunday morning organ concerts," the Harvard astronomer Harlow Shapley wrote to WEEI on November 30. "This series is one of the three or four best musical offerings now on the air." Shapley would become a regular correspondent of Biggs's as the series spread his reputation far and wide. Even the early hours of the broadcast did not deter fans in the West from getting up to hear it at an hour "which seems very early on Sunday morning," as the Reverend Lindsay B. Longacre of Denver wrote to Biggs, "but we set our alarm so that we shall not miss the broadcast." Charles E. Toth, of Hyannis, Massachusetts, wrote, "When you first started on the series, I didn't care for the or-

gan you play on, but the more I hear it the more I like it." Servicemen wrote postcards of appreciation, from Hawaii and Alaska to
New Haven, where W. K. McClelland, of the U.S. Naval Reserve,
wrote in December 1943 to request the F-major *Toccata and Fugue*
and the A-minor *Prelude and Fugue.* The Bishop of Delaware wrote,
showing that he had not missed the real point of the show: "Here is
an opportunity for people to know what real organ playing sounds
like," he wrote in 1942.

ᴏᴧᴏ

Mrs. Coolidge was obviously impressed as well. She wrote to Biggs, in
November 1942, "We are enjoying your broadcasts so much, and
are hearing so many pleasant things about them, that I am wondering whether the Columbia people could arrange to give another series and how the idea would appeal to you. If it could be done in
the same way, I should be very glad to help to the same extent that I
did this year for producing another ten concerts."

So Biggs was launched. In May 1943, he persuaded CBS and Mrs.
Coolidge to carry on for another year, this time with thirteen programs, the standard radio network format, with music for organ
and other instruments as well as solo works. His patroness came
through with a $1,600 guarantee, and now their professional rela-
tionship began to turn into real personal friendship. When she
took ill in October, Biggs sent her a bouquet of roses, and three
months later, he began signing his handwritten letters "Jimmy."
"How very generous indeed of you to suggest continuing further
the CBS broadcasts," he wrote to Mrs. Coolidge then, and her reply
was addressed, like all her letters afterward, "Dear Jimmy." But with
the years separating them and with the respect any artist owes a
generous benefactor, he never addressed her otherwise than as
"Dear Mrs. Coolidge."

"Please give my love to Colette," she wrote "Jimmy" in February
1944, but Mrs. Coolidge was unaware that Biggs's marriage was
falling apart. Perhaps the reason was professional rivalry between

musicians. Biggs's concert promotional literature had occasionally offered two Biggses for the price of one—his transcontinental tour in 1940 had billed him as "soloist with the symphony orchestras of Boston and Chicago," and mentioned that he would be "assisted by Colette Lionne, pianist, in music for piano and organ." But there was not much of that kind of music, and perhaps Colette was tired of playing second fiddle to her ambitious and peripatetic husband. The marriage ended in divorce, and the household was broken up.

But, as biographer Barbara Owen writes, "Biggs was never without female companionship for very long," and soon he was going out with an attractive alto singer in his choir at Harvard Congregational Church—Margaret Allen, a tall, poised woman from Greenfield, Massachusetts, a dozen years younger than himself, with a nursing degree from New England Deaconess Hospital. According to Owen, in March 1945, performing in Chicago with the Chicago Symphony, after Biggs heard that the government was considering drafting unmarried nurses, he immediately called "Peggy" Allen to get on the next train to Chicago, and got a justice of the peace to marry them the following day. They would never have children; Biggs's career and his constant travel made that an impossibility from the start.

Franklin D. Roosevelt's death on April 12 threw the country into a state of shock and mourning. When the president's death was announced, CBS asked Biggs to stand by, and then put him on the air six times to play solemn music. "One short period, immediately following the one minute of silence at four o'clock, went out over all four networks, to an estimated seventy million people!" Biggs wrote to Mrs. Coolidge six days later. He had tried to donate his services, but Fassett told him union roles forbade that: "The simple fact is that we are not allowed to accept your services gratis."

Biggs's ambitions were hardly confined to playing service music, even to a nation enthralled. His premieres of the Poulenc and the Grandjany works led him to think that the CBS program could be a platform not only for his playing but for premiering more new works that he would commission himself, enticing composers with the prospect of a free inaugural performance over nationally broadcast radio.

The Harrison baroque organ must have been the key to persuading Virgil Thomson to compose for the instrument. "The modern pipe organ and its repertory make a strange dichotomy," Thomson wrote in the *New York Herald Tribune,* whose music critic he was for many years.

> The instrument itself is the most elaborate, the most ingenious, the most complex and the most expensive of all instruments. Also one of the most common. Hamlets that never saw a bassoon or a French horn or an Australian marimba or even a concert grand pianoforte will occasionally have a quite decent one. City people give them away like drinking fountains and altars and stained-glass windows. And yet, in two centuries scarcely twenty pieces have been written for the organ that could be called first-class music. . . . The cause of this neglect lies, I think, in the nature of the instrument itself, which has nowadays little but a glorious moment of history to offer. . . . All through the 19th and early 20th centuries it got bigger and bigger. It grew row after row of additional pipes. . . . It plays today the tiniest of roles in the concert hall and in the theater, while attempts to give it a new (and secular) prestige through its exploitation in department stores and cinemas have merely ended by robbing it of what little secular dignity was left to it, after a century and a half of cloistered servitude.

Thomson nevertheless made a contribution to Biggs's radio broadcasts, with a *Fanfare* and *Chorale Preludes* for organ solo.

Other musicians known and unknown were also sending him manuscripts of their work to play, and Biggs was soliciting new concertos for organ as well. He wrote to composers requesting new works of moderate length for organ and small orchestra, and in the first five years of the broadcasts was able, by his own count, to give the first hearing to original compositions by seventeen contemporary musicians, including Howard Hanson, Sowerby (who wrote another work, the *Classic Concerto for Organ and Strings,* specifically for Biggs to perform on the program), Walter Piston, Ned Rorem, and Daniel Pinkham. Pinkham, a Boston composer who was a student of Biggs, wrote a note of gratitude on February 26, 1944: "Maestro: Again my thanks for doing such a splendid performance of my little *Sonata for Organ and Strings.* I listened very carefully on Sunday morning and was extremely happy with the way you and Fiedler made it sound. . . ." Piston produced a *Prelude and Allegro for Organ and Strings,* and Biggs premiered it on the radio program in August 1943; another work by the same composer that Mrs. Coolidge had commissioned, the *Partita for Organ and Strings,* based on Carl Sandburg's poem "The People, Yes," had its premiere with Biggs at the organ in Coolidge Auditorium in Washington in October 1944. Quincy Porter's *Pastoral Theme for Organ and String Orchestra* also got its premiere on the program in 1943, and Roy Harris wrote a *Chorale and Toccata for Organ and Brass,* at Biggs's request, that was first performed in 1944. Biggs was not only performing the classics; he was adding to the organ repertory.

After the war, CBS cut back and Biggs had to play many concerts on the organ alone, supported by Mrs. Coolidge. Biggs had shown that the organist didn't have to follow the audience; if you had good music, and a flair for promoting it, the audience would come. "Skillful promotion was as necessary with the concert patrons of 18th-century England as with the public of this day," he wrote in *Musical America* in early 1945. "London music lovers enjoyed well enough the many new oratorios and operas of George Friedrich Handel, yet, according to accounts of the period, concert halls were filled to overflowing at any announcement of a 'new organ concerto' in which Mr. Handel would play and improvise in person. This was bait indeed. . . ."

Biggs brought his serial performance of all the organ works of Bach on the Harvard organ to the radio audience in 1945, again to national acclaim. "A young man of unaffected simplicity," T. R. Kennedy Jr. described the performer in *The New York Times* on August 5, 1945, "who frankly professes to be amazed by his voluminous mail that denotes a sizable number of listeners on the West Coast get up regularly at 6:15 A.M. to tune in the program. . . . Mr. Biggs has labored in other ways to make the radio audience fully conscious of the organ, its literature and its possibilities. He is forever conducting experiments to achieve the best microphone pickup and is now getting such good results that listeners throughout the nation, and the world for that matter, have written their appreciation. An American 'somewhere in Australia' sent thanks for a 'little touch of home.' A lonely United States Leatherneck on a South Pacific island wrote that the Sunday morning concerts reached him clearly by radio—'It is our musical event of first magnitude.' Mr. Biggs, who has the square-cut jaw of a boxer, but a kindly glint in the eye when the topic is the organ, calls such letters 'my reward.'"

> *He has flutes, he has drums,*
> *He has fingers and thumbs,*
> *He has feet—and they're ready to render ...*

David McCord wrote in a poem called "More E. Power Biggs to You! (9:30 A.M. every Sunday: E. Power Biggs, organist; Station WEEI & a National Network)," published in *The New Yorker* in April of 1948. "Go ahead and play something that is good—and the public will follow right with you," Biggs had told *Newsweek* two years earlier. Biggs had "juice," as RCA Victor had found after it informed him at the end of 1946 that it saw no room on its schedule for organ recordings in 1947 or 1948. Biggs just trotted over to CBS and presented a five-year plan of proposed recordings to Goddard Lieberson, the president of Columbia Records, and Lieberson signed him right up.

Not all of Biggs's organ-promotion schemes worked out so smoothly. Hugh Hooks, the Hollywood agent of Columbia Artists Management, found no takers for a script by Phillips Endecott Osgood, based on a sketch by Biggs, of a film on the life and music of J. S. Bach that was proposed for the 1950 bicentennial of Bach's death. "Reasons why this film should be produced" included "1)

On Records: Bach is a best seller" and "6) The Concert-Going Public (according to a recent poll) is double that for baseball. Last year 30 *MILLION* people attended 'live' concerts, symphonic and concert courses. Sixteen million attended Baseball games." Biggs offered his services, playing with the Boston Symphony in Symphony Hall, and held out the possibility that Walter Piston would collaborate on developing an original musical score. But the Hollywood moguls were unmoved.

Biggs had met with similar resistance in 1945 when he wrote Walt Disney with a proposal for a cartoon featuring Christmas music for organ. Remembering, certainly, how Stokowski had conducted the Philadelphia Orchestra in Bach's *Toccata and Fugue in D minor* in the animated feature *Fantasia,* Biggs appealed to Disney: "The combination of your pictorial genius with this ageless music would be quite irresistible, and I have a plan for a short along these lines. I should like to offer this plan to you, and to play the music." Disney managed to resist.

At this point, Biggs appears to have seen the baroque organ in the Germanic Museum not as an end in itself, but as a vehicle both for his ambitions as a popular concert organist and for his ambitions to expand the repertoire, sometimes with works that had long lain dormant, as he found when he wrote to the great American composer Charles Ives in 1948 asking if he had any organ works that Biggs might play on his radio program. In response, he received a letter from Harmony Twitchell Ives, who reported that her husband was "not at all well" and therefore had asked her to reply.

"He has not composed anything for the organ for over 40 years—and apparently most of it has been mislaid or lost," she wrote. "He can find only two—'Variations on America' and a short prelude—photostatic copies of these will be sent to you under separate cover. . . . P.S. Mr. Ives says the 'Variations on America' are a kind of reflection of youthful days, and the playing of the pedal variation near the end gave him 'almost as much fun as playing baseball.'"

Biggs wrote back with his thanks and told Mrs. Ives that he planned to play the *Variations* on his radio program on July 4. Thus did Biggs resurrect a work that would have been lost to history, "stuck in a pile of music in the barn, back of the old Ives house in Danbury," as Biggs later recalled, "if I hadn't asked him . . . for something to play on the CBS broadcast."

When he resumed his transcontinental concert touring in 1947, he had not become a baroque purist—that would hardly have been possible anyway in America at the time. He was perfectly happy to play on the romantic and eclectic organs he found in Los Angeles, Salt Lake City, Syracuse, and all points in between, many of them by G. Donald Harrison.

Biggs's relationship with Harrison at this time was quite close. Since he and Helen made their home in New York, Harrison often stayed with the Biggses in Cambridge during his abbreviated work weeks at the Aeolian-Skinner factory. He was so frequent a house guest that he wrote his son J. Michael Harrison in England a letter in August 1946 asking him to look for an antique clock to give the Biggses as a present: "They have been extremely kind to me, and I would like to do something for them," Harrison explained.

Biggs made his first recording for Columbia on another new Harrison American Classic organ—a completely rebuilt instrument, originally by Skinner, in St. Paul's Chapel at Columbia University. The work was done during a great blizzard in 1948, the snow-covered stillness of New York City providing ideal conditions for a recording of Bach works in resonant acoustics that were unusual at the time for organ records, since miking techniques up to the late 1940s had required close-in positioning as if in a sound studio. This recording, all Bach, made the organ sound more natural.

"For about a thousand years organs have inhabited cathedrals and other spacious auditoriums, and with a consequent independence the instrument refuses to be thrust into the present day 'acoustically treated' studios," Biggs wrote. "Resonance is the priceless ingredient which gives the organ and its music character and splendor. The measure in which this essential quality can be transferred to records is the measure of the records' excellence." The true-to-life sounds included not only pipes but also the stamping feet of a refugee from the blizzard who stumbled out of the snow into the church during the recording session. In those days recordings were made directly onto wax masters, with no way to splice out mistakes—it was all or nothing, and so the snow boots stayed in.

Ernest M. Skinner could carp all he wanted about what terrible things Harrison was doing to instruments Skinner had installed; at this point, Biggs was firmly on Harrison's side of the argument. "Does Mr. Skinner think that everyone is out of step but himself?" Biggs wrote to the *Musical Digest* in March 1948 in answer to one of Skinner's screeds. "Does he really believe that the fine art of organ building came to full flower in himself and the instruments he built? And that others are now engaged merely in tearing down that perfection?"

The Biggs-Harrison association was still strong in 1947, when the two were involved in another Boston Symphony project, this one the rebuilding of the organ that Skinner had installed for George Hutchings's company when Symphony Hall had been built a half century earlier. The Bostonians were inclined to be parsimonious, at first wanting simply to rebuild the Hutchings or, failing that, to install a used residence organ that one of their supporters was willing to donate. Biggs was for a new organ, and endorsed Harrison's proposal for an eclectic American Classic wholeheartedly. "We know far more today about the musical requirements of an instrument in Symphony Hall than the Hutchings company could know in 1900," Biggs wrote to the symphony's board. "Many of the present stops are thick and heavy in tone, and are not useful in either solo or orchestral playing. It is often impossible to find soft but bright stops to accompany the B minor Mass and other choral works, and Dr. Koussevitzky invariably finds much fault with the organ on these occasions, criticism that is never directed to the Tanglewood organ. At the other end of the tonal scheme, the organ does not have the climax necessary for works such as the Saint-Saëns Symphony or Zarathustra."

The board was finally persuaded by Harrison's estimate that Aeolian-Skinner could build a new organ, using many of the old pipes (and keeping the familiar Symphony Hall organ case, with its Greek key motif, in its place behind the orchestra), for a grand total of $41,420. A contract was signed by Harrison and Henry B. Cabot, the chairman of the Boston Symphony's board, on June 19, 1947, with delivery scheduled "as soon as possible." The stops the organ would have were chosen by Harrison after consultations with Biggs, G. Wallace Woodworth, of Harvard, and Wallace Goodrich, who had been the Boston Symphony's organist for a dozen years and was now at the New England Conservatory of Music. The final list of stops made it clear that this was an organ designed to play music from any period, but it bore the distinctive Harrison stamp, with more treble stops in all six of the organ's separate divisions than Hutchings or Skinner had ever used, a complete positiv division for solo recitals with Bach and other baroque composers, and powerful bombarde and trumpet stops for the full organ with orchestra. Biggs, who had himself contributed $1,000 to the Boston Symphony Orchestra to help raise funds for the organ, had insisted on a thundering thirty-two-foot bombarde for the pedal—and not just for the low C that Skinner had provided a half century before. This expensive stop was finally made possible by the elimination of an elevator to bring the four-keyboard organ console up onto the orchestra's stage. The trustees were unwilling to come up with the extra money Harrison said an elevator would cost, so instead the big console would be rolled on and off the stage with a cable that could be unplugged or plugged to connect it with the organ mechanism under the pipes—an arrangement that would cause untold wear and tear and that Biggs, Harrison, and the orchestra would all come to regret later.

The project attracted considerable attention in the music world, for it was intended to be completed in 1950 and used in observations of the bicentennial of Bach's death. Albert Schweitzer came to Boston to visit the Aeolian-Skinner factory on July 20, 1949; he inspected pipes with Biggs as they were being finished and autographed a plaque that was set into the inside of the console. Harrison took Schweitzer to visit the large organ in the Harvard

Memorial Church. Schweitzer, who was extremely critical of instruments stuffed into chambers, as the Harvard organ was, just poked at a few keys; he was more interested in Harrison's neobaroque instrument in the Germanic Museum. He also made a point of making the acquaintance of Ernest M. Skinner while he was in Boston, but it is not clear whether he tried any of Skinner's instruments.

The work on Symphony Hall and, on its heels, on the huge instrument that Aeolian-Skinner put into the nearby Christian Science "Mother Church" (the First Church of Christ, Scientist) in 1952 was taking a toll on Harrison. After hours of enforced teetotaling in the church, he would hit the Amalfi restaurant on Westland Avenue, his favorite locale, and relax with more cigarettes and Scotch than were good for him, sometimes drinking so heavily that some of his church clients noticed, disapprovingly. "It is bad stuff, particularly over here where if you drink at all, they expect you to go in for it in a big way," he wrote Michael Harrison, describing smoking as "my real bad habit. As a matter of fact, I am just in the act of lighting up a cigarette at this moment. I find that a difficult thing to break." Smoking, hard work, and a heavy travel schedule all took their toll, and sometime in the early 1950s Harrison suffered a heart attack of some kind. Afraid of the effect the news might have on Aeolian-Skinner's fortunes, he kept his condition a secret from all but his closest associates. Soon, however, he was in the grip of degenerative heart disease. Harrison took nitroglycerin pills to deal with the pain but did not change any of his habits.

The Symphony Hall project was finished in the fall of 1949. Koussevitzky had retired by then and Charles Munch was conducting when the organ was first heard on October 7, in a program identical to the first one given in Symphony Hall fifty years earlier, with Biggs as soloist in Handel's *Organ Concerto No. 4* and the orchestra concluding with Beethoven's Fifth. A month later, on November 14, the organ was officially "opened" by Biggs in a benefit concert for Schweitzer's mission hospital in French Equatorial Africa, for which Biggs wrote a gala program recalling the original Boston Music Hall organ that had been built by E. F. Walcker and

*Charles Munch and G. Donald Harrison with E. Power Biggs
at the Symphony Hall organ console*

removed to Methuen as well as the 1900 Hutchings organ, and expressing the hope that Harrison had created "a third organ worthy of the Boston tradition, to last perhaps another half century." "It's amusing that for the past 25 years orchestral conductors and arrangers have been raiding the organ literature, while on the other hand organists tie themselves into knots playing arrangements of orchestral music on the organ," Biggs wrote.

The concert that followed showcased the organ and let it speak in its own distinctive voice, starting with the first American performance of an organ concerto by Haydn in C major, with musicians of the Boston Symphony, and then Paul Hindemith's delightful *Kammermusik No. 7*, a lively concerto for organ and chamber orchestra—with no parts for violins or violas—written in 1928. Biggs then played Bach's *Toccata, Adagio, and Fugue in C*, three chorale preludes, and the warhorse *Toccata and Fugue in D minor* solo, concluding with the Poulenc concerto. "The organ has a certain tight brightness that proclaims its newness from almost every stop," Harold Rogers wrote in the *Christian Science Monitor* the next day. "It is essentially the baroque organ of Bach's era in effect, or so it would appear with Mr. Biggs at the console. When let loose, it is almost unbearably loud." But, Rogers reported, "a full house enthusiastically approved the new instrument and Mr. Biggs's performance."

Biggs gave all the credit for the organ's success to Harrison. "The idea of the organ really grew from the famous Harrison organ in the Germanic Museum in Cambridge," he told the *Boston Sunday Post.* In the program he wrote, "Design and specification of the instrument have been left almost entirely in the hands of one man— G. Donald Harrison, head of the Aeolian-Skinner firm. Organ 'architects' and other side-walk superintendents were kept at arm's length. Too many cooks can easily spoil the tonal broth." As for the eclectic design and the electropneumatic action, Biggs observed, "The instrument is a perfect medium for any music, classic, romantic or contemporary. Mechanically, everything is right up to date. . . ." The organ was tuned slightly sharp—the A above middle C was set at 444 cycles per second instead of the international standard pitch of 440 cycles per second at 70 degrees Fahrenheit, because Koussevitzky, like many other directors, had sharpened his orchestra's pitch to make its playing sound brighter and clearer.

Biggs loved the organ, as well he might since he had been its midwife, and showcased it himself at the American Guild of Organists national convention in Boston in 1950, when he served as program chairman and persuaded Aeolian-Skinner and three other organbuilding companies, Wicks, Estey, and M. P. Möller, to bring stock pipe organs to the ballroom of the Copley Plaza, the convention headquarters, where one evening Biggs and three other organists played them all in a rendition of "I'm Looking Over a Four Leaf Clover." At no time during the convention was an electronic organ allowed to make an appearance. After it was over, Biggs and his wife, Peggy, celebrated with a trip to England, where he played an all-Bach recital in Westminster Abbey and was finally able to perform the Sowerby Concerto in a "Proms" concert at Royal

*G. Donald Harrison, Margaret and E. Power Biggs,
and Joseph S. Whiteford of Aeolian-Skinner celebrating
the new organ at Symphony Hall, Boston*

Albert Hall, just as Sir Henry Wood had promised him all those years ago.

For the first few years of the 1950s, Biggs made the Boston Symphony Hall instrument his new recording mistress, and from all outward appearances, all seemed well between Biggs and Harrison. Their careers had been so closely intertwined for a decade and a half, one former Englishman advancing the other's prospects in what appeared to be an ideal symbiosis of organist and organ-builder. After a concert on the new Harrison masterpiece at the Mormon Tabernacle in 1949, Biggs told the *Deseret News,* "Everything needed to play the works of the classic masters as well as the compositions of the modern composers with their delicate shades of tone color is there, perfectly balanced."

Biggs had been teaching for many summers at the Organ Institute that Arthur Howes ran in Methuen, and he returned to the Methuen Memorial Music Hall organ in 1953 to record two big romantic works. This famous organ, though, was no longer the Teutonic import it had been when first set up in Boston in 1863. Ernest Skinner had removed or altered some of its pipes when he owned it, and when Harrison was asked by the Methuen Memorial Hall Music Foundation to rebuild and restore it, he changed it into a largely American Classic instrument. Emerson Richards, who disliked mid–nineteenth century German organs, didn't think Harrison had gone far enough. "Don has contrived a silk purse out of the sow's ear, but you can still smell the hog and hear the grunt," he wrote.

Nevertheless, the instrument's German-romantic origins were probably one of Biggs's reasons for recording Reubke's *Sonata in C minor on the 94th Psalm* and Liszt's *Fantasia and Fugue on B-A-C-H* on the Methuen organ in 1953. In Barbara Owen's judgment, the recording was one of the best ever made on that instrument, and Biggs's playing was brilliant and vivacious. Edward Flint, a trustee of the Methuen Hall who had encouraged Biggs to do it, was ecstatic at the result. He wrote to David Oppenheim, Columbia's music director: "For ninety years this organ has been a headache to its various owners; and if tomorrow it should go up in smoke I should feel less badly than I would have a fortnight ago."

In Harrison's own estimation, about 44 percent of the 112 sets of pipes were completely new by the time he had finished rebuilding it in 1947. "Most of the other work including all the mixtures have been rearranged and worked over as to be unrecognizable, [and] there is really little of the old quality of sound left," Harrison wrote to an organ historian, William King Covell. "I think you will agree that it takes on generally an Aeolian-Skinner flavor." But in the jacket notes that Biggs wrote for the recording for Columbia, no mention was made of what Aeolian-Skinner or Harrison had done to alter the organ.

Something had soured their relationship. Emerson Richards thought it might have been Aeolian-Skinner's decision in 1948 fi-

E. Power Biggs at Methuen Memorial Music Hall

nally to demand payment for the Germanic Museum organ, which it had been subsidizing and maintaining for more than a decade. Harvard wasn't interested in buying it, and Biggs had tried to round up other donors to put up the money, but not enough were interested. Yet he needed the organ for his CBS radio broadcasts. "Compelled to purchase it," he fumed, but paid the $8,000 Aeolian-Skinner wanted. It hadn't been Harrison's idea to ask for the money, but perhaps Biggs's falling out with him began with that.

The growing distance between them was also due to Biggs's dawning realization that Harrison, who had awakened Biggs to the intrinsic polyphonic nature of the baroque organ, did not share Biggs's ideas about what use should be made of these ideas in new organs. While Harrison had been interested in incorporating baroque sounds into his own American Classic concept, Biggs had become more interested in the neobaroque on its own terms. Harrison had started something that Biggs was determined to take further, and their friendship cooled. Harrison moved his personal effects out of the Biggs house at 53 Highland Street in Cambridge, and the distance between the two men widened.

In April 1953, an exchange of letters between Harrison and Biggs over alterations and other work on the Germanic Museum and Symphony Hall organs betrayed Biggs's growing disenchantment with Aeolian-Skinner and its work. Biggs had requested changes in the Germanic Museum organ, but he wasn't satisfied with the results. When Harrison sent him a bill for the work, Biggs complained, "I'd be glad to pay for anything that represents progress for the organ, but its shortcomings won't be cured in this way. I should think that the company would have the artistic interest to improve the instrument, and it's too bad if this isn't so." Biggs was also unhappy about mechanical troubles with the Symphony Hall organ. "We can hardly depend on it when scheduling broadcasts or a recording session," he complained.

Harrison's reply began "Dear Jimmie," but the tone was wounded: "Some of the things you say may be justified. However, other things hurt me not a little." Biggs apparently felt that Aeolian-Skinner had overbilled him for tuning the Symphony Hall organ for recording sessions the previous October, but Harrison, learning that Biggs would be billed personally for these, had cut the cost, he explained. "It seemed to me that you could probably use this expense against income. However, you told me over the telephone that it was too late for that," Harrison wrote. "Frankly, I would rather write off these amounts than have any hard feeling about them." There were troubles with the cables that connected the Symphony Hall console to the organ mechanism, Harrison conceded, but they would be replaced. "You know the way the console is banged up and pushed around there are bound to be some troubles." As for Biggs's unhappiness with a new stop he had wanted for the Germanic Museum organ, Harrison expressed exasperation. "I certainly agree that you must have exactly what you want," he wrote. "If we could get together and decide exactly what it should be for your purpose, we can make another swap. Perhaps you will let me know about this." He signed the letter, "Very sincerely yours, Don, President."

But it was not long before word spread that the friendship had ended. Biggs got the maintenance contract for the Symphony Hall, Tanglewood, and Germanic Museum organs changed to another company, and in late 1953 Walter Holtkamp wrote to him from Cleveland: "Jimmie, me boy,—there is too much talk going around about the parting of the ways of one E.P.B. and G.D.H. I don't like it. You both have too much meaning for each other and together, you have too much meaning for the American organ scene to so upset your public. If I may, I would suggest an arms around the shoulder picture" in *The Diapason,* then the official journal of the American Guild of Organists. "You are clever. You can contrive it."

Perhaps the truth was that, for Biggs, Harrison and Aeolian-Skinner had served their purpose. Harrison's Germanic Museum organ and Mrs. Coolidge's sponsorship of the radio broadcasts on it had launched him to national fame, and like the discarded stages of a rocket, Mrs. Coolidge (who died in 1953) and Harrison had both fallen away behind Biggs's rising star.

In the fall of 1952, he had become impressed with the work of Herman L. Schlicker, an Alsatian immigrant who had set up an organbuilding shop in Buffalo. Biggs eventually placed an order for a neobaroque small portable organ that he wanted to use both for practice at home and to take on tour, for which he was now getting up to $500 per engagement. This meant, he told Schlicker, that it would have to be pitched above A-440, like the Symphony Hall organ, so that it could play with orchestras that used the higher pitch.

Schlicker built his organs with electropneumatic action, which was still fine with Biggs at this point. Biggs's Schlicker organ, after further alterations, was dubbed "the Cambridge Portative" and, in December 1953, he had a trailer built to haul it behind his Studebaker.

In March 1954, Biggs appeared with the portable organ in the Coolidge Auditorium in Washington, D.C., for a concert of chamber music for organ and strings. "The organist seemed a part of the proceedings, not like a player in a large church who presses the keys and after a lapse of time listens to a reflection of the music he has made," the *Washington Evening Star* observed. Piston's 1944 *Partita,* played on the 1923 Skinner organ, in marked contrast, sounded "hollow and muffled," the sound of the organ seeming to come "from the green room, rather like the ghost of Hamlet's father on strike." A year later, the trustees sold the Skinner.

By that time, Biggs and Harrison were speaking to each other only through lawyers. Biggs heard that Aeolian-Skinner was spreading rumors that Schlicker had charged Biggs nothing for the portative organ, in return for free publicity for Schlicker's organbuilding business. "I'm all prepared to punch someone on the nose," Biggs assured Schlicker, "if we can be sure who's the right one to punch." He instructed his attorneys that he had "always paid full professional price for all instruments, including our present Schlicker, also the Aeolian-Skinner in the Germanic Museum, and contributed a thousand dollars . . . towards the Aeolian-Skinner organ in Symphony Hall. . . . I assume that officials at Aeolian-Skinner are gentlemen, not given to irresponsible statements! Yet in addition to this, there is their very concrete and unauthorized use of my picture in their advertising, and it seems time to call a halt to some of their business practices." This was a reference to a picture in an Aeolian-Skinner publicity brochure that showed Biggs, Harrison, and Albert Schweitzer at the factory in 1949 with pipes of the Symphony Hall organ.

Harrison, for his part, had turned to Aeolian-Skinner's lawyers to get legal satisfaction for Biggs's failure to credit Harrison and the company on the Methuen recording jacket. Biggs and Harrison confronted each other at a meeting with their lawyers present, and Harrison settled without payment of damages after Biggs agreed to amend the jacket notes in any future reissues of the recording, giving the poorest of excuses: he hadn't been given enough space on the jacket to tell the full story.

In June 1956, Harrison was working feverishly to complete one of his company's largest projects, the rebuilding—in fact, largely the replacement—of the Skinner organ in St. Thomas Church on Fifth Avenue in time for a national convention of the American Guild of Organists. Biggs was scheduled to appear at the convention too, but not to play on any Aeolian-Skinner organ. Instead, he demonstrated his portable Schlicker at Hunter College.

On June 14, a stiflingly hot day, Harrison set off at the end of the afternoon for his apartment on Third Avenue, but because of a taxi strike had to walk the eight blocks home. On the way, he was overcome by a feeling of exhaustion and stopped in a drugstore for a dose of smelling salts. Reaching home, he was able to eat dinner with Helen. Afterward, they sat down in front of the television set to watch Victor Borge clown around at the piano. At 11 P.M., Harrison suffered a sudden and instantaneously fatal heart attack.

Harrison was buried on Long Island on June 18. His instrument at St. Thomas was completed by his assistants, who finished installing and voicing most of the 8,905 pipes over the next seven days. The organ was an ambitious project that included an entire baroque-style "positif" with seventeen stops. The other six divisions included shimmering célestes and powerful romantic French-style trumpets, bombardes, and mixtures. Like all of Harrison's work, it could play any kind of music, with tones as clear and piquant as an Arp Schnitger organ or as majestically stentorian as one of Cavaillé-Coll's. Except for the lack of a resonating cathedral echo, it sounded convincingly French when Pierre Cochereau, the organist of Notre Dame in Paris, opened the convention with a recital in St. Thomas on June 26. The church was packed to the galleries, with people even sitting on the floor as Cochereau played. He concluded with an improvised symphony on themes submitted to him on the spot. Its last movement was a dirge to Harrison's memory.

Peggy Biggs was present at the funeral and at the memorial service at St. Thomas, but her "Biggsy" stayed away, apparently with no sentimental feelings left for either Donald Harrison or the Aeolian-Skinner company. In a letter written to Eugene Ormandy four months after Harrison's death, Biggs recommended Schlicker Organ Co., Walter Holtkamp, and M. P. Möller as possible builders of an organ for the Philadelphia Academy of Music. "You might expect me to add the name of a Boston firm for your consideration," he wrote, "but to my regret there's nothing in our experience at Symphony Hall or in other recent installations that enables me to say anything in recommending them!"

Time magazine in 1954 reported Biggs's disapproval of "ever bigger and boomier organs, trying to compete with the symphony orchestra" and commented that a recital in Westminster Abbey that spring had disappointed British listeners who had expected something more romantic and thunderous. "Every instrument you approach is different. A pianist can be reasonably satisfied that most pianos will be about the same. An organist has to climb up to his instrument; he's got to make friends with it," Biggs told *Time* before heading off to what the magazine said would be "a rugged two-month tour of Europe for a series of 30-odd concerts."

It was this 1954 European tour that marked the next major turning point in Biggs's life and career. The organs he saw in Europe were an epiphany that revealed to him a new vision of the organ as a musical instrument and of himself as the leading American evangelist of that vision—and, as such, the polar opposite of Virgil Fox, the American organist who was his main rival for the public's affections.

"The Fox"

Virgil Fox—love him or hate him, nobody who cared anything about organ music in America during his lifetime could be indifferent to him, and E. Power Biggs certainly was not. Two more contrasting personalities would be hard to imagine.

Fox's flamboyant style and his willingness to employ any device, from rhinestone-studded organ shoes to smoke and lights—anything that would open people's eyes and lure them into churches, concert halls, or rock auditoriums where they could then have their ears opened to the power and the beauty of Bach and other composers for organ—infuriated those who deplored his vulgarity as poor taste or thought that organists should remain proper and dignified in their console alcoves and choir lofts, heard but not seen.

Not Fox, as Albert Fuller, a classical harpsichordist, discovered turning pages for him (a rare occasion, since Fox almost always played from memory) at a recital on the Ernest M. Skinner organ in the Washington National Cathedral during World War II. Fox was wearing the uniform of a staff sergeant in the Army Air Force in those days, with modifications. "When he was finished, I saw that he was soaked with sweat, and his army uniform was covered with wet splotches," Fuller said. "He turned to me and asked me to hand him the pile of dark cloth lying on a chair nearby. When I picked it up, I found it immense. One side was covered in scarlet silk, and I wondered what the devil it was. He instructed me to hold up one end and put it around his shoulders. Aha! Now I realized it was a cape! I instantly asked, 'Sergeant Fox, Sir, why do you wear a cape?'

He looked me straight in the eye and said, 'Honey, they see you before they hear you!'"

Fox was a showman; that was the one thing both his detractors and admirers could always agree on. The showmanship was calculated. The gay sensibility that defined it was not. It was even naive, in those days, long before the Pentagon applied the policy of "Don't ask, don't tell" to people like Fox who were routinely drafted into the military ranks. Fox did not hide his sexuality. With Fox there was nothing to hide, no shame in coming across as who he was, as a man and as an artist. "I can outplay any organist living," *The New York Times* quoted him saying many years later, in 1974; the "purists" he so scorned (and who so detested him) sneered, but in fact most of them knew that his boast was true. "There is this about Virgil Fox," Harold C. Schonberg wrote in *The New York Times*. "When his hands are on the console, there are two of them; and when his feet are engaged in pedal work, there also are two. They can be counted. Two hands, two feet. But when the famous virtuoso organist is busy adjusting stops, and he is always busy adjusting stops, he has many hands. He must have. Fingers and wrists are incessantly darting out of nowhere, there is a constant blur, and one gets the impression that Mr. Fox has as many hands as he has teeth."

Fox was, as Jonathan Ambrosino has pointed out, a throwback, an organist who affected late nineteenth-century romantic style when the American musical establishment and most organists were scorning it and rejecting the orchestral organs Fox needed to show it off.

Fox's playing of Bach was amazingly facile and fluent, dazzlingly so, but it was also orchestrally conceived, with rubato and registrations that were far from orthodox in the 1950s and were considered fundamentally flawed by the proponents of "authentic" performance in the 1970s. "His ideas about Bach have nothing to do with what today is considered the correct style," Schonberg wrote in 1974. "Indeed, there are those who would be so unkind as to call his Bach appallingly vulgar." It was vulgar only in the literal sense. Fox was always willing to stoop to the mass audience he wanted so badly. He had to stoop, he believed, to pitch Bach to the crowd, and Harold Schonberg saw exactly what he was doing: "He showed himself to be not only the Stokowski and P. T. Barnum of the organ, but also its Billy Sunday."

Virgil Keel Fox was practically born into show business in Princeton, Illinois, on May 3, 1912. His father, Miles S. Fox, owned a movie theater, where Virgil's mother, Bird E. (Nichols) Fox, ran the box office. Birdie Fox, who sang alto in the First Presbyterian Church, was descended from an Illinois pioneer, Abigail Nichols, a doctor and a teacher who according to family lore had brought one of the first pianos to the prairies. Fox's father played the harmonica with such rhythm and verve, his son boasted later, that he could get 150 couples swaying enthusiastically at a barn dance. Virgil Fox received his first piano lessons from the organist of his family's church, a woman who, in his recollection, never changed the stops, making everything she played sound alike. At about age eight, he was given a chance to sit down at the same organ and play it, Fox once said, and after that, "my existence took on another plateau." More piano and organ studies followed with Hugh C. Price, a teacher in nearby Lasalle. As a young prodigy, Fox played piano in his father's movie theater, keeping audiences entertained while the hall filled, and he occasionally took over from his old piano teacher at the church. By age fourteen, he was giving organ concerts; 3,000 people came to hear him play that year at Withrow High School in Cincinnati, and he began studies in Chicago with one of the leading Bach performers of the world, Wilhelm Middelschulte.

A composer as well as an organist and harpsichordist, Middelschulte played with the Chicago Symphony. Fox went for his first audition with this formidable German professor to the Church of the Redeemer on the south side of Chicago. "When I got to the loft and climbed the stairs to the organ," Fox remembered later, "he took off these great pince-nez glasses and said, 'This is the most mechanical of all instruments, and if YOU can go beyond those mechanics and make great music upon it, you will do what few organists ever have done or shall do!' Then he put out his hand and said, 'How do you do, Mr. Fox?'"

Fox won national recognition in 1929 as the best player at a competition of the National Federation of Music Clubs in Boston, and he graduated from Princeton Township High School as salutatorian of his class in 1930. What Middelschulte thought of his protégé's successes can be surmised from his decision in later years to dedicate to Fox a piece called *Perpetuum Mobile*. This is a fiendishly difficult exercise, played by the feet alone on the pedalboard, and when they were Fox's feet it was dazzling, as one of his own protégés, Ted Alan Worth, later remembered:

> It started out light, delicate, and soft, but soon the feet were flying and I noticed that Virgil Fox was actually playing "thirds" (pedal notes that were two notes, or a third, apart) with his right foot while the left played single notes. All the while his hands continuously manipulated the stops and couplers (in order to connect the keyboards with the pedalboard), adding stops gradually, one by one. The volume built. Then the left foot started playing thirds. I thought, how is it possible? By this time, the volume and tempo were increasing, and the two feet were a blur. The organ roared! Then the pedals stated the original theme "wide open" [Fox's usual term for triple-fortissimo full organ]. Both feet played crunching chords: three notes with the right foot and two with the left. Then, for the first and last time in the three-minute piece, the right hand, on a manual keyboard, made a glissando and struck the final chord. I couldn't believe my ears or eyes, although the ovation was deafening all around. . . . Few organists in the world could copy his virtuosity, although he eventually published his edition of the music for any that dared to try.

After studying with Middelschulte, Fox won a full scholarship to the Peabody Conservatory of Music in Baltimore, where he studied with a Dutch organ master, Louis Robert. In a single year there, he played five recitals from memory, completed all his diploma requirements and won the school's award of $100 for the student achieving the highest examination grades.

In the fall of 1932, Fox was determined to set off for Europe to study with Marcel Dupré in Paris, but his father wouldn't give him the money. As Richard Torrence, later Fox's manager and one of his closest friends, wrote, "He went to his 'Mama.' 'Come here, boy,' she said. They went to the piano in the parlor. She opened the front of the instrument and took out a roll of bills. She asked how much it would cost. 'Two thousand dollars, Mama.' She peeled off the exact amount (it hardly made a dent in the roll) and said 'Don't you tell Papa!'"

To be twenty years old and an organist in Paris in 1932 must have been bliss. "Paris is the promised land for an organ student," Fox wrote in a brief "Paris in Review" letter to *The American Organist*. Not only could he revel in the cafés, drinking cups of hot chocolate thick enough to eat with a spoon, but he could also hear the great romantic organs of Cavaillé-Coll and learn the exciting modern music that was being written for them from the composers themselves. Charles-Marie Widor and Dupré were both playing at Saint-Sulpice, Sunday after Sunday; the nearly blind Louis Vierne, composer of six organ symphonies, was still doing his inimitable improvisations at Notre Dame. Fox took instruction from Dupré and reported hearing Widor and Vierne; he could also have heard Olivier Messiaen at La Trinité, Charles Tournemire, one of the greatest masters of organ improvisation since Bach, at César Franck's old post at Sainte-Clotilde, and the young Maurice Duruflé, who had just composed the first of his organ masterpieces, the *Prelude, Adagio, and Choral Variations* on the medieval plainsong theme *Veni Creator Spiritus*, at Saint-Etienne-du-Mont.

In Paris, he practiced his French, more prairie than Saint-Germain-des-Prés, and learned that he didn't know everything there was to know about organ playing. At his first lesson, Dupré asked him what he would play. The Bach *Prelude and Fugue in D major* (BWV 532), Fox replied, one of Bach's most vivacious showpieces, with a dazzling pedal part in the fugue that fairly dances, and proceeded to play it—flawlessly, he thought—for the master.

"Too fast, too detached!" commented Dupré, whose own playing was often exceedingly staccato. "Where did you get that idea of pedaling? You must buy my editions of pedal scales with my markings for exactly how to pedal, the heel and toe, and so forth, and prepare them for me—just one or two scales before each lesson."

Fox was furious, his feelings hurt, but he did as he was told; he bought Dupré's edition and performed all the scales for him, just as marked, at the next lesson. As Worth recalled, "Virgil said Dupré never asked to hear another scale; and Virgil said that he never again followed Dupré's markings!"

Fox returned to the United States via London, where he played a recital at Kingsway Hall in mid-1933. He made his New York debut on the organ at the Wanamaker store on lower Broadway. His first American concert tour followed, and apparently Fox pushed the envelope where the fees were concerned; a church in Madison, Wisconsin, balked at paying the $50 fee he demanded. The following year, he was appointed organist at St. Mark's Lutheran Church in Hanover, Pennsylvania, where he met the man who would be his companion for nearly thirty years—W. Richard Weagly, the church's choir director, already widely admired in his own right in sacred music circles. Fox and Weagly, who was three years his senior, moved together to Brown Memorial Presbyterian Church in Baltimore in 1935, where Fox was appointed organist—on a four-keyboard instrument built by the Skinner Organ Company—and Weagly became choirmaster. Three years later Fox succeeded his old teacher at Peabody Conservatory as head of the organ department. He was then twenty-six years old.

Fox was not a gifted sightreader, nor was he especially talented at playing by ear. But he had phenomenal self-discipline and an ability to put in hours of hard work, practicing pedal scales, piano exercises in velocity, and Bach, Bach, Bach. His technique allowed him to race through virtuoso Bach pieces like the *Toccata and Fugue in D minor* (BWV 565) far faster and more flawlessly than most of the people he later dismissed as "purists" could, but more often Fox tried to make Bach sound like a romantic composer. Invited to play on the Wanamaker organ at an American Guild of Organists convention in Philadelphia in 1939, Fox chose a rich setting of a chorale notated by Bach, *Come, Sweet Death,* an orchestrated arrangement that Leopold Stokowski had recorded for RCA Victor with the Philadelphia Orchestra, and transcribed it from the record. It took Fox eight separate trips to Wanamaker's to get the music just right and to choose the stops that could milk every drop of pathos from both the music and the instrument, whose 6,000-pipe string division "wraps its sound around you—and squeezes," in the words of an enthusiast who heard Fox play. The assembled organists gave Fox's performance a standing ovation.

Come, Sweet Death as arranged by Virgil Fox propelled him right to the top of his field. Two years later, he published the score and RCA Victor produced a recording of him playing it on the equally lush 1933 organ in the chapel of Girard College in Philadelphia, an organ that is largely Ernest M. Skinner's work—"hands-down, the *finest* thing on *this great earth,*" as Fox described this great instrument to a fellow organist, Carlo Curley. "Virgil Fox at Girard College," the first of more than sixty records Fox made during his long career, came out just before the Japanese attack on Pearl Harbor thrust the United States into war.

Fox took leaves of absence from Brown Memorial Church and Peabody in 1942 when he was drafted into the army, which did not suspend his career but drove it right along. No basic training for Fox; his duties were confined to the chapel at Bolling Field outside Washington, D.C., where he played five services a week as a chaplain's assistant. He also provided musical therapy for injured servicemen at Walter Reed Hospital in Washington, and played piano and organ at fund-raisers for the Air Force Aid Society, a charity that was run by the wife of General Henry H. "Hap" Arnold. The army also let him play organ recitals, and when he appeared at the National Cathedral to play on the great Skinner organ, the audience filled the apse and transept (all that was completed of the church at the time), much to the delight of the organbuilder, who took Fox's success as his own. "The Cathedral is *packed* when Virgil Fox plays my organ there," Skinner wrote in 1943.

Fox had also learned with his mother and her sister, Fox's doting

Aunt Etna in Princeton, how important it was for a great artist to have a patron—or, more often in his case, a matron. In Washington, his work with the Air Force Aid Society brought him into contact with its wealthy sponsors, women who were attracted to him by his talent, not his sexuality, and wanted to nurture his reputation. One of them was Anne Saunderson Archbold, heiress to the fortune of one of John D. Rockefeller's original partners in Standard Oil of Ohio, John D. Archbold. Anne Archbold had built "Hillandale," a thirty-four-room Italianate villa on thirty acres of land off Reservoir and Foxhall Roads in the Georgetown section of Washington. In an enormous music room, she had installed a two-manual pipe organ built by the Aeolian Company in 1923. There she invited guests such as Eleanor Roosevelt, Leopold Stokowski, and Margaret Sanger to hear music. Fox entertained people like them regularly, and Mrs. Archbold showed her gratitude by giving him the run of the estate. "Fox was able to live at her house, provided he got back to the base at Bolling by 6:30 A.M.," according to Jane P. Boutwell, who as a child was often invited to Hillandale with her family and recalled that Private Fox got around Washington in a Cadillac even then. As Fox put it to Ted Alan Worth, "I slept between satin sheets in Annie Archbold's palace the entire time I was in the service!"

At dinner at the Boutwells' one evening, Fox came in with his freshly cleaned uniform from the dry cleaner's. Augustin M. Prentiss Jr., an Air Corps captain at the time, remembered him as "a charming, exuberant young man" who played the piano as beautifully as he did the organ. "He was a brand new private with no idea how to wear his insignia," Colonel Prentiss discovered, and he helped Private Fox pin brass badges and ribbons in their proper places.

By 1945, he had become Staff Sergeant Fox, and on April 29 of that year he played a recital on the huge M. P. Möller organ at the United States Military Academy at West Point. Soon afterward, he was invited by the noted organist David McK. Williams to play a concert at St. Bartholomew's Episcopal Church on Park Avenue, on the largest pipe organ—a Skinner—in New York City. Fox looked to Williams as a sort of role model. Williams, too, wore a cape and was gay, and Fox and Weagly later often traveled to New York City to hear Williams and the choir perform in Sunday afternoon oratorio performances. For his concert, Fox had worked up Vierne's *Second Organ Symphony*, written in 1903, a work that had earned praise from none other than Claude Debussy, who had said of its sonorities, "Old J. S. Bach, the father of us all, would have been pleased." Fox planned to introduce it with one of the little inspirational talks that he liked to deliver with the music. "I have to tell them all about this wonderful symphony!" he told Williams, whose imperious reply was "Say nothing. We will have no speeches during concerts at St. Bartholomew's Church. People will come to hear you play, dear boy, not to hear you speak!" But of course Fox did speak. The Vierne symphony, with its agonized minor-key chromaticism and its E major conclusion, must have seemed most appropriate as the end of the long war in Europe approached.

Fox was discharged from the Army Air Forces half a year later, and in February 1946, again a civilian, he performed a series of three organ recitals in the Coolidge Auditorium of the Library of Congress under the auspices of the Elizabeth Sprague Coolidge Foundation, again to full houses. Fox was taking aim at E. Power Biggs's spot as the leading American concert organist of the day, and here he was playing in an auditorium whose benefactress was sponsoring Biggs's weekly radio broadcasts from the Germanic Museum at Harvard University on CBS. Perhaps Fox intended to show that anything Biggs could do, he could do better—Bach, of course, starting with the brilliant *Prelude and Fugue in A minor* (BWV 543), and a solemn piece by the eighteenth-century French court musician Louis Marchand. The program does not say whether Fox gave one of his little lectures, but if he did, he would have pointed out that Marchand was the musician who, challenged to an improvisation contest with Bach during a visit to Dresden in October 1717, lost his nerve and left town at the crack of dawn instead. Fox performed the Middelschulte pedal dazzler too, and concluded the program with the rip-roaring opening Allegro of Widor's *Organ Symphony No. 6*.

Dick Weagly was also discharged early in 1946 from military service in Germany, where he was assistant to the air chaplain of the Army Air Corps in Europe, and he and Fox resumed their musical and personal relationship at Brown Memorial in Baltimore. But they had set their sights on bigger things. Six months earlier, Anne Archbold had written to her friend John D. Rockefeller Jr., the chairman of the board of trustees of Riverside Church in New York City and its principal benefactor, that "Sgt. Virgil Fox" had talked with Harry Emerson Fosdick, the chief minister of the church, about a position there. "I feel that he is not only an unusually fine musician but has great ability to interest people in music and to arouse and secure their cooperation," Mrs. Archbold told "Dear John." In May, Dr. Fosdick, Rockefeller, and the Riverside Church trustees took Mrs. Archbold's advice and decided on Virgil Fox. They wanted him so much that they agreed when he insisted that his demanding concert schedule would require the church to split the job into two pieces, and they also hired Weagly to train the choir.

Together, the two set out to create an ambitious church music program to rival the one at St. Bartholomew's, with stirring service music on Sunday morning and, three times a month, Sunday afternoon performances of cantatas and oratorios by the choir, with Fox playing the orchestral accompaniment on the organ, a Hook & Hastings installation completed in 1930 that left Fox dissatisfied from his first days on the job. Its faulty playing action constantly produced ciphers, and the four keyboards and pedalboard and limited stop-combination controls of the console made playing awkward. "Mr. Virgil Fox wants to see you specifically about the organ," Rockefeller was informed in a memo by one of his office assistants at the end of 1947. "The situation regarding the organ as it stands at the church is almost impossible. The man who takes care of it is beginning to lose his courage. . . . The organ is so bad that when Mr. Fox invites people to hear him play he has to go out to another organ—this just as an illustration of its condition. He wishes the whole Board would come to hear it. . . . Everything about it is wrong." Quite possibly, the main thing that was wrong with it in Fox's eyes was that it was not an Aeolian-Skinner.

Rockefeller asked Archer Gibson, who had often played the house organ at the Rockefeller family estate in Pocantico Hills, to come in and make an appraisal. Gibson agreed that the organ had major shortcomings and recommended various organbuilders, not including Aeolian-Skinner, but Fox successfully steered the church authorities to G. Donald Harrison in Boston.

Fox was on the way to getting the new organ he wanted, but only in stages. Rockefeller and the trustees gave the go-ahead in 1947 for Aeolian-Skinner to construct a new console. Fox was not shy about telling the company exactly how he wanted it designed, with five keyboards, row upon row of toe-studs—buttons the organist hits with the feet to change stops in the middle of a piece—and no fewer than seven footpedals, lined up side by side in the center of the baseboard, for controlling the various swellshades. The maze of stopknobs on the jambs on either side of the keyboards was so vast that it looked like a Seurat canvas.

"The new console at Riverside for Virgil Fox is, in my opinion, the ugliest, and unhandiest, large drawstop console to which my attention has been drawn," Henry Willis III wrote to Harrison after receiving a photograph of it in 1948. "Of course, this is Virgil Fox's design—not yours—and I suppose you took the line that he could have what he wanted. But I think that no organist should be allowed to impose his own pet idiosyncrasies on an instrument over which he, temporarily, presides."

Fox made so many suggestions and changed his mind so often, in fact, that Aeolian-Skinner later complained that it had taken a loss of $8,000 in building the console. It was an investment, perhaps, in a potentially much bigger job, but with the postwar economic outlook unclear, the Riverside trustees decided to wait a few years before deciding to give Fox the new organ he wanted to go with the new console.

Fox kept agitating, annoying Rockefeller no end. "Perhaps we should make Mr. Fox either a deacon or a trustee, in addition to our organist; he would then be looking at his requests from a point of view other than an unlimited desire for an ideal organ," Rockefeller wrote to Dr. Robert J. McCracken, Fosdick's successor, in 1948. Harrison came from Boston to appraise the organ in 1949 and recommended replacing all of its leaking windchests, reducing the air pressure, and redesigning the "very dull and heavy" tonal scheme, though he thought he could save and reuse pipes from many of the "beautiful string tone stops and some flutes." Whatever the organ's shortcomings, Fox played fortissimo too often for Rockefeller's taste, apparently, for he wrote to his fellow church trustee A. LeRoy Chipman, "It seems to me that we will never have any peace or quiet—and I use the word 'quiet' from the musical point of view—at Riverside Church until Mr. Fox's successor is found and installed."

Fox, who had taken the job on condition that he could continue his active concert career around the country, needed an assistant who could substitute for him at rehearsals and services, accompany the high school choir, and deal with his concert managers in New York.

At a recital at the Municipal Auditorium in Minneapolis in mid-1949, he found the person he was looking for—Roberta Bailey, a recently graduated University of Minnesota organ player who had organized the program, part of a regional convention of the American Guild of Organists, and had been swept off her feet by Fox's musical genius. "What words could ever tell you the thanks I sincerely feel for making that concert go as you did?" Fox wrote to "Bobbie" Bailey on July 13. "I certainly am pleased that you are coming to New York and you know where to check in as soon as you arrive!" She arrived at the church to take up whatever duties Fox would assign to her on September 25, a Saturday, when she found him playing in one of the Riverside Church side chapels for a wedding—in sandals, since the console of that organ was out of sight of the participants.

"One of the first things I did for him was to look at folding cots downtown after morning working hours," Bailey wrote in her diary. "He needs a new one for his office, so he can rest between the morning church service and the 5 P.M. oratorio service." Fox had a high-ceilinged fourth-floor office in the church tower, with a library and a piano that was constantly out of tune and two Gothic windows looking out on Grant's Tomb, the Hudson, and the George Washington Bridge. Here he could retreat to nap or simply to avoid tedious staff meetings from which he exempted himself because he liked to do so much of his practicing late at night. He paid Bailey $15 a week and threw in organ and piano lessons, but he required her to drive him to the airport Sunday nights when he flew off to concert engagements, and to pick him up Fridays when he returned to Riverside for choir rehearsals.

Fox had other assistants who were unpaid, young men usually. Foremost among them was Robert Hebble, whose talent for harmony was his ticket to a seat with Fox at the console on Sundays. "Although Virgil was a supreme musician, his harmonic flow was, in a word, 'basic,'" Hebble wrote. "In other words, it was a bit cornball. Enter me at age sixteen, cute and brimming over with colorful '$50 chords.' Harmony had always been 'my thing.' Thus, I could really help him while he improvised during a service and he'd ask me under his breath, 'What chord should I play now?'"

Fox had the use of a church car, but soon he got a new Cadillac, one provided by another rich lady friend—Florence Candler, the second wife of Asa Griggs Candler Jr., the son of the founder of the great Coca-Cola Company of Atlanta. The Candler family were good customers of the Aeolian company, commissioning and buying four different house organs in Atlanta over the years. Asa Candler Jr. had installed an eighty-seven-stop, cathedral-sized Aeolian instrument in 1925, and after his death Florence Candler continued to invite great organists to give house concerts. Fox became one of her favorites. Seventeen years his senior, she, like his own mother and like Anne Archbold, doted on him. "Oh, you have to help these poor starving artists out," she told Carlo Curley, who had become a protégé of Fox's and whom she took under her wing. Fox often stayed with Mrs. Candler when he went to Atlanta, and in 1950 he flew there to take delivery of a new white Cadillac convertible she had bought him from the Capitol Automobile Company in Atlanta, her favorite dealer. Fox had his assistant go down to Atlanta by train to meet him there. He and Bailey took turns driving the Cadillac, with the top down, to New York, at breakneck speed when Fox was at the wheel.

Now young Miss Bailey found that she would also be expected to drive the car out to Tenafly, New Jersey, where Fox and Weagly shared a house, to pick up Weagly's mother for the Sunday afternoon oratorio performances. One Sunday in 1950, Bailey also had to play for the entire Sunday morning service, because, as she wrote to her mother in Minneapolis, "Virgil is in Nassau with Mrs. Archbold." Anne Archbold sponsored a concert series in the Bahamas, where she wintered, and she wanted Fox there to attract a big audience.

Another one of Fox's artistic admirers and sponsors was Emilie Parmalee Spivey, an Atlanta organist who, with her husband, a dentist, had become wealthy through investments in real estate. Mrs. Spivey arranged prestigious concert engagements for Fox whenever he came to Georgia, and he reciprocated by presenting a recital for her at Riverside, perhaps with an ulterior motive in mind. "If you needed to, exactly how much cash could you lay your hands on in the space of 24 earthly hours?" he would ask his wealthy friends, but usually the answer was something evasive like "I have no earthly idea." (Anne Archbold left him $10,000 in her will when she died in 1968.)

The concerts at Riverside and around the country continued to build Fox's reputation, and in 1950 he was invited to a convention of the American Guild of Organists in Boston that was being organized by Biggs. Fox's rival had scheduled playing time for him, but on an organ Fox considered inadequate for the display of his virtuoso talent. Roberta Bailey called Joseph Whiteford, Harrison's assistant at Aeolian-Skinner, and asked him what could be done about it. "He said Biggs really gave VF the worst organ in the city and he is trying to get it changed, but Biggs had just said that VF either plays on it or not at all!" Bailey wrote her mother. "I hope Whiteford has a brilliant idea or maybe VF should show Biggs what can be done with a lousy instrument."

It was an organ at Emmanuel Church in Back Bay, one that had been designed by Lynnwood Farnam, the American virtuoso to whose memory Louis Vierne dedicated his *Sixth Organ Symphony* in 1932, and built in 1917 by Casavant Frères Ltée of St. Hyacinthe, Québec, one of the leading organbuilders of the day. But it was not an Aeolian-Skinner, in the city where Aeolian-Skinner was king.

Fox's reaction set off Weagly, who at times succumbed to feelings of inadequacy and rivalry toward his companion. "VF was really up-set about it all and had decided not to play and then Dick Weagly made one of his usual nasty remarks and then they were off!" Bailey wrote. "The three of us were going downtown for supper and VF asked me what I thought he should do and I said that if he didn't play in Boston and show everyone what could be done, I would be disappointed in him forever and that I was disgusted with both of them and was going back to the club and not to supper with either of them! The next morning, Saturday, Dick took the bus into Man-hattan and when VF came in while I was practicing the piano in his office, he said, 'Let's go to lunch and send Biggs the telegram that I'll play on 'junk.'"

The concert that June was, in Bailey's estimation, a "big success," although Fox, in front of so many fellow professionals, seemed more nervous than she had ever seen him. *The Diapason,* the official journal of the Guild, reported that there was standing room only in the church. Fox's friends, led by Anne Archbold and her delegation from Washington, were all there. The program included Satie's aus-tere and plaintive *Messe des Pauvres,* a work seldom heard then or since, with the flavor of medieval plainchant spiced occasionally with dissonant chords. Satie was followed by the Bach *Toccata in F* (BWV 540) and the *Introduction, Passacaglia, and Fugue,* a "monu-ment of organ literature," as Fox explained, by Healey Willan, a contemporary Canadian composer.

After a lively rendition of the Bach *Trio Sonata VI* (BWV 530), Fox stepped before the audience to deliver a talk and made the assembled organists and other musicians stand up to sing the rousing Welsh hymn Hyfrydol, "Alleluia, sing to Jesus." A chorale-prelude by Ralph Vaughan-Williams on the same tune followed, along with *Come, Sweet Death* and Bach's *Prelude and Fugue in D major.* Played on "junk" or not, the whole performance earned Fox a standing ovation.

Fox's convertible, though, was stolen from the nearby parking lot of the Ritz-Carlton Hotel, where Bailey had driven and left it before going off to the less expensive hotel she had booked for herself. The police found the car the next day in one of the Boston suburbs, unscratched and in good repair, as undamaged by the episode as Bailey's relationship with the maestro. Fox appointed her his concert manager in 1951, breaking with the established house of Bernard Laberge, where he had been only one artist among many—including one of Fox's greatest rivals in the world of organists, Claire Coci, who was married to Laberge. Fox always felt that he was nonpareil, a feeling no doubt reinforced when the American Guild of Organists elected him that year to its national board for a three-year term.

Fox's new concert manager had discovered that he was not only demanding but "selfish," requiring her to delay her own departure to Europe for the concert tour she had arranged for him in the summer of 1952 because he needed her to attend to details in New York. Both Bailey and Weagly were with him nonetheless in England and in Switzerland, where he made an appearance at the Lucerne Music Festival in August. Anne Archbold also arrived, on the 20th, and, as Bailey wrote in her diary, "took over the Fox! Didn't see him rest of the day—he slipped a note under my door late, but I didn't get up to get it."

From Lucerne the entourage moved to Bern for the International Church Music Conference, where Fox's playing rocked the reviewer for the local newspaper, *Der Bund,* on his heels: "A huge reputation preceded the American organist Virgil Fox (New York).

But that he would offer a concert of such technical perfection was probably unexpected by almost everybody. Here and there it could be asked whether his playing was really any more than just outwardly perfected technique—extraordinarily masterly though it was—accompanied by an equally extraordinary virtuosity and even a kind of theatricality, which dealt with the stops of the Bern Cathedral organ like a juggler. But then came chorale preludes and the F-major *Toccata* of J. S. Bach, which Fox performed with deeply affecting sensitivity."

ᑯᓭᑐ

Fox and Weagly took summer vacation trips to Europe every other year; Weagly attended choir festivals in England while Fox returned to Paris and toured famous European organs. Otherwise, they took car trips at home in one of Fox's Cadillacs. There was a new one every couple of years, always a convertible, and when General Motors offered Cadillacs in lavender, Fox went for one. Off the two men would go, disregarding all speed limits, to the West Coast, where Bird Fox had been living in Pasadena since her husband's death in 1950. Fox usually made it a point to go by way of Salt Lake City to hear the great Aeolian-Skinner organ that Harrison had installed in the Mormon Tabernacle. He still had his heart set on getting one just like it.

Fortunately for him, the Hook & Hastings organ in Riverside Church cooperated, growing steadily more troublesome, with loud notes ciphering in service after service. Fox tried to minimize these failings, but when

*Virgil Fox with a new Cadillac
at LaGuardia Airport in 1953*

all else failed, Roberta Bailey more than once had to climb the ladders in the organ chambers, much to the amusement of members of the congregation, to pull wailing pipes out of holes.

On Easter Sunday of 1951, calamity struck again. "More than 4,000 people were crammed into the church (including President and Mrs. Eisenhower! the guests of Mr. and Mrs. John D. Rockefeller Jr.) with loudspeakers blasting out on Riverside Drive to the overflow crowds," Robert Hebble recalled.

> As the choir finished a glorious anthem, three notes on what was then the loudest stop in the organ—the Solo Tuba—continued to play what was definitely not one of my famous "$50 chords." I was about to reach over to Virgil's left to shut off the organ motors when Virgil blocked my hand and said, "Don't touch a thing! This is the answer to a prayer!"
>
> Dr. McCracken was unable to begin his sermon because of the raucous-sounding ciphers. Virgil started walking down the center of the chancel in full view of the congregation, down the steps, and over to the side door to the organ chambers where he turned on three floor levels of fluorescent lights. It wasn't pretty. He climbed up two separate ladders while the whole congregation watched, disconnected the offending pipes at the very top level, then climbed back down.
>
> At the end of the service, Mr. Rockefeller bolted through the curtained doorway behind the console. "Virgil, what is it we need?" he asked. "A new organ!" was Fox's response, as it had been so often before.

Fox had been assiduously cultivating Rockefeller ever since his arrival at Riverside. Abby Aldrich Rockefeller, John D. Jr.'s first wife, had died in 1948, and Martha Baird Rockefeller, his second wife, was a former concert pianist who called upon Fox several times to help her pick out new pianos for the Rockefeller homes on Fifth Avenue and at Kykuit, their estate in Pocantico Hills, New York. The Rockefellers also had the three-manual Aeolian organ at Kykuit regularly maintained and tuned by Aeolian-Skinner, and they occasionally invited Fox to the estate to play for their soirées.

Fox drove his Cadillac up the Hudson one moonlit summer night in 1951, strolled through the gardens, looked out over the great river below the hills, and then went inside to regale his benefactors and their guests with soothing and relaxing selections, both Bach and romantic music—the Rockefellers did not care for loud, dissonant showpieces. The next morning, he found that the house staff had washed and polished his car and filled the gas tank for the return drive to New York City. He was almost beginning to believe he was considered a member of the family.

Rockefeller thanked Fox for his playing and his help in selecting pianos for three of the Rockefeller homes in a letter a few days later. Enclosed was a check for $500. Fox responded with effusive and obsequious thanks, but he was also shocked back to reality enough to fracture his French: "I really hope and pray that the arrival of such a completely generous check does not mean a 'faite accomplis' and the end of music together in your house! For I would rather, a thousand times, make music for you in the inspirationally beautiful setting of your rooms and gardens—feeling the warmth of your friendship and the keen pleasure of your personality (even if we do not speak of world-shaking matters, ho! ho!) than to be a part of the furniture, carefully screened behind potted palms, engaged at a flattering fee!"

Nevertheless, he kept testing the Rockefellers' generosity. More than once, he asked for permission to take his mother to Kykuit to show her the gardens, and he was infatuated with the indoor swimming pool. "In a former life I think I must have been a *fish*!" he wrote to the Rockefellers in November of 1951. "If there were some times when none of your family were using the pool at Tarrytown, might I be permitted to motor up and have a swim? I would promise to make no fuss (will gladly take my own towel!) and would be more grateful than words can tell. Pools in the city have such an excess of chlorine in them and to last the entire winter with no swimming is a let-down." Rockefeller replied cordially that Fox should just write the housekeeper at Kykuit "whenever you feel like a dip," but wrote separately to the housekeeper: "Mr. Fox is a delightful young man. He has done much to help us with the organ and our various pianos and, while boyish and enthusiastic, will not I am sure take advantage of this permission to use the swimming pool." Rockefeller was wrong, though, if he thought Fox wouldn't use the pool at all. Two weeks later, he got a letter from Fox saying "I've already had one delicious 'dip.'"

Fox's relations with other trustees and the church elders continued to have occasional rough spots. Dr. Norris L. Tibbets, one of the most dignified senior ministers at Riverside, was once startled by a greeting from Fox at the organ console, "How good to see you, Honey!" Dr. Tibbets replied, offended, "I'm not your honey, and kindly never address me that way again!"

Finally, all the organ ciphers and the attendant theatrics persuaded Rockefeller and the trustees to go ahead and order a new organ from Aeolian-Skinner. Fox was working with Harrison's assistant Joseph Whiteford, whom he had met in Washington at one of Anne Archbold's galas, and in early 1952 Whiteford sent a proposal to build a new organ that would "solve all problems" for the church for $105,000, as he told the church's business manager, George J. Heidt. "We discussed informally Mr. Fox's relation to the rebuilt organ and I could easily see that Mr. Whiteford hoped that some system could be worked out whereby new ideas would not be introduced from week to week as the organ was being rebuilt," Heidt wrote the trustees in April. The following month, the trustees and Aeolian-Skinner agreed on a $104,000 contract, with a $25,000 pledge from John D. Rockefeller Jr. to encourage donations from other wealthy backers. Once the funding was assured, the public announcement of the plans that October made news in the New York papers. "Please know there is one human soul who is 'walking on air' in anticipation of the day when this needed thing is accomplished," a grateful Fox wrote to Rockefeller then.

The "new ideas" Whiteford had feared were not long in coming. Less than two months after the announcement, Fox wrote to another trustee with some of them. "There are several more things that I would like to have in the organ in order to present my music most effectively to the Congregation," Fox said. "I have talked with Mr. Harrison about suggested changes in the specification and he has agreed with them as being practical. In some cases they cost more money; in others no expense is involved. . . . The items I am thinking of now, however, cost approximately $10,000 addition in the cost of the organ." The main addition was to be an unenclosed positiv division, with pipes visible to the congregation instead of placed behind the chancel screens with most of the rest. "In Mr. Fox's travels he has noted that in many of our big organs we do have this unenclosed positiv division and it is certainly very effective for the Classic literature when it is properly physically placed," Harrison wrote to one of the trustees. "You can realize that all good organists have certain things in an instrument that they feel are indispensable for their type of interpretation and, of course, in the case of Mr. Fox (who is a very brilliant player) such desires are very real and, therefore, worthy of very careful consideration." But the trustees balked and Harrison backed down (though Fox had cleverly provided for stopknobs for a positiv division in the 1948 console and, after he left the church, one was added in 1967).

What Fox wanted from Aeolian-Skinner was an organ capable of lushness, of brilliant power to accompany choirs with more than a hundred voices, and of the clear, bright sounds needed for Bach, all of which were evident in the specifications. But that was on paper. Fox's admiration for Harrison was enormous, but he also had his own definite notions of what a "string" stop should sound like and what coloration the tone of an "oboe" or a "trumpet" should take on. Fox's notion of just how many beats per second there should be in the tremolo device that made a flute pipe play with vibrato like a flautist's was legendarily fussy. "The same vibrato that Kirsten Flagstad has on high F-Sharp in *Tristan und Isolde* is the effect I'm after," he would insist, for he went to the Metropolitan Opera to hear her in Wagner's opera every time the great soprano came to New York to do it.

Harrison soon wearied of dealing with the temperamental Fox and left the job of coping with his ever-changing demands to Joseph Whiteford. The huge rebuilding project required Aeolian-Skinner to do the work section by section, so that services would never be completely without organ music. The work went on in stages through 1953 and 1954, and there was apparently enough organ in early 1953 for Rockefeller to warn Fox again that his music was often too loud and dissonant for his and Mrs. Rockefeller's taste.

"Mrs. Rockefeller, as your friend and admirer, has written you on the artistic and professional level about the organ playing in the Riverside Church," Rockefeller reminded Fox. "I am writing you on a solely material and business basis. To make clear my thought, let me use a very simple illustration. Suppose you tell your cook you want your eggs *soft* boiled and she persists in serving them to you *hard* boiled and when you speak to her about it, she tells you *she* knows how eggs should be cooked and in what form they are most appropriate for your table. Would you not feel that since you were paying her salary, you should have the eggs as *you* wanted them irrespective of her judgment in the matter? Does this homely illustration have any bearing on the situation under consideration?"

Fox was not about to let his relationship with the church's biggest benefactor be scrambled—not while Aeolian-Skinner was finally installing the new organ Fox wanted so badly. He fumed inwardly and may even have drafted a combative reply rejecting Rockefeller's implication of a master-servant relationship. But in a letter that Rockefeller did receive and file away that spring, Fox was quite conciliatory: "On Easter Day, if the organ at Riverside seems fuller than usual, please don't think I've gone back on my promise of 'eggs to order.' It will be momentary and not permanent, I assure you!" Rockefeller's reply after Easter was terse but complimentary. "The services of the Riverside Church yesterday were supremely beautiful in every respect," he wrote.

Before the new organ could be completed, there was a problem that worried Harrison as much as the pipework. That was the "dead" unreverberant acoustics of the Riverside sanctuary, the fault of the sound-absorbent Guastavino tiles in the vaulted ceiling that Rockefeller had insisted on in 1930 to make Harry Emerson Fosdick's sermons clearly audible to the congregation. An echo might be good for an organ or for the choristers, in the widespread American Protestant view, but not for the speaker of a sermon, and the Word, nothing else, was to be the centerpiece of the service. That, needless to say, was not how Fox viewed matters, and it took all of Harrison's diplomatic tact to persuade the church's trustees to spend the money necessary to treat the ceiling of the apse and part of the chancel with sealant that gave the music a little more breathing room.

The organ, as it was when finished in 1955, bore testimony to the American Classic ideal, a success despite the acoustical problems, with pipes at both ends of the church. Fox now had an instrument capable of playing music from any age, as he insisted he should have, with individual voices to produce all his favorite kinds of sound: a distant "voix humaine" high up the gallery organ for the ethereal mystery of a warbling register, often called for in the works of Franck, that is vaguely suggestive of the human voice; a cor de nuit, a concert flute, even a zauberflöte in the choir organ division, and a viola pomposa, one of Harrison's trademark stops, doubled with a viola céleste to produce lush undulations; flutes and strings galore in a huge swell organ division with powerful mixtures and trompette, hautbois, and oboe d'amour, and a "menschenstimme" stop, the German variation on the voix humaine; a solo organ division with orchestral flute, English horn, orchestral oboe, and French horn, along with chimes, harplike celesta, and a stentorian English-style tuba mirabilis; and a powerful independent pedal organ division—Harrison always insisted on that—with not one, not two, but four mighty thirty-two-foot stops that could set the entire auditorium to rumbling. Capping it all was a "celestial organ" division, speaking from above the altar with pipes that pointed directly out at the congregation—a piercing trompette at unison pitch and a French-style clairon an octave higher, complemented with a huge mixture to reinforce the harmonics and dominate the full organ.

The 193 sets of new and reworked pipes had taken more work, and labor had cost more, than Aeolian-Skinner had estimated, Whiteford later advised the church. The result was a $14,540 net loss on the contract, he claimed to the church's business manager, who reported to the trustees one of the reasons why: "Mr. Fox has a much more critical ear than most organists, and his demands are therefore more exact." With Aeolian-Skinner claiming serious financial trouble and a net loss in 1955 of nearly half its capitalized valuation, the Riverside trustees eventually agreed to pay an extra $7,500. But John D. Rockefeller Jr. sent a check for $7,000 to make up the difference.

On the great new Aeolian-Skinner instrument in the church—"that gorgeous organ of mine," Fox called it—over the next decade, Fox performed all kinds of music, running the gamut from austerity to schmalz, and orchestral transcriptions, to show off all those lush solo stops Harrison had made for him. And as for the meager reverberation, despite the treatment applied to the vault in the nave, Fox compensated with what he called an "acoustical release" technique, ending big chords on the full organ by letting go of the top notes first and the lowest note last, a kind of reverse arpeggio to create the illusion of the rich reverberation that so greatly enhanced the organ sounds he had heard in French cathedrals.

The big console that Fox had designed was tucked away on the left side of the chancel, near the altar behind the massive choir stalls, the keyboards and organist out of view of the pews in the nave, as church organ consoles so often are. But Fox had had it placed on a movable platform, so that when he gave recitals it could be rolled out in front of the altar to put the performer at center stage, turning the church into a concert hall. But the church leadership balked when he tried to put the plan into action. "Rubinstein doesn't play behind a potted palm! Why should I?" Fox argued to the trustees, who were unmoved. Fox strained his relations with the church music committee almost to the breaking point as the March dates approached for his opening solo recital and a concert with the Philharmonic-Symphony Society of New York under Dim-

Virgil Fox at the console he designed for Riverside Church

itri Mitropoulos—the conductor insisted on by one of the Riverside trustees who was on the board of the Philharmonic, although Bailey had originally approached Stokowski instead. With the need to place 100 musicians and their instruments on the chancel, the church officials eventually decided that they had no choice but to let Fox move the organ console. Finally they gave in, allowing the wooden choir stalls to be moved and the console wheeled out as well for an opening recital before the orchestra concert, on March 25. Four days earlier, at a Sunday morning dedication service, Dr. McCracken may have tried to remind Fox of his proper liturgical place: "Music rendered for its own sake, however fine it may be, is not worship," he said. "A church is not a concert hall. . . . Music has no place in worship if it is designed merely to call attention to itself or to entertain."

Fox's solo recital included a warhorse of the organ literature that was, for once, entirely appropriate for the occasion: the *Toccata and Fugue in D minor* that Bach had used to "test the lungs," as Bach put it, of a new organ using all the stops. The high point came with the Philharmonic concert, underwritten by many of Fox's musical friends, including Florence Candler. The centerpiece was the *Symphonie Concertante* by the Belgian organist and composer Joseph Jongen, a work Fox had first performed in 1952. He liked it so much that he transcribed its last movement for organ solo, and made sections of it staples of his itinerant concert programs. Written in 1926 in a postromantic style fusing elements of Dukas, Debussy, and Respighi, the *Symphonie Concertante* was conceived expressly for one of the musical extravaganzas in the Wanamaker store in Philadelphia, although the concert it was written for had never come to pass. The work concludes with "a wild toccata in which everything at once goes on," as Harold Schonberg put it, with heroic solo melodies, crashing orchestral chords, and the organ part racing a mile a minute through it all.

Triple-fortissimo, orchestra and organ combined in what Fox knew would be a guaranteed crowd-pleaser, and Fox's performance at the Riverside dedication brought the audience to its feet, including Florence Candler, who found it "a mighty loud concert" and told Carlo Curley, "I could just as well have stayed in Atlanta, left the windows open, and avoided all those damned Yankees." But when the applause died down and the festivities were over, the console was rolled back into its niche on the side of the altar, never to emerge again. Fox had to content himself with a large mirror placed behind the console for organ concerts, tilted so that the audience could see the keyboards—but not Fox's dancing feet on the pedals.

In their tenth-row pew, John D. Rockefeller Jr. and Martha Baird Rockefeller began to develop the conviction that their organist, and

their church, might be better off if he devoted full time to his concert career. Only a few weeks later, Rockefeller drafted a letter to
Fox complaining about "the excessive volume of sound and often—
I use the word advisedly—the noise, which comes from the organ,"
and sent a copy to Dr. McCracken. The minister wrote back, advis-
ing Rockefeller against sending the letter to the organist: "I can
conceive of him showing the letter to his supporters in the congregation and in that case there might be some dissension." Rockefeller filed it away, having gotten the matter off his chest. But
neither did he send another, shorter alternative letter he had prepared, congratulating Fox on the concert with the Philharmonic.
"Standing alone it would seem to represent a complete and whole-
hearted approval of Mr. Fox' organ performances which I do not
feel," he confessed.

Fox's salary at Riverside was not exactly a pittance for those
days—he and Weagly had been hired for $10,000 between them—
but it was not enough to support his lifestyle. His concert career
made the difference, and it was thriving. "Virgil Fox flies thousands
of miles each year, playing over 80 concerts which are crowded into
a tightly planned concert season," Bailey wrote in his promotional
brochure. "Each Sunday Fox not only plays the morning service at
the famous church, but also accompanies a complete oratorio presented by The Riverside Choir each Sunday afternoon. And almost
every Sunday night Virgil Fox flies off to another city, gets acquainted with another organ, plays it in concert, flies to another
city going through the same routine and then flies back to New
York in time for the Friday night choir rehearsal. This is a schedule
few people would wish to have. It is the yearly timetable of Virgil
Fox." Bailey was also successful at booking record contracts for Fox
with Capitol and RCA Victor. Fox would give them Christmas carols,
hymns, reveries—whatever they thought people wanted to hear.

Fox's concerts were bringing in $500 a throw, a large sum for an
organ recital in those days. Bailey toyed with the idea of asking
Rockefeller to buy Fox a movable organ, pipe or electronic, that he
could take with him on the road, but thought better of it; Fox's fre-

quent absences, though agreed to by the church elders when they hired him, were a growing irritant. But in 1953, Fox was doing well enough to move with Weagly from their house at 3 Brook Road in Tenafly to a twenty-six-room gray stone mansion in Englewood, also on the New Jersey side of the Hudson, that Fox bought for $68,000. Their new home, at 394 East Palisade Avenue, a twenty-minute drive from Riverside, was hardly a castle—it was set back only a hundred feet or so from the busy thoroughfare—but it had space enough, on two acres, and eventually Fox added an indoor swimming pool to get his favorite form of exercise and "clean the pores," as he put it. Inside, the house was capacious enough for separate suites for Grace Weagly and her son, whose blue bedroom was opposite Fox's pink one on the first floor, and there was room in the basement for a pipe organ underneath the main room on the ground floor. Fox later opened most of the floor to the basement with a grillwork over a home organ assembled from bits and pieces of old instruments. An Aeolian instrument, Opus 1377, originally built for a residence in Cleveland, Ohio, with a finely carved oak console, was the core. Over the years, the organ grew, taking over parts of the solarium and some upstairs rooms, when Fox added pipes from an E. M. Skinner organ that had been built for New Old South Church in Boston in 1915.

On this, his own house organ, Fox could practice music as loudly and as late as he liked, which had been a problem at Riverside, where the giant instrument was on the other side of the wall from a dormitory for students of Union Theological Seminary. Fox felt that he did his best work at the organ after dinner. But when the theological students complained about the racket, the church ordered Fox to pipe down after 10 P.M. Usually, but not always, he complied.

In the mid-1950s, Fox shared the spotlight with Biggs at the top of the American organ world. Roberta Bailey was program chairman of the convention the American Guild of Organists held in New York City in June 1956, when Fox played the American premiere of Duruflé's *Suite, op. 5, Prélude, Sicilienne, and Toccata,* written

Fox in his home in Englewood, New Jersey

in 1933 and dedicated to Paul Dukas. The virtuosity, the drama, and the sheer drive of Fox's playing of this dense but eloquent work, redolent of Duruflé's fascination with Gregorian modes, brought the audience at Riverside, which included hundreds of organists, to their feet. Then Weagly conducted the Riverside Choir in the American premiere of Ralph Vaughan Williams's choral masterpiece *Dona Nobis Pacem*, with Fox playing the orchestral parts on the organ. Thus did Fox and his partner bring two magnificent works triumphantly into the American repertoire—in a concert dedicated to the memory of Harrison, whose unexpected death had come just two weeks earlier.

Fox was a throwback to a heroic age of high-romantic organ playing whose reverberations were still resonating with the broad pub-

Virgil Fox and Roberta Bailey in Methuen

lic. Roberta Bailey could see that, but she also saw that Fox was completely self-centered and that his selfishness would end up consuming her unless she could somehow escape his orbit. Her success with the 1956 convention program encouraged her to broaden her concert management career, booking more American engagements for Pierre Cochereau and other artists of his stature, such as Karl Richter, the organist and conductor of the Munich Bach Orchestra. Soon after the 1956 convention, she became engaged to Richard F. Johnson, who lived in Westborough, 180 miles away, in central Massachusetts. Their wedding in Riverside the following year was a musically splendid occasion, with a march improvised in person by Cochereau and the rest of the music performed by Fox and the Riverside choir. But after Roberta Bailey Concert Management moved to Westborough and later to Worcester, Massachusetts, Fox began to feel a bit neglected, no longer able to summon his concert manager at any hour of the night to tell her to reserve airplane tickets, make arrangements for out-of-town recitals, drive him to the airport, or just go to dinner with him at his favorite restaurant,

Schrafft's on Forty-sixth Street, for ice cream with plenty of choco-late sauce.

With Bailey out of reach, Fox began to rely more heavily on the young organists who worshipped at his feet at Riverside—Hebble and Worth, whom Fox dubbed his "chicks," and then Frederick Swann, whom he had met in Chicago before Swann came to New York. Swann performed so well, and effaced himself so gracefully while accompanying Weagly and the choir when Fox was away, that Weagly began to look forward to the absences. Fox's accompani-ments at times seemed more like contests for the choir's attention, and frequently the choir found itself witness to vicious spats be-tween him and Weagly. "You know, Virgil, we don't need a crucifix in this church," the choir director said before a rehearsal of the Brahms Requiem. "You crucify me and the music every time you play the organ." Louise D. Maxwell, an aspiring soprano soloist, re-called, "If you have never been part of a musical tug-of-war, you can't possibly understand the situation. The singers had to keep their eyes on the movements of the director's arms, that were not aligned with the tempo of the organ!" Usually Weagly brought Vir-gil to heel, as Ms. Maxwell put it, but not always, and once there was very nearly a disaster.

"In 1957, the senior minister of the Riverside Church, Dr. Mc-Cracken, asked if I would come to his office at the conclusion of the service," Swann wrote later. "I walked in to see not only Dr. Mc-Cracken, but also the chairman of the Music Committee and sev-eral church officials. In a rather blunt manner, I was told that because of the legendary feuding between Virgil and Richard Weagly, and the uproar it was causing (sometimes even during a church service!), the church would not renew these two men's con-tracts—and, by the way, would I agree to take over? Of course I would not!"

Ruffled feathers were smoothed, the prepared memos dismissing Fox and wishing him well in a concert career were filed away, and Riverside kept both Fox and Weagly—but later gave Swann the same title Fox had, since it was Swann who henceforth was expected to play most of the services and oratorios. Each of them, Fox and Swann, was now "organist"—not "the organist"—of the Riverside Church.

After the dust settled, Fox did have more time for concert tours, on which he often took his "chicks" along, letting them ride in the back of the Cadillac while he drove at eighty to ninety miles an hour and regaled them with off-color limericks:

> A gay lad and lass from Rangoon
> Stayed up one night in their room.
> At a quarter-to-two, they were still wondering who
> Would do what, and with which, and to whom.

Swann remained a part of the inner circle despite his promotion. "We all became Virgil 'groupies,'" he wrote. "Bob and Ted were closest to Virgil—almost his shadows."

After Bailey moved to Massachusetts, she had a baby girl in 1960 and two more children, a son and a daughter, soon afterward. She continued to manage Fox's concerts, but she had her hands full with the children, as her husband had a full-time job with his family's pressed metal company, and no doubt she was not as responsive as she once had been to Fox's late-night telephone calls and his incessant demands.

Fox's impatience was growing when he heard about Richard Torrence, an unemployed young friend of Worth's in San Francisco who had a talent for business as well as an appreciation of music, and who would consider relocating to New York if he could get a job. Fox asked if Torrence would be willing to become his personal secretary—he wouldn't need to pay him much money, Fox thought, if Torrence could keep collecting unemployment from California.

Perhaps Roberta Bailey should have seen what was coming next. When she pointed out the risks of raising Fox's standard concert fee from $500 to $750, as he wanted to do in 1962, calling it "suicide" (although she did as he asked), Fox wrote her that he was "in a quandary about the financial end of my career." She was giving him inadequate "promotion," he complained, not enough publicity, apart from occasional mailed notices to organists' magazines, and she never traveled, as his previous manager, Laberge, had done to promote him and his concerts around the world. "The only way I can see clear for me to hire somebody is for the Management to take a *little* less percentage," he wrote. "You have demands upon your time and strength (and I wouldn't have it otherwise for the world) and the things my career needs because you cannot promote me are being neglected."

There it was, the selfishness Bailey had always found Fox's most annoying personal trait. She had just received a letter from Riverside Church complaining that Fox was letting newspaper articles describe him as "the" organist of the church, slighting Swann. "For practical purposes, he sometimes seems to be an occasional organist," Carroll B. Fitch, of the church, wrote on April 24. "I go weeks without seeing him. He never attends a staff meeting. His relationship with what goes on here is minimal." Bailey defended him and pointed out that neither she nor Fox could control what newspapers wrote about him.

She also understood that, in Fox as in every great artist, his ego was part of what made him so great, but now it was to cost her. Could she take 15 percent instead of 20 percent commission, he asked. "I'm going to talk with a San Fr. boy, Richard Torrence who is a 'natural' for this job, when I'm there on this trip," Fox wrote. "He has been a banker up 'til now—is a *gentleman* (good appearance)— meets people well. . . . You will like him, I think."

At first, the new arrangement worked well enough. The late-night phone calls stopped; Concert Management Roberta Bailey at 15 West End Avenue in Westborough, Massachusetts, kept arranging engagements, and Torrence took care of matters involving publicity and contracts with record companies in New York City. Capitol Records, Inc., for which Fox made ten records between 1958 and 1962, was leaving the classical music field, but Torrence successfully negotiated a deal for a three-year contract with Command Records in New York City in 1963.

Soon afterward, on May 1, Fox's lawyer, James F. Hoge of Rogers, Hoge & Hills of New York City, wrote informing Roberta Bailey that his client intended to terminate his professional relationship with her. "It is very difficult not to become quite bitter over this," she wrote to the lawyer in June, but she was bitter—"I know he is not a forthright person—even to me after 14 years of work together," she complained in July. But by then Richard Torrence was Fox's concert manager, not Roberta Bailey.

Torrence—"the sweet child that has the face of a cameo," Fox had described him to Ted Alan Worth—immediately jacked up Fox's standard fee to $900, and at first the raise seemed to be accepted without much protest. "My new man, Cameo—there's no one like him," Fox boasted.

Everybody wanted Fox, it seemed, including Lincoln Center, the vast new performing arts complex built on Manhattan's West Side with donations from the Rockefellers, where the auditorium nearing completion for the New York Philharmonic was to have a fine Aeolian-Skinner pipe organ that would be dedicated by three of the greatest American organists of the day—Biggs, Fox, and Catharine Crozier, a well-known teacher (at the Eastman School of Music and, later, Rollins College) with a successful concert career that had begun before World War II on Ernest M. Skinner's great organ in the Washington National Cathedral.

The Philharmonic Hall organ was designed by Joseph Whiteford, who had become head of Aeolian-Skinner after Harrison's death, and its installation was a musical event in a city that by that time had no concert venue with a functioning first-class pipe organ. But the work had been difficult. Philharmonic Hall's acoustics turned out to be a nightmare, requiring engineering changes even before it opened. "The organ was actually built last year and we delivered it in June," Whiteford wrote Biggs at the end of August, "but subsequent acoustical changes in the Hall have created so much dust that it has been impossible for us to put pipes in and thus to do the finishing and tuning. The Union situation aggravated the problem considerably because the men simply didn't know what they were doing, as you can imagine, and practically everything had to be done over again. . . . Last week, just one month away from the opening, the entire interior of the auditorium is filled with scaffolding and there are two inches of dirt all over everything. You can imagine what a mess it is." The organ was not finished when Philharmonic Hall opened in September 1962, but by December the 5,498 pipes were finally ready to speak, as Whiteford showed a reporter for *The New York Times* by demonstrating it at full volume. "Mr. Bernstein and the Philharmonic will have their hands full trying to match that sound," he boasted.

Aeolian-Skinner's Opus 1388 was unveiled on December 16, a Saturday afternoon, to an invited audience that included the composers of three works commissioned for the event, Virgil Thomson, Henry Cowell, and Vincent Persichetti. "Before the concert began," Ted Alan Worth wrote, "no one was aware that there was an organ in the hall—except, of course, for the imposing four-manual ebony console in the center of the stage. Just before Biggs came onstage, the house lights dimmed, and from behind the metal and wood screen above the stage, the great organ gradually came into view. Shades of blue, purple, and red made the silver pipes shimmer, and showed off the gold-leafed positiv division casework and the gilded 32-foot Kontre Geigen stunningly. It was breathtaking!"

Biggs performed Thomson's *Pange Lingua* and delighted his audience with a lively rendition of Charles Ives's *Variations on America*, whose high-spirited dissonance, good humor, and rollicking rhythm were then still unfamiliar to American audiences. The composer and educator William Schuman, sitting in the audience, was so impressed that he made an arrangement of the piece for band; Biggs himself rode it for all it was worth for years, although at the one performance that he gave of it in Canada, a music critic condemned it as a "tasteless parody on the British National Anthem."

When Biggs was finished, the lights dimmed, and during the forty-five-minute intermission, the stop combinations were rearranged for Miss Crozier, who impressed *The New York Times*'s critic with her "quiet warmth and sensitivity," playing Cowell's *Hymn and*

E. Power Biggs, Catharine Crozier, and Virgil Fox
at the inauguration of the organ in Philharmonic
(now Avery Fisher) Hall, New York City, 1962

Fuguing Tune No. 14 and Franck's *Choral No. 2 in B minor* among other works. After the applause for her died down, the hall was dimmed yet again for another forty-five minutes to set up the organ for Fox's performance. He had insisted on being last because he thought he would upstage the others; instead, he found himself coming at the end of an already long afternoon when most people, even organists and organ buffs, were ready to call it a day, and some had made liberal use of the bar during the intermissions.

Fox, who never drank what he always disgustedly referred to as "booze," had spent close to three hours biding his time in the Green Room. The tension burst out in an explosion of speed and virtuosity in his opening number, Bach's *Toccata in F major*, with its towering broken chords and running pedal part, all played by Fox, in the words of Mary Monroe, an organist who was present, "at absolutely blinding speed, but with every note in place."

"All went well," Ted Alan Worth wrote, "until, during a decrescendo midway in the work, Virgil closed the crescendo pedal (the device that automatically adds and subtracts stops), only to find that no other stops were on! There was dead silence for a second or two, as Virgil's fingers and feet continued to fly over the mute keyboards. He recovered miraculously after this minor train wreck, and finished the work in record speed. The audience roared its approval, but Virgil was shaken and definitely not pleased with his performance so far." Next came the Franck *Choral No. 1 in E major* and the Persichetti work, *Shima B'koli, Psalm 130*, whose musical point Fox had never understood; he called it "Scratchings at Random" and, according to Torrence, played it that way—"That's awful," Persichetti told Torrence after it was over. Fox raced on with the concluding work, giving the *Toccata* from Duruflé's *Suite No. 5* probably the most rushed and unimpressive performance he would ever give it. By the time the recital was over, half the audience had left.

Three weeks later, on January 7, 1963, Fox appeared at Philharmonic Hall again, solo this time, in a performance that may have marked the apex of his career. With the sweep of wood and metal pipes behind the stage and the console illuminated for the occasion, he performed, first, the Bach *Passacaglia and Fugue in C minor*, after telling the audience that although many of them might have heard it before in Stokowski's famous orchestrated version, they were now going to hear the *Passacaglia* "in a concert hall in New York on the instrument for which it was composed." Worth later wrote, "I don't exaggerate when I recall that even with every stop drawn on that large instrument, and the mighty roar that it produced, Virgil could not drown out the frenzied standing ovation that occurred during the final chord! It was as if the audience could not contain itself."

Even allowing for sycophancy, Fox's playing that night of more Bach works—the contrapuntal filigree of the *Trio Sonata VI* for organ, followed by the majestic pedal scales of the D major *Prelude* and its drumroll *Fugue*—must have been masterly. After the first intermission followed the romantic harmonies of Franck's monumental *Grande Pièce Symphonique*, a truly symphonic essay from the 1860s, and, from three-quarters of a century later, Messiaen's *Dieu Parmi Nous* ("God Among Us,"), the fortissimo coronation of that composer's series of nine meditations on the mystery of the Nativity. And then a second intermission, and a third section that finished with what Albert Fuller called a "hugeosity," the nineteenth-century German composer Max Reger's *Fantasy and Fugue* on the Christmas chorale *How Brightly Shines the Morning Star.* This was a piece that Fox had practiced late at night at Riverside, playing fiendishly difficult passages twenty or thirty times in succession and pounding his fists on the chancel floor in frustration until finally mastering a work that had, as he told Carlo Curley, "the mathematics and complexity of Sebastian Bach *times five!*" But one of the things that made Fox's performances so amazing was that he punished himself and did the hard work so that in the end he could play it perfectly, and musically, as he did that night in Philharmonic Hall. Afterward there were more ovations, encores, still more ovations, and then a greeting line that stretched from the Green Room nearly to the lobby.

Fox later recorded part of this program in a Command Classics album, despite the early-morning recording date—cajoled into a good mood by a practical joke that may have been by Joe Whiteford. Fox had complained to him that Biggs's name seemed to be "on every piece of toilet paper" at Philharmonic Hall. Sure enough, when Fox went to his dressing room and pulled on the toilet paper, "E. Power Biggs" had been printed on every sheet.

A year later, on January 21, 1964, Fox returned to Philharmonic Hall for another eclectic and equally challenging program, received with equal enthusiasm. But, as *The New York Times*'s critic, Raymond Ericson, noted, "As last year, the audience was primarily made up of organists, and one wondered why it should be such an intramural affair." Fox seemed bent on changing tonal colors far too often, the critic found. "A good part of the evening, which should have provided musical substance, ended up as a succession of moods and sonic fireworks."

Fox's insistence on keeping up a heavy concert schedule had become a major distraction from his musical duties at Riverside, continuing the tensions that had led the trustees to promote Fred

Swann and creating intolerable pressure on Fox's relationship with Weagly, who felt that even when Fox was in town and accompanying the choir, he often seemed bent on stealing the limelight with loud playing and inappropriate registrations. Weagly's life had reached a crossroads after his mother died in her room in the house on Palisade Avenue. With her moderating influence gone, Fox and Weagly bickered and sniped, their great art no barrier to the corrosion of petty egotism. Fox was now insisting on presenting himself as "Dr. Fox," since Bucknell University had awarded him an honorary degree in 1963; when his coterie kidded him about it, he defended himself: "Dr. Fox" would get better service from travel agents and hotels than Mr. Fox would, he decreed, and so Dr. Fox it would be.

And now Weagly found himself being replaced in Fox's affections by a young man in his twenties named David Snyder, an admirer Fox had met at a concert in Kitchener, Ontario, and brought home for a visit in mid-1963. Snyder's age, thirty years younger than Fox, was a shock to Weagly, who was offended: "Why, the boy could be his grandson! Has he gone mad?" A few months later, Fox announced that David Snyder was joining the household as a permanent guest. Weagly moved out, hoping to shock Fox to his senses. But the new infatuation snapped the few remaining threads of the emotional bond that had kept the two men together for three decades. Never again did Weagly return to Palisade Avenue.

By this time, the personal nastiness between choirmaster and organist was evident to every member of the Riverside Choir and the congregation, which had split into Weagly and Fox factions. One spring Sunday in 1964, after Weagly and Fox had, in Swann's words, a "super altercation," Fox drew all the stops on the organ and, as Swann tells it, "launched into a fiery toccata during the choir's a cappella benediction response (a soft, ethereal series of Amens) from the north ambulatory. At that point, two prominent female members of the congregation who hated Virgil charged up to the organ, one to beat his back with her umbrella, and the other to pull him backwards off the bench!"

Fox's position at Riverside was now gravely compromised. When Torrence suggested that Fox take a sabbatical leave of absence to work on memorizing Francis Poulenc's *Concerto for Organ, Strings, and Tympani* for an engagement in California, the church agreed. The sabbatical began in September and was to end the following June, and at Fox's suggestion was without salary, but midway through it, Torrence received a letter addressed to Fox from the church's music committee, informing him that his resignation was accepted "effective immediately." Fox, vacationing at Anne Archbold's estate in the Bahamas, returned for a confrontation with the committee's chairman, a prominent New York banker who told Fox that he had grown "too big for Riverside." Fox, in tears, agreed that the time had come to leave. At the end of his sabbatical, June 1, 1965, the church announced, Virgil Fox was formally retiring. "The date coincides with the termination of a seven-month leave granted him last November," *The New York Times* reported. "He will be succeeded by Dr. Frederick L. Swann, co-organist since 1958. Dr. Fox . . . will devote a major part of his time preparing an extended repertoire for his recital and concert work."

By that time, Weagly, too, was on leave, in London recovering from nervous strain. After he returned, he took refuge in the Greenwich Village apartment of Anna Brandt, an alto and the choir librarian. His formal departure from Riverside came in 1967; later, he moved with Brandt to California—and married her!

Professionally, Fox was now on his own, ready to make his living as E. Power Biggs had been doing for nearly a decade, solely as a concert organist, without a church position either to lean on or to hold him back. If people would not come to churches or concert halls to listen to him play, he would go where the audiences were, he decided, thus launching his career on a trajectory that took him beyond pipe organs altogether.

"The Way God Intended
Organs to Be Built"

E. Power Biggs became a spokesman for a return to the organbuilding principles of the classical and baroque period after taking a tour of historic European organs in 1954. The trip became a turning point in a journey that took him, literally and figuratively, to places he had never been before.

Shortly before Biggs and his wife embarked for Europe, David Oppenheim, Biggs's producer at Columbia Records, suggested they take a small tape recorder. "Let it run while you play," Oppenheim said. But Biggs had never been one for half-measures. He and Peggy took along 500 pounds of tape recorders, generators, cables, and microphones, billing Columbia for the excess baggage in the $2,739.95 of trip expenses.

The first stop was Portugal, where Biggs was fascinated by the horizontal "royal trumpets" pointing out like machine guns, as he put it, from the façade of the 200-year-old organ at the National Conservatory in Lisbon. After Portugal, the tour went to England and then to Holland and North Germany, but it was in Holland that Biggs's ears truly began to open. "What a tremendous revelation these Dutch organs are!" he wrote. "Here surely in the organs of Holland . . . is the great tradition of organ building in its clearest form." At the Oude Kerk in Amsterdam, climbing up the same stairs to an organ loft that Jan Pieterszoon Sweelinck had used almost four centuries earlier, Biggs thought, "How magnificent are

"Biggsy" and Peggy Biggs embarking for Holland
in the 1950s

the sonorities of Sweelinck's music as heard in his own church! One seems never to have heard the music before." The sounds Biggs heard there were not those that Sweelinck heard, however; the instruments of Sweelinck's time had long since been replaced, and even the 1738 Caspar Müller organ in the Oude Kerk had been tonally "modernized" in 1869. Biggs, like so many other visitors to old organs, modified or not, was thrilled by the idea that he was hearing sounds that seemed to speak down through the centuries.

Biggs followed Bach's footsteps to the church of St. Jacobi in Hamburg, where Bach had auditioned on the large 1693 Arp Schnitger pipe organ whose preservation had been a cause célèbre of the German organ reform movement in the 1920s. Here again, Biggs could not hear exactly what Bach had heard in 1720. German authorities had requisitioned the largest pipes of the organ during World War I and melted them down for their tin. Later, in the Allied bombing that destroyed much of Hamburg in 1944, the building, with the original organ framework, burned to the ground, but the church had foresightedly removed all but a few of the pipes and the essential mechanisms of the organ, which Albert Schweitzer considered "an irreplaceable monument to the perfected tonal character-istics of the instruments of the classical period of organ music," to an underground bunker. Biggs gave his recital in Hamburg in the partially reconstructed nave on the organ as reconstituted by the German organbuilder Emanuel Kemper, but it was not authenti-cally restored until forty years later. Biggs also played and saw other Schnitger organs in Steinkirchen and Neuenfelde, and visited the Johanniskirche in Lüneburg. The organ Bach had heard in 1700 no longer existed there, but Biggs could imagine how the sonorities of the church had inspired the young composer to the flamboyan-cies of the *Toccata in D minor.*

Biggs was inspired, certainly, by one of his guides: Dirk A. Flen-trop of Zaandam, Holland, whose organbuilding firm, Flentrop Orgelbouw, had restored some of the Schnitger organs. Flentrop, whose father was also an organbuilder, was building modern instru-ments using the old mechanical and tonal principles, though not the old unequal temperament tuning system that limited the music organists could play to only certain keys. Biggs and Flentrop, four years his junior, mounted winding stone staircases that led to organ lofts, crawled into dusty organ cases, stepped onto the walkboards between pipes of organs all over northern Europe. Now they were on "Biggsie" and "Dick" terms.

"Playing the great historic organs of Europe had, for me, the im-pact of a revelation," Biggs wrote later. "For the first time, I became aware of the enormous reservoir, the sum total, of the art of the or-gan in its building and tonal aspects from five or six centuries. The sound of these instruments was so enormously different and supe-rior to what we were accustomed to, and the instruments, despite their age and different playing dimensions of the console and ped-alboard, were so much more responsive. Many things thus suddenly came into focus—the importance of tracker action, of articulate voicing, of the organ case, of the windchest, and so on and on; and particularly the complete interaction of playing action and pipe sound."

He returned to the United States full of fresh ideas about playing and interpretation—and about how to make himself spokesman and personification of these ideas. In February 1956 he was on national television, in black tie, on the Sunday afternoon Omnibus program with Alistair Cooke, explaining the history and the workings of the organ with his Schlicker portative and with a half-scale model of an ancient precursor of the instrument, a Greek hydraulis that was borrowed from the Boston Museum of Fine Arts to make a favorite Biggs point—that the organ is among the most ancient of instruments.

Biggs shared what he had learned, and recorded rather primitively, on his European tour with his American listeners in an album called "The Art of the Organ" that Columbia released in 1955. That was followed the next year by Bach's "Eight Little Preludes and Fugues," recorded on historical organs in Alsace, Germany, and Austria, and "A Hi-Fi Adventure," with the Bach *Toccata in D minor* played on fourteen different organs, and its *Fugue* played on the modern British-built neobaroque organ at Royal Festival Hall in London. "The older organs," *The New York Times* wrote in its review, "take the laurels from the new ones when it comes to beauty of tone."

In August 1955 Biggs was back on "A Mozart Organ Tour," as a subsequent recording was entitled, on the trail of organs Mozart played or might have heard. At Salzburg Cathedral, where Mozart had carved his initials into the organ case backwards, Biggs recorded Mozart's "Epistle" sonatas for organ and chamber orchestra, with the Camerata Academica under Bernard Paumgartner. "Cathedral authorities and the Salzburg police obligingly rerouted all traffic from the Cathedral Square so that we could have complete quiet, and the drama of the great Cathedral at night during these evening performances is something long to remember," Biggs reported in an organists' quarterly that fall. "At St. Thomas, in Strasbourg, I asked the caretaker whether Mozart had played there," Biggs told the *New Yorker*, "and he said, 'Not last year or this.'" But the recordings were a success: "To misquote Frank Buck, we brought 'em back aloud," he declared.

By this time, he was able to make a comfortable living from his recording fees and concerts alone. Year after year, music critics and editors voted him America's foremost organist in Musical America's poll, and now that his managers, the Independent Concert Bureau of Mercury Music Corp., were able to get him $300 to $500 per concert, he was finally able to get along without a regular Sunday church job. This time, he wasn't fired. He resigned from Harvard Congregational Church in Brookline at the end of 1956, pleading "the pressure of other work."

At the organists convention in New York earlier that year, with its memorials to G. Donald Harrison, Biggs had persuaded his new Dutch friend Flentrop to come over to give a lecture on trends in European organbuilding. Biggs, now fully engaged by his quest to reveal to modern American listeners the secrets that had made baroque organs so appealing, proposed a recreation of the idea that had brought Harrison's neobaroque organ to the Germanic Museum twenty years earlier.

"Would you like to consider the idea of building a new organ for the Museum?" Biggs wrote Flentrop after the convention. "It seems to me that there could not be a better spot anywhere over here in which to set forth your philosophy!" Biggs would sell the electro-pneumatic Harrison instrument to pay for a new mechanical-action organ if Flentrop would agree to build one, he wrote. "Naturally it would be tracker!" Biggs enthused. "If your organ can have a persuasive, outgiving mellow quality, and a rich but never 'hard' ensemble (yet very articulate in speech beginnings) I think it will just bowl people over! They will say THIS IS IT! It will be nothing less than an earthquake, for which America is ready *right now!*"

How could Flentrop not be interested, after an invitation like that? And now that Biggs was entirely free of church duties, he and Flentrop had plenty of time to work out a design. Flentrop accompanied Biggs and his wife on part of the next European recording tour, in the spring of 1957. This time, they had packed a workhorse Volkswagen minibus with 178 reels of tape, two 28-pound Ampex speakers, a 29-pound Ampex 350 tape recorder, a Telefunken condenser, microphones, 500 feet of microphone cable, 200 pounds of power units, and much else, shipping it off to Amsterdam at Columbia Records' expense.

The Biggses' Volkswagen bus became famous in Columbia lore. Their plan was to do most of the recording themselves, with occasional on-scene help from sound engineers on contract to Columbia. But they had their hands full with technical difficulties— buzzing in the speakers, short-circuits, and other problems that spoiled some of their recordings. "I guess our lesson is that we must never attempt any such expedition without technical help all the time!" Biggs admitted later.

Technical difficulties of the bureaucratic variety also came up. Biggs wanted to go to Communist East Germany to visit Leipzig and the Thomaskirche, where Bach had been cantor for so long; Handel's home town of Halle; and Freiberg, in Saxony, where one of the greatest eighteenth-century organs by Gottfried Silbermann had survived intact in the cathedral. The United States did not recognize East Germany at that time except as the "Soviet Zone." When Biggs asked the State Department about getting sponsorship from the International Exchange Program for a trip, Robert C. Creel, an official of the Office of German Affairs, wrote Biggs all sorts of dire warnings. "If you do travel to the Zone," the official wrote, "the United States Government will not be in a position to extend to you the protection and assistance which it is normally able to provide to United States Citizens traveling abroad. Every foreign traveler in the Zone is exposed to the hazards of a powerful police regime whose actions are arbitrary and unpredictable." Traveling with all kinds of recording equipment would pose problems, Creel warned. "Furthermore, if you do travel to the Zone, there is a risk that the Communist authorities might try to exploit the presence of an American citizen of your prominence there to give the population of the Zone the impression that your visit indicates a changing attitude on the part of the United States Government or people toward the recognition of the Soviet Zone government." But Creel's letter left the ultimate decision up to Biggs, observing that if he did manage to avoid being exploited by the Communists, he could also help undermine them by showing understanding and sympathy for the plight of the oppressed East German population.

Communist bureaucracy rescued the State Department from the potential embarrassment it feared by denying the Biggses permission to travel to Leipzig, Halle, and Freiberg, places in East Germany where he had planned concerts, or for that matter anywhere beyond East Berlin. "Instead of making a record on this trip to Germany I've broken one!" Biggs wrote Columbia. "And that's the record of never having missed an announced concert or broadcast. Now I've missed three."

But the tour had its compensations elsewhere, notably in Holland, where Biggs discovered the 1720 organ by Arp Schnitger's sons Franz Caspar and Johann Georg Schnitger that Flentrop's firm had restored in the Grote Kerk in Zwolle. Biggs's Columbia recording, "Bach at Zwolle," in 1958 had enormous impact on the American organ world, although Flentrop's restoration of the instrument, which had been substantially altered over the centuries, was not without its critics.

The Biggses continued to England to do a recording, in the Parish Church of St. James in Great Packington, of the sixteen organ concertos of Handel with the London Philharmonic under Sir Adrian Boult. The organ was an authentic instrument from Handel's time, and its bellows had, Biggs observed, "handles Handel handled." Here again, there were technical difficulties to be overcome. The church, on the private estate of the Earl of Aylesford, had no electricity, but Lord Guernsey, the earl's son, got an underground power line laid to the church, at Columbia's expense. The company had initially balked at the musicians' fees demanded by the orchestra and negotiated them downward. The organ, on the other hand, would have to be tuned up a half-step to be able to match the London Philharmonic's standard pitch, and doing this would require altering the lengths of the pipes. But the Earl of Aylesford raised no objections, and, astoundingly, neither did Biggs. One wonders what he would have said if the organ had been, say, the one Bach had actually played in the Jacobikirche in Hamburg. As it was, Noel Mander, one of the best British organbuilders, came to Great Packington, removed the pipes, cleaned them, shortened them to tune them sharper—but then fitted them with tuning slides, sleeve-like fittings at the top of the pipes that would allow them to be returned to their original lengths and thus returned to their original, flatter pitch. Nevertheless, British organ preservationists grumbled about the vandalism Biggs, Columbia, and the orchestra had inflicted on Handel's organ for the sake of a record.

The organs Biggs heard on these European tours had clearer tone, greater articulation, and more incisive speech, he believed, than most of the American organs he played on his concert tours. Listeners began to notice little changes in his style to compensate for these differences. Biggs's playing had always been "correct" and his rhythms steady, without melodramatic effects like exaggerated rubato—so correct, in fact, that it was sometimes criticized for being bland. But there had always been wit and energy in his playing. He wheeled on and off the organ bench on the concert stage, feet in the air. Now his touch became increasingly staccato, as if he were trying to beat European-style articulation out of lazy American organ pipes, his feet slapping the pedals audibly.

His professional ambition was focused on the revolution he expected to begin after he unveiled the new Flentrop organ at Harvard, in what had been renamed the Busch-Reisinger Museum. The new instrument was nearly finished by early 1958, when Biggs sold the Aeolian-Skinner for $11,500 to Boston University for the auditorium of the School of Fine and Applied Arts (where an arsonist destroyed it in 1971). Only many years later did Biggs acknowledge gratitude to G. Donald Harrison for the "wonderful opportunity" that this earlier groundbreaking instrument represented. "It took a little while for the lessons, both positive and negative, taught by the instrument, to be learned," Biggs said. "All in all, the organ was quite playable; it sounded extraordinarily well—bright tone, outgoing, very persuasive."

The Flentrop organ that replaced it was not the first "reform" instrument from Europe to be imported to America, nor even the largest—a four-keyboard mechanical-action instrument by Rudolf von Beckerath of Hamburg had been installed in Trinity Lutheran Church in Cleveland the previous year. But the Flentrop's arrival in Cambridge in the summer of 1958 was a signal event. While encased like a baroque organ, the design and ornament were modern. The organ pipes of the "hoofdwerk," or the main section, the "pedaal" or pedal section, and the softer-sounding "borstwerk" (meaning, roughly, "breastworks," and in fact the pipes are at about chest level of a person standing directly in front of the organ) were contained in a shallow mahogany case, entirely unenclosed in front. There was a separate, free-standing section whose pipes and case sat right over the museum balcony, in front of the organ from the perspective of a listener below but at the organist's back, since the keyboard was built into the main organ case. This was the "rug-positief," Dutch for rückpositiv, meaning a positiv in back of the player. The wind pressures were low because Flentrop and Biggs believed that would make the speech of the pipes sound unforced. It was not a huge or overpowering instrument, with the same number of stops as the one it replaced. The goal was an organ that suited the hall, with stops that would have been familiar to Sweelinck or Bach or any of their contemporaries. The pipes ranged from eight feet to a few inches in length, and the tonal ensemble was bright, clear, singing, yet solid.

Harvard was probably only too happy to have Biggs install this new organ at his own cost (and, as the university authorities may have expected, he later donated it to them). He threw a big party to inaugurate it in September, and most of the Boston organ world came to the museum for the festivities. Cocktails came first; then the assembly moved into Adolphus Busch Hall to hear Biggs play works by Sweelinck, Franck, Vaughan Williams, and Bach, demonstrating his belief that music from any period could sound good on a "classic" organ. Finally came the baptism: Flentrop poured wine from a display pipe into glasses up in the gallery where the organ stood, and Peggy Biggs passed them around, for a toast. "The taped-up mouth of the pipe leaked, the wine tasted of pipe size, and almost as much went onto the floor as into the glasses," Barbara Owen wrote. "But the mood was ebullient and nobody minded that the ceremony lacked the solemnity it doubtless had in ancient times."

Almost simultaneously, Columbia Masterworks issued "The Organ." This, the "talking dog record," as Biggs dubbed it, was a manifesto that had an enormous impact on the American organ scene. With the record were articles by Biggs, Flentrop, Emanuel Winternitz, a leading organ historian, and John McClure, Biggs's producer at Columbia, along with photographs of organs old and new and illustrations of how they worked. On the long-playing record, Biggs's English-accented voice introduced snippets of music played on instruments in Europe and America and explained the complexities of organ tone, mechanics, and registration.

"The Organ" was only partly a manifesto against the electronic organs, whether by Hammond, Rodgers, Conn, Allen, or any of the other builders who sold them on the premise that they sounded as good as pipe organs but cost far less and took up less room. These creations Biggs waved off dismissively: "Though well adapted to night clubs, they are all inadequate for presentation of organ music," he wrote. "No church or auditorium should seriously consider these make-believe devices."

It was the pipe organ that Biggs wanted to save, from all the notions that had degraded it over the years. It was not sufficient for an organ to have pipes to produce authentic organ tone. "Articulate and beautiful pipe tone is the first musical essential in an organ," Biggs said. "Music as speech must be set forth with natural accent. The bite of a bow on the string, the point of woodwind tone, the percussive quality of a harpsichord—all these articulate sounds express the musical sense of a phrase. A well voiced organ pipe also has a natural accent, a consonant before the vowel of sound, a sort of 'chiff.'"

Louis Marchand had called the organ "of all instruments the king," Biggs said, "yet compared to their illustrious ancestors, most of our modern monarchs have lost a courtly grace of speech." For a century and more, modern organs, Biggs said, had had pipes whose mouths were "nicked," notched so that they wouldn't chiff or chuff when the air first blew through them but, instead, ease in and blend smoothly, as romantic builders had always believed good organs should do, but they sounded "woolly." Pipes had been put into chambers with shutters to make the volume swell and fade, but the result, in Biggs's words, was tone that was "trapped, absorbed, jangled and scrubbled up. A pipe in the open is worth two in a box." Remote electropneumatic connections between key and pipe valve, Biggs often quipped, were "a fine way to ring a doorbell," but no way to make music. For playing an organ, there was nothing like tracker action, direct connection by a system of levers between key and pipe valve, which made keys "an extension of one's own fingers, and responsive to touch."

In his essay explaining the record, Biggs challenged modern American organbuilders to see the light and change their ways. "The organ appears to possess a fatal appeal to ingenious but not necessarily musical minds," he observed. In the nineteenth century, "the organ, previously as responsive as a harpsichord, was turned into something approaching a machine. Its measure came to be volume and number of stops. Voicing ideals were based largely on imitation of the orchestra. Pneumatic and electric actions provided the player with a set of telegraphic ivories instead of the sensitive keyboard of direct tracker action. . . . There is, of course, no reason why we today cannot build organs as well as, or better than, the men of the 18th century. . . . To build tracker-action, slider-chest organs again is not to go back, but rather to put one's feet on firm ground in order to go forward. A return to basic principles could mean that organs built in the coming decades will stand for centuries, as have their European counterparts."

Ringing declarations like these in "The Organ" had all the effect Biggs had hoped for. "Heard at a quarter century's remove, Biggs's voice is the voice of a prophet—one who, fortunately, lived to see his prophecies come to pass," Barbara Owen wrote later. But Biggs was preaching to people whose ears had been prepared for the sound of the "true" organ by what Harrison, Holtkamp, Schlicker, and other pioneering American builders had done over preceding decades.

For Biggs, 1958 was a turning point for the worse in other respects. The first setback came from CBS Radio in a November 7 letter from James Fassett, who announced Biggs's weekly radio broadcasts and was CBS's supervisor of music. "For some time I have seen the handwriting on the wall and now at last has come the final blow," Fassett wrote. "As of the first of the year, the CBS Radio network will vastly curtail the daily number of hours it will service its owned and affiliated stations, and all but the commercially sponsored programs and a few traditional public service broadcasts like the Philharmonic will cease to exist as network programs. Your weekly broadcasts, I regret to say, are among the many casualties, and the final broadcast will be that of Sunday, January 4th."

Biggs, on a concert tour in Mexico City, got the news from his wife and phoned Fassett to protest, offering to reduce his fee if that would keep the broadcasts going. "He said—yes, & unfortunately they wouldn't pay even *that*!" Biggs reported back to Peggy. There was nothing to be done.

As his wife knew, Biggs had suffered an even more bitter blow that year. He developed rheumatoid arthritis—"a cruel disease for any musician, but particularly so for an organist," as Peggy Biggs wrote to Barbara Owen later. "Only constant practice despite pain kept his hands and feet limber. . . . He was most grateful to his orthopedic surgeon, Dr. Theodore Potter. . . . Once, when Dr. Potter showed X-rays of his hands, and pointed out the new joints that constant practice had worn in, Biggs quipped that that picture would make an interesting record sleeve cover. . . ." Biggs also began taking corticosteroids to try to slow down the disease, but the treatments had deleterious side effects on his liver and kidneys, caused swelling of his tissues and puffiness in his face and wrists and made his bones fragile.

If the radio broadcasts were over, Columbia Masterworks was still interested in his recordings. "Music for Organ and Brass," with the Boston Brass Ensemble under Richard Burgin playing Frescobaldi and Gabrieli, and "Joyeux Noël" in 1960, with Biggs playing Daquin's eighteenth-century elaborations on French Christmas tunes, were the first of many issues that were made on Biggs's new Flentrop organ.

For all his trips to Europe to play historic instruments, Biggs had never gone looking for early American instruments. But in 1956, he went to a dinner at St. Bartholomew's Church in New York City with a new group called the Organ Historical Society, whose members were trying to save old American organs from destruction. Were there any that were worthy of being recorded? Biggs asked Barbara Owen, who was seated next to him.

There were plenty, Owen assured him, and promised to help him organize a tour like the ones he and Peggy Biggs had done in Europe. By July 1959, she was ready, and the Biggs microbus was loaded up again with tape recorders and microphones—and, this time, also with a sound recording engineer from Columbia.

The trip produced another seminal recording that had enormous influence, "The Organ in America," released by Columbia Masterworks in 1960. Heard here, for the first time on a nationally released record, were organs built by George G. Hook in 1827, by Thomas Johnston in 1759, and by David Tannenberg in 1804. "Its tonal excellence is apparent the moment you hear it," Biggs wrote of the Tannenberg organ in *The Diapason* in September 1960, "and its playability the instant you set hands on keyboard. Here, in short is an organ built in America a century and a half ago that in its variety of musical possibilities, achieved through the simplest of means, carries a vital lesson and indeed poses a challenge for us today."

"These early American organs reinforce the basic tonal truths so apparent in the great organs of Europe," Biggs wrote on the record jacket. "The best way—in fact, the only way—to build an organ which is to be a responsive and artistic musical instrument is in the classical way, perfected by centuries of experiment and experience."

Biggs, by now able to command fees of $650 to $750 per concert, made Peggy his manager and, in January 1961, started planning

The Biggses at the Arp Schnitger organ of St. Jacobi, Hamburg, in 1954

another European tour, with John McClure as his producer and engineers from Philips recording in Holland and Germany to record on Schnitger organs in Cappel, Germany, and Alkmaar and Zwolle in Holland. A request to make a recording at St. Jacobi in Hamburg was denied by the church's organist, who as Philips informed Biggs, had written "a nasty letter . . . saying that he has a contract with the church giving him exclusive right to make recordings of the church's Arp Schnitger organ, and he has no intention of giving up any of his rights." Biggs was incensed. "A historic organ such as that does not belong to the organist, but to the musical world at large!" he fumed. Three years later, a record, "The Golden Age of the Organ," appeared, with Biggs performances on thirteen Schnitger organs, including St. Jacobi. But the performance, of the Bach *Toccata in D minor,* was one that Biggs had recorded in 1954. "Mr. Biggs takes advantage of his opportunities as guide and demonstrator; the role inspires some of his best playing, and it seems less impersonal than usual," *The New York Times* commented on this recording, which, like all others with Biggs billing, was guaranteed to sell well.

Although his relationship with Aeolian-Skinner was by now a thing of the past, Biggs was pleased to be associated with the inauguration of the new Aeolian-Skinner organ in New York City's Philharmonic Hall in 1962. Five years earlier, when Philharmonic Hall was still on the drawing boards, Biggs had written to an officer of the New York Philharmonic-Symphony Society, who had asked whether an electronic organ might be acceptable for the auditorium being planned for Lincoln Center. "Today's electronic 'organs'—all of them—are totally inadequate for the presentation of organ music, or for playing the organ parts in orchestral scores," Biggs wrote. "Lacking pipes, they lack the first essential of an organ, and no amount of electronic juggling will produce the characteristic speech and tone of organ pipes. . . . Electronics may serve for night clubs and skating rinks but would be totally inadequate for the Philharmonic Orchestra!"

Just a few weeks before the inauguration of the Aeolian-Skinner, Biggs was scheduled to play in the hall with the New York Philharmonic in Richard Strauss's *Festival Prelude for Organ and Orchestra* and with the Philadelphia Orchestra in Barber's *Toccata Festiva*. As those concert dates approached, it became clear that the pipe organ would not be ready in time, and Biggs found himself forced to make a choice between eating his words about electronic organs or canceling the orchestra concerts. The Allen Organ Company was willing to lend Lincoln Center a two-keyboard electronic instrument so that the concerts could go ahead, and reluctantly Biggs consented to play it. He soon regretted his decision. "From the raucous blasts of the electronic organ to the din of the supplementary brasses stationed in the second terrace, this was an ordeal," one newspaper wrote of the Strauss performance, and Allen annoyed Biggs by trying to use the performance as an endorsement by him of its products. "What the concert did show was that *certain* repertoire was almost acceptable on the Allen," Biggs halfheartedly conceded.

Better nothing at all, Biggs believed, than music that was not the real thing, as he made clear to Eastern Air Lines, United Airlines, and Delta Airlines in identical letters sent on April 17 of 1963. "May I please suggest that the canned music you inflict on your captive audience during the half hour or so of loading is really most unwelcome. As you must know, it's just musical drivel, from which, unfortunately, there's no escape," he fumed. "You really should have no music at all during the period, for a very obvious reason. And that reason is this—there is usually a loud note from a generator or some other piece of machinery that cuts through the music with a constant dissonance. The whole effect is most irritating and unpleasant and does not produce at all the effect you perhaps think it does." So much for the soothing effect of Muzak.

"Poor old Jimmy! He's been dead from the neck up and the waist down for years!" Virgil Fox sneered. Yet Biggs was not all fuddy-duddy by any means. He had always cut a trim, debonair figure on the concert stage, with his jaunty bow ties and never a hair out of place, and in some venues, he had feminine admirers attentive to his every need, particularly in New York City, where he came year after year to play the 1958 M. P. Möller organ at St. George's Episcopal Church at Christmas.

Despite his arthritis, he was keeping up an ambitious concert schedule, although at times, as Lorene Banta observed in a review of a Biggs concert on the Methuen Memorial Music Hall organ in the fall of 1960, "Organ students who were present must have been comforted to observe, from several slips in the Bach pieces, that even Mr. Biggs is human." He returned to the symphonic splendor of Methuen—and filled the hall to capacity—year after year. Large audiences would come to hear him whatever he played on—1,800 people attended the inauguration of another German tracker-action organ by Rudolf von Beckerath in Pittsburgh in 1962, and 1,500 Maine music lovers braved a blizzard in February 1963 to hear him on the old Austin-built Kotzschmar Memorial Organ in Portland.

That November, Biggs's doctor, Carey Peters, urged him to slow down. "I wish you could arrange to take some time off," he wrote. "The constant pressure and always being on the production line certainly is a stressful situation." But for Biggs there was just too much work to be done for the tracker-organ cause. He and Flentrop achieved a signal victory in 1965, with the dedication in Seattle of a four-keyboard Flentrop tracker organ in St. Mark's Cathedral; the organist there had gone to Boston planning to order an Aeolian-Skinner but had been smitten by the Flentrop sound in the Busch-Reisinger Museum. Two years later, in 1967, at Biggs's urging and with his advice, Harvard replaced the 1932 Aeolian-Skinner organ in the Memorial Church with a modern American-built mechanical-action organ by Charles B. Fisk.

By this time, the revolution that Biggs had encouraged was in full swing. He continued his systematic exploration of historic organs of Europe, making more than a dozen recordings for Columbia in France, England, Holland, Austria, Germany, Spain, and Portugal from the mid-1960s to the early 1970s. Columbia clearly considered Biggs as close to a household name as a classical organist could ever come. It declared March 1968 "E. Power Biggs Month," releasing six albums over the course of the year, most of them reissues. A recording of organ, brass, and strings that Biggs did in the sonorous Cathedral San Marco in Venice with the Edward Tarr Brass Ensemble from Germany and the Gabrieli Consort La Fenice from Italy won a Grammy award as the best chamber music performance of 1968. In 1969, Columbia issued an "E. Power Biggs Greatest Hits" album that included a new recording of the Ives *Variations on America* performed on the new Fisk organ at Harvard. "It is bright and gay, far better than the previous version," Biggs himself commented.

By 1970, he had recorded or at least heard and played most of the surviving baroque organs in western Europe—but none in Bach's stomping grounds in Saxony, then still part of Communist East Germany, which had denied Biggs a visa in the 1950s. The Silbermann organ that Bach had played in Dresden's Frauenkirche, with its distinctive stone cupola, had been destroyed with the church in the firestorm of Allied bombing in 1945, but other Silbermann works had survived, notably the instrument in the royal chapel in Dresden and two Silbermann organs in the cathedral in

Freiberg. The Thomaskirche in Leipzig, where Bach had been cantor, no longer had the organ Bach knew (he had never liked it much, anyway), but for Biggs, just to walk on the same stones Bach had stepped on would be a thrill. Now détente was beginning to thaw the cold war, and even though the United States had not yet recognized the German Democratic Republic, a visit became possible. In 1970, VEB Deutsche Schallplatten, the "German Records People's Factory," finally invited CBS to have Biggs do recordings in Leipzig and Freiberg that would be released jointly by the two recording companies. In May, Biggs and Hellmuth Kolbe, a recording consultant for CBS, were met at Checkpoint Charlie in Berlin by Reimar Bluth, the director of VEB Deutsche Schallplatten, and set off on the two-hour bumpy drive down one of the original Hitler autobahns to Leipzig. "As we came near the center of Leipzig, Herr Bluth turned and said, 'In a moment you will see the Thomas-kirche,'" Biggs wrote later. "He had sung there as a choir boy, and he knew the place inside and out, yet he could not have said it with more excitement—not even if he were proposing to show us the celestial regions."

"Here, surely, is the Mecca of all Bach lovers," Biggs wrote on the jacket of the recording he made in the Thomaskirche. "A thousand thoughts go through one's mind as one walks about the place— some jubilant, some sad, some amusing. A wall tablet proclaims that Richard Wagner was baptized in St. Thomas's. (Bully for him! you think.) Grim portraits of church council members, with whom Johann Sebastian was so frequently at loggerheads in an effort to maintain his musical authority, gaze down upon you. . . . All such thoughts, however, are swept up into a triumphant realization that it was here, within these four walls, that so many of Bach's greatest works were first heard. . . . This is the place, one feels. This is where so much happened. This is where Bach's auditors, privileged beyond their comprehension, experienced the first hearing of the powerful music that has conquered the Western world."

There were two organs in the church, the larger of the two a late nineteenth century romantic instrument that occupied the gallery where Bach had conducted his cantatas. Biggs chose instead to record on the other, a small 1967 neobaroque tracker instrument built in East Germany by Alexander Schuke of Potsdam, placed in the north gallery of the nave. For several nights, while he recorded the *Toccata and Fugue in D minor,* the *Passacaglia and Fugue,* the *Prelude and Fugue in G major,* and the *Prelude and Fugue in C major,* the Leipzig People's Police rerouted traffic around the church so that the records would not be marred by the sounds of automobiles or the occasional Red Army convoy. "When our week of recording was finally over, it was difficult to take leave of the place," Biggs wrote on the jacket. "Reluctantly, when the last session ended—at three o'clock in the morning—we stepped out into the misty night. The impressive statue loomed high above, a figure of a man both familiar and unfathomable. Even the director and personnel of the East German recording company, certainly no strangers to this scene, felt the magic of the moment. To have been in 'Bach's Church' is to know a deep joy in the continuity and close presence of the past, and to realize anew that Johann Sebastian Bach is a true 'Ambassador Extraordinary' to the world." To John McClure, Biggs reported after the recording sessions were over: "Playing at the Thomaskirche was really high drama, and I feel the record will catch this!"

Catch it the record did. The recording, "E. Power Biggs Plays Bach in the Thomaskirche," issued by Columbia Masterworks in 1971, was one of his most memorable. "First recording by an American in this historic building," the jacket proudly boasted, Columbia's dig, perhaps, at Virgil Fox's own boast that the recital he had given in the Thomaskirche in 1938 had been the first ever by an American organist there—both claims omitting the detail that neither musician had played the organ Bach had known in the Thomaskirche. Biggs, normally the most straightforward of players, indulged himself in a brief improvised cadenza that seemed to have been inspired by his thoughts of the great master. "The power of Bach's music on the instrument in these authentic surroundings is undeniably impressive," Igor Kipnis wrote in *Stereo Tape.* "So, too, is

Biggs's playing. It has real propulsion, power, and drive, and I am inclined to think that this is the American organist's finest recording of his long career."

Biggs liked baroque best, but he still had a spot in his heart for the best romantic organ music, and, perhaps despite himself, Biggs was still part showman. "In general, we should graduate back to large instruments—window rattlers," he suggested to McClure in early 1970. Although his arthritis was bothering him, and the steroids he took for it were causing his bones to become brittle and his body to swell, he appeared at St. George's in New York in November 1972 with an orchestra conducted by Maurice Peress in a performance of two organ concertos by Josef Rheinberger. The following March, Biggs even appeared on the "mighty Wurlitzer" theater organ in Radio City Music Hall in a program organized by Columbia Records in hopes of attracting youthful listeners. Biggs played works by Soler and Bach, Hewitt's *The Battle of Trenton,* and the Ives *Variations on America* on the seat-shaking Wurlitzer, finishing up with ten pianos in a rendition of *Stars and Stripes Forever.* That appearance earned a favorable mention by John Rockwell in *The New York Times,* although the critic noted that Biggs "may not be the deftest organist in the world in matters of fingering," the arthritis by now obviously affecting his playing.

Biggs had made himself an instrument of the baroque revival, but unlike many otherwise like-minded pedagogues, he was determined to make music an enjoyable experience whatever it was played on. Biggs had acquired a harpsichord with pedals just like an organ's from John Challis in the mid-1960s and made a Bach recording on it. In 1973, Biggs had a new idea after hearing a physician friend playing Scott Joplin rags on the piano. "She suggested that I try them on the pedal harpsichord, and the pedal harpsichord took them up as if they had been written for it," Biggs wrote. He persuaded Columbia to do a recording and suggested a way to promote it: "After 25 years with Columbia Records, E. Power Biggs is in Rags!" The record, "E. Power Biggs Plays Scott Joplin," featured Biggs in a zoot suit on the cover standing in front of the riverboat Peter Stuyvesant—on the Hudson, not the Mississippi. Biggs's Joplin was like his Bach—the rhythms were a little too strict, the playing a little too strait-laced—but his obvious enjoyment of this music, and his respect for it, shone through.

In early 1974, Biggs fractured an arm in a fall. He had to cancel his concert engagements, though he was able to keep up a recording campaign that included a quadraphonic release of Bach toccatas and fugues played on the four different organs in the cathedral of Freiburg, West Germany. As always, he did much of the recording and editing himself—"the Compleat Record Man," Pierre Bourdain of Columbia affectionately dubbed him. But, now in his late sixties, he was fighting off other ailments of advancing age. His left eye was still bloodshot from a cataract operation when he went to Ohio in November 1974 to receive an honorary doctorate from Oberlin College, where a Flentrop tracker organ was being installed in Warner Concert Hall. With Flentrop and Fisk standing beside him, Biggs found himself the center of attention, stunned by "long and roaring applause which held him speechless on stage," *The Diapason* wrote later.

Biggs recovered and issued a blast on what he called "the carnage at Carnegie"—the Carnegie Hall trustees' refusal of a large Flentrop organ that had been offered by Mrs. Leo Simon, a wealthy philanthropist, and the installation in its place of a five-keyboard electronic Rodgers Organ Company instrument that Fox had helped to design, and had inaugurated. Biggs fumed for a long time over this affront to every principle he stood for, at various times saying that the Flentrop organ had been lost to the hall "through stupidity" and referring to the Rodgers as merely a "synthetic object."

"The electronic sound is still pudgy, inarticulate, the flutes without character (unless you consider the tremolo to be character) and the ensemble becomes more turgid as it gets louder. . . . Where is the symmetry of organ pipes, the beauty of an organ case, where, in fact, is any *identity*?" he asked a group of organbuilders in Albany in 1975. His campaign would be to no avail as long as Isaac Stern lived. Stern, the great violinist who had almost singlehandedly rescued Carnegie Hall from demolition after Lincoln Center was built, had vetoed the Flentrop. A large, freestanding pipe organ could interfere with the acoustics, Stern felt, and this one would go into Carnegie Hall over his dead body.

"Short of putting up the organ, or a dummy case, that question can't be proved one way or another," Biggs was still grumbling the following year, "but I must mention that we have had an organ for 76 years in Symphony Hall in Boston, and no one has ever said it spoiled the acoustics. And think of the Concertgebouw in Amsterdam, and a score of other European concert halls with their wonderful acoustics and their organs." By that time even Philharmonic Hall was again without a pipe organ, after the removal of the Aeolian-Skinner organ when the auditorium was torn apart in one of its periodic acoustic convulsions and renamed Avery Fisher Hall.

Biggs had enjoyed a small moral victory in the spring of 1975, however, when Alice Tully donated a four-keyboard tracker-action organ made by Orgelbau Kuhn AG, a Swiss builder, in the smaller Lincoln Center auditorium that bears Miss Tully's name. "Dear Miss Tully," Biggs wrote enthusiastically before the inaugural concert. "Here truly, and at last, for New York is an instrument 'built the way God intended organs to be built!' And we are all not only greatly in your debt for your generosity, but also for your keen judgment in the whole matter. The organ is going to cast a long shadow—an illuminating shadow." As a gift of appreciation, he said, he was sending his St. Thomas record—"And I cannot resist putting in a little Scott Joplin also!"

Poignantly, Allen Hughes wrote in his review of the performance in *The New York Times*, "Mr. Biggs, who is nothing if not consistent, chose stop combinations that made the Tully Hall organ sound like Busch-Reisinger. He may not have the dexterity now that he had then, but his performances were characterized by the professionalism and integrity that have been characteristic of his work from the very beginning."

Biggs had had another cataract operation, this time on his right

Biggs autographing a record jacket at the
Harvard Cooperative Society, Cambridge, 1975

eye, in February, but three months later, he collapsed before a concert with Maurice Peress and the Kansas City Orchestra in that city and had to be hospitalized. He recovered enough to fly to Germany at the end of May for another recording at the Thomaskirche in Leipzig, with the Gewandhaus Orchestra under Hans-Joachim Rotzsch, of the six concerto sinfonias from Bach's cantatas 29, 35, 169, 146, 49, and 31—"one-movement organ concertos" in Bach's words. Issued at the end of 1976, it was Biggs's last.

That March, Biggs had turned seventy. Daniel Pinkham had organized a concert in his honor at King's Chapel, with a reception, and Columbia and its people had cabled congratulations. Biggs and Arthur Fiedler were planning a performance of Rheinberger's *Organ Concerto No. 2* and a Mozart sonata at Symphony Hall for a convention of the American Guild of Organists in Boston, at which Biggs was to be honorary program chairman. But two days before the concert, he broke his left elbow. Biggs had to have it strapped into position so that he could play as scheduled on June 25. "If the elbow was stiff," Peggy Biggs said, "the fingers were not." The audience cheered the performance, but the next day, Biggs went straight to the hospital.

The night before, he had been made an honorary member of Boston's prestigious Handel and Haydn Society. "E. Power Biggs plays the organ," was the only introduction he had needed from Thomas Dunn, the society's conductor, who went on: "Countless listeners having their first love affair with music cherish that fact in their hearts. Few in the history of performance leave indelible marks on their art; of them, none rivals him in the affection and respect of layman and colleague alike. He is the rollicking forward scout of scholarship. . . ."

In October, Biggs suffered a broken leg that forced him to cancel all concerts. He still wanted to record Liszt, Franck, and Rheinberger at Methuen, more Bach in East Germany, Pachelbel in Lübeck. He had plans for a record, the "reverberation of 3,000 miles," that would combine Biggs playing at St. Thomas in New York with the choir of the Thomaskirche singing in Leipzig. None of it was to be.

By early 1977, his whole system was failing. To try to save him, his doctors performed an emergency operation on March 10, but it was unsuccessful. Ellison C. Pierce Jr., the attending anesthesiologist, an admirer of Biggs since his high school years in the 1940s, wrote to Margaret Biggs a few weeks later, "We did try very hard to pull him through." Another of the doctors who operated on Biggs tried to console her by saying that he "wouldn't have had much of a life" if he had survived.

Biggs would have been seventy-one years old on March 29. George Wright, the great theater organist of the time, wrote to Mrs. Biggs, "Attached is a letter I had meant to write to your husband for five or ten years. And now he is gone." Undated, it read in part, "I love your adventurous registration and the way you get the most out of all those smaller two-manual organs you play. I long ago tired of the bizarre grotesqueries of Virgil Fox and the runaway tempi of Richard Elsasser," another contemporary virtuoso. "There are two outstanding instances of big talents gone wrong. You're quite a swinger on the harpsichord, too!" Wright's letter continued. "My mother would have approved of that. She always maintained that ragtime is basically whorehouse music and the limpwristed approach of Joshua Rifkin, for instance, drove her round the bend."

Biggs was buried in Mount Auburn Cemetery in Cambridge, Massachusetts, after a service in Harvard's Memorial Church on March 27. The church was packed. Members of the Boston Symphony Orchestra, with Daniel Pinkham conducting, played some of Biggs's favorite pieces from Georg Philipp Telemann and Bach, including the *Sheep May Safely Graze* from the *Jagdkantate* that Biggs had played on the organ at the end of every one of his hundreds of radio broadcasts. John Ferris and the Harvard University Choir were all there, and workers from Fisk's workshop and members of the Harvard-Radcliffe Organ Society served as ushers. Edward O. Miller, the Rector of St. George's in New York City, spoke for the assembly: "With humor, with gaiety gladdened by goodness, he transmitted serenity to make our spirits rejoice."

Peggy Biggs received letters, Barbara Owen reported, from everybody from the president of Harvard University to the UPS delivery man. Columbia Records paid tribute, in an advertisement in *The New York Times:* "E. Power Biggs became an artistic legend in his own lifetime. He was a man cherished for his great warmth and wit, his indefatigable spirit. . . . We rejoice in the life of E. Power Biggs." More memorial concerts and tributes followed as the months rolled on; 3,000 people came for a tribute in Oakland, California, in September.

"In a way," Owen wrote, "Biggs created his own memorial in the records he made, the music he edited, the students he helped, and the untold number of organs his influence helped to save or to bring into being." Not the least of these, she said, was the Flentrop instrument still heard regularly in Adolphus Busch Hall. The Flentrop stands as a monument to Biggs and to the cause of the organ-building reform in America that both Biggs and the Flentrop instrument had done so much to advance.

"Heavy Organ"

After Riverside Church severed ties with him in 1965, Virgil Fox was making a lot of money as a concert artist, playing to audiences in cities large and small all across America. But to develop his concert career to its full potential, his manager Richard Torrence thought, Fox needed to develop a younger following. With a touring organ—not a cumbersome collection of pipes, but an electronic organ—Fox could broaden his audience beyond the church circuit and eventually take his music to popular venues where youthful audiences were. Eventually, these arguments convinced Fox. So began the phase of his career that came to be known as "Heavy Organ"—anathema to most of his fellow organists at the time.

Like them, Fox had always hated the idea of what he insisted on calling "electric" organs. But when electronic organ manufacturers turned out to be willing to pay him to play, he overcame his objections. Rodgers Jenkins, the head of the Rodgers Organ Company in Oregon, was eager to demonstrate that his company could produce sound with transistors and speakers that, at least for some kinds of music, was every bit as good as a pipe organ's. Rodgers was ready to design a large instrument to Fox's specifications if he would consent to take it on demonstration tours for the public. Fox finally agreed, but insisted that Rodgers send someone to New York City to listen to him play the pipe organ at Riverside and then try to match its sounds electronically. In due course, a junior executive arrived and joined Fox at the Riverside console, but the meeting was a near disaster. In Torrence's words, "The young man said nothing while

*The Rodgers Organ Company's electronic Virgil Fox Touring Organ
stopping off in the 1960s near the George Washington Bridge*

Virgil proceeded to dazzle everyone with outstanding demonstrations of virtuoso German and French music. Finally, visibly moved, the young man said, 'Gosh, I had no idea you could really play! I always thought you were just a showman!'"

Rodgers developed a "Virgil Fox Touring Organ" with three keyboards and full pedalboard, but the project very nearly died a premature death because the company let an obscure organist give the instrument its first tryout at a concert hall in Montreal, wrongly assuming that Fox would never hear about it. When he did, Fox flew into a rage. Torrence calmed him down and persuaded him to go ahead with a series of grassroots concerts.

The Rodgers was serious business. The console weighed 1,800 pounds and was connected through sixteen amplifiers to fourteen individual speaker cabinets and two large bass cabinets, which Fox pointed directly at the audience when he played, to maximize the sound. The organ had been designed, at his demand, to produce an immense volume of sound, just as "his" Riverside organ did. But

Virgil Fox and Liberace with Mike Douglas on NBC,
stealing his show in 1973

when the first reviews were in, they were critical, along the lines of "Electronic Device Deafens Audience." As Ted Alan Worth wrote, "It sounded ugly, loud, and definitely 'electronic.' Virgil was mostly to blame. In Merion, Pa., there were perhaps 1,600 seats in extremely dry acoustics. Virgil had turned up the organ way too loud, with every tweeter at its highest level. The sound was dreadful and unmusical. No one could stand it for long. . . . It was like a hammer that bludgeoned. It did anything but thrill the audience."

Fox took the Rodgers with him for a television appearance on the *Ed Sullivan Show,* playing successfully even though a donkey in the show's animal act that Sunday night had trodden on one of the main speaker cables. He appeared more than once on the *Mike Douglas Show* as well; in 1973, he appeared on the show with Liberace, with whom he dueled in a duet on *Tea for Two.* It was hard to tell who outshone whom—Liberace, with rhinestones glittering on his dinner jacket, or Fox, whose organ shoes had rhinestones twinkling on the heels.

Fox played sixty concerts a year, often to houses between 300 and 1,200 people, always playing the music of Bach, Franck, Vierne, Jongen, and classical organ composers. But on the matter of loudness, Fox was intransigent. He was also furious when Torrence told him that Rodgers wanted to make the organ available to other organists to demonstrate. "That's my organ, and no one else will touch it!" he raged, but finally had to acquiesce when Torrence persuaded him that it was, after all, Rodgers's organ.

Richard Torrence and his collaborator Marshall Yaeger convinced Fox that to reach a younger audience, he needed to appeal to them on their terms. Fox had always had a histrionic side, tending toward vulgarity, that sometimes sent him "over the top." To his detractors, he was all too ready to cheapen himself. Worth remembered that at the concert in the municipal auditorium in Worcester, Massachusetts, in the 1950s, Fox, playing with the Philadelphia Orchestra, had constantly drawn attention to himself (in a gray silk tuxedo that stood out from the white tie and tails the orchestra wore) with musically unnecessary theatrical flourishes. When he needed to push stops in, he lunged like a wild animal, throwing his whole body against the side panels with the stopknobs, though he could have quietly pushed an automatic general-cancel button to do the job. At a later concert with the orchestra in Philadelphia, Fox refused to sit idle at the console during the many long measures of the Saint-Saëns *Organ Symphony* that precede the instrument's first entry; he made a dramatic entrance by tip-toeing across the stage and then swinging onto the organ bench just in time to start playing.

Torrence felt that David Snyder, Fox's new partner, encouraged this undignified slapstick. It became more and more evident after Snyder began accompanying Fox on tours, helping to produce them and even weighing in on financial matters, much to Torrence's annoyance. Snyder experimented with lighting effects at concerts, using spotlights to bathe Fox in rotating colors as he played. Snyder had replaced Dick Weagly in the mansion in Englewood with Fox and had his ear. Torrence, who lived with Yaeger in a sort of carriage house on the grounds, began to feel second-guessed, and threatened to leave. But Fox, whom Torrence was now booking for fees of $900 a concert, the highest of any American organist, dismissed his objections. David could do no wrong in Virgil's eyes.

When Snyder urged Fox to use a Canadian organbuilding firm, Keates Organ Company (for which Snyder just happened to be the American agent) to add a section of baroque-sounding pipes to Fox's home organ, Fox happily agreed. "There were divisions in the sun-porch, the attic, and also the basement," Carlo Curley wrote. "A large lattice grille had been installed in the living room floor. Homes with pipe organs often had similar arrangements and one could walk over the grilles without comment. To do so at Englewood was to court disaster, since the apertures were large enough for toes, heels, pieces of china and small children to fall directly through. For safety's sake, a narrow wooden plank was placed across, so that one could walk from entrance hall to living room without incident."

"Outside the thick stone walls of his 26-room house—silence," the *Christian Science Monitor* wrote of the place. "Inside his baronial living room—chandeliers sway and china rocks." Showing off the organ to a reporter for *The New York Times* in 1968, Fox called it a "Heinz 57 varieties." "Up on the third floor," the *Times* wrote, "at the top of the central stairway, a rectangular hole has been cut through the wall. The bedroom on the other side will soon be transformed into the pipe chamber of the Echo division of the organ, and the hole in the wall is to permit the sound to drift down the stairway into the music room."

Organists willing to pay for the privilege could take summer master classes at the mansion. "They all want to see the house, they can swim in the pool, gawk at the grounds, and pay me a fortune for the privilege!" Fox told his friends. Guests were warned that peeing in the pool would turn the water red around offending bathers, and soft drinks were available—at 50 cents a bottle. And at the end of the summer, Fox threw a barbecue banquet in his dining room, with hamburgers and hot dogs served on the best house china, but asked Torrence and Worth to pass around a paper cup for contributions to defray expenses.

Fox had not become a nightclub performer in his attempts to popularize organ music. He seasoned the classical repertoire with sentimental dollops and played baroque music in a romantic style that made no concession to "authentic performance." For that he had only contempt. "Fox has long been at odds with the instrumentalists who insist on playing in the baroque style on baroque organs—those whom he calls 'the baroque boys,'" the biographical sketch he approved for *Current Biography* proclaimed. "In Fox's opinion this is a backward move, since it imposes on new instruments the limitations inherent in the early baroque organs. Modern organs, he feels, are equipped to range over the entire repertoire; they retain the intimate ensemble needed to play the classic works of Buxtehude, Bach, and Couperin, and they also have the extended tonal range, modulation, and mechanical versatility to perform the organ literature composed since the classic period."

"I do not cram down the throats of the concert-going public morsels of choice music that have been shrunken and dried by dull, lifeless, and colorless interpretations," he proclaimed in "My Credo," written for *Music Journal* in February 1967. "Music has not been the only victim of the radical new movement that is sweeping the world. Art, literature, drama—they are all involved in a common set of changes which I call a preoccupation with the *letter* rather than with the *essence* of the law. Now don't get me wrong. I am not against the discipline of learning the law. I am, however, against those who possess little talent (totally lacking imagination) and those incapable of playing with virtuosity hiding behind abstract ideas and the limitations of a certain historic period." Fox made clear to friends that one of those he was talking about was E. Power Biggs, whose approach to the organ, Fox said, was about as interesting as "dried owl shit."

The baroque organs Biggs championed, Fox told Richard Dyer in *The New York Times*, "are monotones because they have no ability to alter the volume or quality coming from the pipe. . . . Unless the pipes are enclosed in a chamber and you have those three pedals that open up the chamber, you cannot make the sound come or go. . . . I notice that these baroquists do not ride in oxcarts; I notice that they do not use outdoor toilets," he sniffed, sounding very much like E. M. Skinner half a century before him. A baroque organ, said Fox, was "fine if you intend to wallow around with Pachelbel, Couperin, Scheidt, Franz Tunder or any of the rest. . . . That's all very interesting for the first piece on a historical program. But I want my immortal soul cleaned out, and my position in life given a little inspiration."

Well, tell that to the baroque boys. "Listening to Virgil Fox's organ recital at Philharmonic Hall last night was like turning the clock back 30 years," Allen Hughes wrote in a brief review in *The New York Times* in 1969. "It was as though the great renaissance in organ-building of the past three decades had not happened, that organ-playing styles of the same period had not undergone vast transformation, that time had done nothing to tarnish the music of French composers such as Vierne and Tournemire and had done nothing to brighten Franck's *Grande Pièce Symphonique*, either." But, as Hughes noted, for all Fox's violation of musical correctness, "He has many loyal followers, who turned out in good numbers for this recital, and they clearly approved of every note he played. Performers are few indeed who claim as much."

"Organ aficionados turn out en masse for Mr. Fox's recitals," Harold Schonberg wrote of a program of organ concertos. "Last night's audience identified with him and the music. During the Jongen there was an empathic wave that passed from Mr. Fox right into the bodies of his listeners. There were smiles, becks and nods from everybody. People were nudging each other as a difficult passage approached, grinning as it was successfully hurdled. And at the last measure of the Jongen, before the sound died away, there were yells and a rising ovation. Mr. Fox deserved every bit of it."

Fox shrugged off the critics; if his public liked what he was doing, that was good enough for him. When he produced a two-record album in 1969 for Decca entitled "Here Comes the Bride," with twenty-one songs that included "I Love You Truly" and "Because," packaged in a jacket festooned with pink hearts and a photograph of a veiled bride in profile, and priced at $9.58, he was deliberately mocking all that "the purists" stood for. Fox boasted to Judy Klemesrud of *The New York Times* that he could ask $1,000 for a wedding gig. Could any of those Fox-hating dried-prune organists fixated on De Grigny and Sweelinck do the same?

While other organists might be retreating into baroque "authenticity" in concerts where—as Fox liked to put it (elaborating on an observation made by Saint-Saëns)—fugue subjects entered one by one as the audience left two by two, he was getting young people to listen to Bach and to like it besides.

But playing in Philharmonic Hall in those days was like preaching to the converted. What Richard Torrence and Marshall Yaeger wanted was for Fox to take the message of Bach on the organ to young audiences mesmerized by an altogether different kind of music. They conceived the idea of an all-Bach concert with a psychedelic light show, in a place where no one would ever expect a classical organ concert—the Fillmore East, a theater remade into a movie house and rock concert hall on the then-funky lower east side of Manhattan. Israel Horowitz of Decca Records was immediately taken with the idea. "I'll record it live," he said. "I'll call the album 'Heavy Organ.'" So the Fillmore East was booked for December 1, 1970, with Joe's Lights, the hall's lighting experts, bathing the performer in psychedelic colors as he played the Rodgers Touring Organ.

Approaching the hall and seeing the old movie marquee outside the theater before the first concert, Fox thought back to the days when his mother ran the box office at his father's movie house in Princeton, Illinois. "I feel like I've finally come home," he told Torrence. The hall had dead acoustics, and Fox was worried about the lights and about the exotic smells that wafted through the auditorium even before the audience arrived: "Is that marijuana?" he gasped, clapping a handkerchief over his face. (Fox was as death on drugs as he was on drink.) But he wanted that audience. "If I were to play Bach the way they did 200 years ago, I wouldn't reach the people today," he told the *New York Post*. Torrence had put tickets on sale for $3.50 to $7.50 a seat—high at the time—but the ticket line went around the block. The house filled to its capacity of 2,650, and 600 people had to be turned away. "The auditorium was filled with a blue haze of smoke, most of which was you know what," Worth wrote. "The concert began thirty to forty minutes late because of the huge, sold-out throng settling in. Virgil walked out on the stage in a splashy dinner jacket and new silk shoes with rhinestone buckles that caught the light in a super-dramatic way. I don't recall a word he said before launching into the hushed, rhythmic opening portions of the A-minor Prelude and Fugue. But I understand that he actually did speak."

"Sebastian Bach is delighted you are here," he told the audience, who cheered "Go-o-o-o Virgil" when he launched into the opening mordant of the *Toccata in D minor*. As Carlo Curley, who took Fox's and his patroness Florence Candler to the concert, recalled Fox's performance, "He looked like the Elton John of the organ. . . . Behind the console came the light show, the different hues swirling in all directions and even Bach's stern features popping up occasionally. The final coup de théâtre was achieved by clouds of artificial smoke which billowed forth most noticeably from beneath the pedal-board, all over the stage. At the end of the final encore, the console was again engulfed in smoke, completely obscuring Virgil." Florence Candler thought Fox had caught fire. "Holy Smoke!" she whispered into Curley's ear. "No, dear," he replied. "Dry ice."

William F. Buckley Jr., the conservative columnist and editor, had been impressed enough on hearing Fox in Philharmonic Hall to get tickets to the Fillmore East. "We arrive, and there are hippies and non-hippies trying to get in, a sell-out," he wrote later. "We are astonished by the crowd, only a minority of which is Woodstock Nation. We learn that that is because the prices have been raised by 25 per cent." But Buckley was disappointed by what he heard after Fox started playing: "The performance is god-awful, because Fox clearly wants to impress the kids by a) the noise, and b) his virtuosity. At one point during a prelude, I am tempted to rise solemnly, commandeer a shotgun, and advise Fox, preferably in imperious German, if only I could learn German in time to consummate the fantasy, that if he does not release the goddam vox humana, which is ooing-ahing-eeing the music where Bach clearly intended something closer to a bel canto, I shall simply have to blow his head off. . . . After the intermission, Fox introduces the *Passacaglia* at Wagnerian length, almost but not quite to the point of causing mutiny in the audience, whose stirrings become discernible after the fourth or fifth minute. The maestro then turns and snows them with his dexterity, which is undeniable, the problem being that it will be ten years before I can appreciate again the music he has played, so over-loud, so throbby, so plucky-wucky the portamentos, so Phil Spitalny the cantandos." Torrence felt that Fox had played terribly, distracted by the lights and the fumes. Two weeks later, on December 13, despite another one of New York's periodic taxi strikes, the second concert drew 2,000 people, and this time, to Torrence's ears, Fox played beautifully.

Heavy Organ took to the road, with Fox commanding rock-musician-size fees, $5,000 a concert, the most a classical organist had ever been able to get. He traveled with the Pablo Light Show until it was replaced by "Revelation Lights" under David Snyder's direction, and gave concerts from San Diego to Boston, where the audiences loved the show even though the *Boston Globe*'s critic found the light effects "spermy," describing the show as a "mixture of showmanship, Bach, lights, slightly tattered virtuosity, homoerotic fantasies, animadversions on religion (pro) and drugs (contra)." John Rockwell, in *The New York Times,* later cleverly adverted to the same theme, alluding to Fox's "homey-eccentric spoken remarks."

At Carnegie Hall, he asked the crowd, "Is there anybody in the room old enough to remember Judy Holliday? She made a marvelous remark—'If you'll come across, I'll come across.'" Then, to introduce Bach: "I have just one question I'd like to ask you—can you whistle?" Bach could write catchy tunes, too, and Fox invited his audiences to clap and stamp their feet to Bach's rhythms, sneering

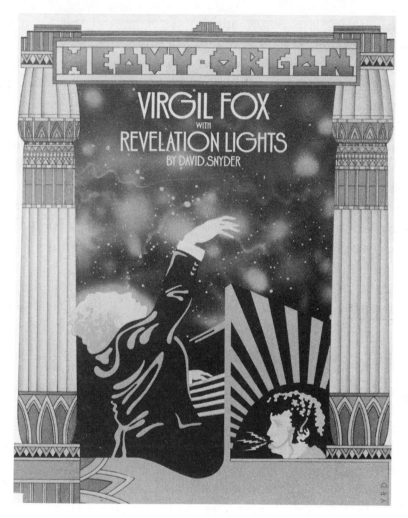

Fox's "Heavy Organ" tours started in 1970, and David Snyder's
"Revelation Lights" joined them in 1972

at the "baroquists" as he did so: "Most of you know what I think about the purists—the ones who TALK about it all the time and can't DO it."

Not since the orchestral organ heyday of the 1920s had so many people been drawn to what remained, for all the lights and all the hoopla, serious business—organ recitals of classical music by a solo organ performer. Fox did the impossible, the unheard-of, and soared off the charts. At an outdoor concert at Wolf Trap Farm outside Washington, D.C., 6,500 people came to hear him in 1973, more than came to see the Bolshoi Ballet or listen to the Cleveland Orchestra or the Preservation Hall Jazz Band. In the back of the lawn was a large group of Hell's Angels, resplendent in leather motorcycle gear.

Fan letters poured in to Fox's home in Englewood. One student at Peabody Conservatory, where Fox had studied the organ in Baltimore, wrote in 1974 that hearing Fox play confirmed his view that "sterile, academic performers had cut down the organ as a breathtaking, noble instrument, and robbed it of its fire, beauty, and power of communication. They had traded all of these in for what they thought were 'historically correct' methods of performance. . . . It was then that I discovered that someone else had reached these same conclusions, and was literally giving 'the proof of the pudding' in his performances. That person is, of course, yourself, Mr. Fox."

Paul H. Alex, a young fan who said he had attended nine Heavy Organ concerts, wrote with a timid complaint. "I have never but in the last concert seen any great variation in your program," he wrote as he made plans to attend his tenth concert. "I hope this time we will have something new and even more moving and inspirational."

In 1974, Carnegie Hall asked Fox to inaugurate its new five-keyboard Rodgers organ, which was twice as versatile and powerful as the one Fox used on tour. The old Kilgen Organ Company pipe organ on which Fox had made his Carnegie Hall debut in 1936 had long since been removed. Fox had been proud of that concert his whole life—it had been the first organ recital in the hall that people had actually paid to attend, his promotional materials boasted. Fox of course had no interest in reversing the decision of the trustees to turn down a baroque-style Flentrop pipe organ that had been proposed for the hall, and he had been only too happy to help Carnegie and Rodgers decide what sorts of sounds the electronic organ that would take its place should be able to produce.

So there was great anticipation before the opening concert, on

October 1, 1974, when Fox was to show just how close to a pipe organ the Rodgers could come. He chose a program of big organ works by Bach, Dupré, Vierne, and Franck. "No wonder the hall was buzzing with excited comment," Schonberg wrote in *The New York Times*. "Every second person in the audience was an organist. Presently Mr. Fox appeared to give his noted vaudeville act. He talks, acts, defends his interpretations, casts aspersions on musicologists, pleads for emotion in music making, plays with exaggerated motions, slides off the stool to take his applause, meanwhile mouthing the last phrases of the piece he has just played. He is a virtuoso in all directions." Schonberg concluded, "It was a magnificent demonstration by a supersalesman. In things like this Mr. Fox is indeed unique."

Fox also demanded his tribute from Rodgers—a five-manual touring organ for himself that would be an exact duplicate of the Carnegie Hall instrument. This, the "Royal V," made its debut in 1975 before an audience of 3,000 people under the stars at the Concord Pavilion in Concord, California, and crisscrossed the country with Fox for about a year, drawing big audiences and publicity for Rodgers everywhere it went. But with Rodgers demanding a fee of $1,000 a concert for the Royal V's use, relations between performer and builder deteriorated.

Fox and Snyder began looking at the competition for a better deal, finally finding one with Allen Organs of Macungie, Pennsylvania. Fox signed a contract to buy a four-manual Allen touring instrument in the summer of 1976. Rodgers belatedly offered to sell him the refurbished original touring organ for $1, but by then he had already signed the contract for the Allen, which he used on tour until the end of his concert career. With four keyboards, 150 stops, and 12 computers programmed with simulated pipe organ tones, Fox's concert programs boasted that "The Aristocrat," as the new organ was called, had 2,700 watts of power capable of producing as much sound as the Mormon Tabernacle organ. But in truth, Fox had never been truly converted to the electronic cause. He needed a big pipe organ to truly express himself, one that could attract big audiences, but unlike most organists, Fox had no home base, no church.

He was also growing uneasy about living in racially tense New York City. Riots broke out even in Englewood. "Our town has a large Negro population," he told one audience. "We could hear shots being fired and people being killed." Urged on by David Snyder, he began looking at properties in Maine, in Arizona, and in the Hudson Valley.

And then he found a castle in Massachusetts.

The castle that the inventor John Hays Hammond Jr. had built overlooking the reef of Norman's Woe on the North Shore in Gloucester had an organ of 10,000 pipes that Hammond (an inventor with no connection to the organ company) had assembled over the years, and Fox had recorded one of his first RCA Victor albums on it just after World War II. He had gone back to the castle to record three more RCA albums in 1954, with the eleven chorale preludes for organ that were the last works of Johannes Brahms, and two grand romantic pieces, Julius Reubke's *Sonata on the Ninety-fourth Psalm* and the Franck *Grande Pièce Symphonique*.

Hammond had kept the castle open to the public as a museum of Medieval art, and when he died in 1965, willed it to the Roman Catholic Archdiocese of Boston. The castle is, as *The New York Times* described it in 1954, "a great gray granite pile, with battlements, towers, a drawbridge, iron entrance doors, narrow winding stone staircases and parapets," and a Great Hall, 100 feet long, 25 feet wide, and 58 feet high, dominated by the organ. But the estate, exposed to the ocean, was about as expensive as a cathedral to maintain and keep open to the public, as Hammond's will required. After sinking more than $250,000 into the castle, the archdiocese put the trusteeship up for sale.

Now Fox was seized with the idea of acquiring the castle, grounds, and organ and turning them into a center for performing arts that would include a residence for himself, Snyder, and their entourage, and a resident International School of the Concert Organ that would train organists to play expressively, with spirit and verve that would turn on the public, not "authentically" like the purists Fox deplored. He would teach, alongside other great performers like Pierre Cochereau from Paris, M. Searle Wright, a distinguished American church music composer and organist, and Alexander Schreiner of the Mormon Tabernacle.

Fox dreamed of making the organ that Hammond had built even larger by adding the 8,600 pipes of G. Donald Harrison's 1932 Aeolian-Skinner organ from Harvard University's Memorial Church, one of the instruments that had been so important to E. Power Biggs's early career. Fox had acquired this organ for $32,000 a few years after the university had replaced it with the Fisk instrument in 1967. Here was a way, Fox must have thought, to stick it to both Biggs and Biggs's favorite builder, Fisk, in the eye, right on Fisk's home turf in Gloucester besides.

Fox needed local allies in Massachusetts, and he found them in the summer of 1973 in Roberta Bailey Johnson and her husband, Richard, who by then had recovered enough from the wounds inflicted by Fox's past treatment of her to consider a new association with a project both of them found exciting. Roberta rented a house near Gloucester to work on the project and try to raise money from foundations and businesses. Fox went back to Florence Candler and Emilie Spivey and pleaded for the $250,000 the archdiocese was asking for the trusteeship of the castle and the museum, but they turned him down. Bird Fox, who owned two farms in Illinois, came to the rescue with a loan, but there were other obstacles to be overcome.

One of these was a competing proposal from a local group called the Gloucester Committee for the Hammond Museum, Inc., which claimed that it would operate the place "as Mr. Hammond instructed"; one of its members was Corinne Witham, who had been curator of the museum for thirty years. In the late summer of 1974, this committee sounded an alarm familiar to anyone who has ever attended a town meeting in New England—the tocsin warning of a threat from "people from away."

"Mr. Fox," the committee wrote in a form letter that landed on Biggs's desk, "would install the Harvard Memorial organ in the museum, put another organ console on the main floor, install Revelation Lights, and the museum would become his home because where his organ is, that is home. . . . We felt his intentions did not meet with Mr. Hammond's plan to perpetuate the museum for all people," the committee wrote.

Biggs might have acted anyway, but a month after he received the letter, Fox did something else that sent him into a towering rage. This was the interview with Richard Dyer published in *The New York Times* on September 29, with Fox's boast that he could outplay any organist living and, even more outrageous, an attack on the neo-baroque pipe organs for which Biggs had become the leading American champion, and on the leading American builder of this school, Fisk—a risky move on Fox's part, given Fisk's ties to Gloucester, but Fox just couldn't help himself. "I loathe what that man stands for," Fox told the readers of *The Sunday Times.* "A Fisk organ can scream out Messiaen with all those bird calls, but it cannot play Mendelssohn; it cannot play Franck, Brahms, Schumann, Elgar, Reger. It is totally inexpressive. It cannot play Bach. Bach was a ROMANTIC composer."

That was all it took to set off Biggs, who fired off a letter to Boston's Cardinal Humberto Medeiros on October 9:

"By his long established habits and manner, and just recently by his statements as quoted in *The New York Times* (enclosed), Mr. Virgil Fox is totally disqualified as a tenant or possessor of the Museum," Biggs wrote. "Particularly objectionable to everyone is Mr. Fox's vicious attack, in *The New York Times,* on Charles Fisk, Gloucester organ builder—and one of the country's most respected and best!"

"I suggest to you," Biggs concluded, "that if the Museum were in his hands, relations between Museum and town would be unfriendly and abrasive, and the future of the Museum would be in serious jeopardy."

Fox and the Johnsons met with members of the Gloucester Committee twice. "I, the Fox, have no intention or desire to own this property," he tried to reassure them, but nothing would allay the group's suspicions, which were far-ranging and highly imaginative.

Fox's plans to enlarge the castle organ would ruin it, they argued. His concerts would lose money—local people would never pay $7.50 apiece for tickets to hear him play. People raised ethical and moral issues: Fox was known for playing in the nude in public, they had heard; was it true that on his Heavy Organ tours, he was known to drop his pants in performance, and that in the 1950s, after giving a recital at the castle, he had jumped naked into the indoor pool, uninhibited even by the presence of Mr. Hammond? If Revelation Lights were allowed in during concerts, would there be monkeys swinging from trapezes above the castle floor? And so on.

Fox issued a statement, published in the *Gloucester Daily Times* on August 29, 1974, assuring townspeople and archdiocese that his intentions were entirely high-minded. "A research center will be established for the correlation of light with music where the further enunciation of the great masters can take place on a level of aesthetic and artistic integrity," it said. "Qualified persons in all of the areas of the museum activities will make up the staff."

"I quite candidly admit that I bring to this task a well chosen flamboyance as alleged once again 'in and out of print,'" he added. "It is my intention to return the life of this castle to a level of creativity that its founder gave it."

But Fox had influential backers as well as local detractors. One of his friends who had pull with the Catholic Church was Catherine Filene Shouse, heiress to the Boston Filene's department-store fortune and founder of the Wolf Trap Farm Park for the Performing Arts outside Washington, D.C., whom Fox had approached for money. Mrs. Shouse provided something he needed even more than money in Gloucester—moral support, in a letter to Cardinal Medeiros that heartily endorsed his plans.

In February 1975, the archdiocese gave Fox what he wanted. After payment of $250,000 to the church, a nonprofit organization with Fox as board chairman and Richard and Roberta Bailey Johnson as directors took over museum operations, fired the longtime director, Corinne Witham, and instituted the Virgil Fox Center for the Performing Arts on the grounds.

The plans were truly grandiose. The castle organ, Fox told Shirley Fleming, editor of *Musical America*, would become the "largest instrument on the face of the earth. I will make the definitive set of recordings of my life the moment that organ is finished." The center would be for "all kinds" of music, he said, and the organ school would emphasize an "expressive musical approach"—no cold-fish neobaroque academics here. And Revelation Lights, which Fleming said had been drawing young audiences to his organ concerts like bees to honey, would be at the heart of a research center to explore the relationship of light to music and to education. "It's a hell of an agenda," Fox boasted.

The housewarming party came on May 10, with herald trumpeters on the turrets over the moat to welcome the guests—a spectacular party that was covered even by the *Washington Post*'s Judith Martin, who noted the satin-and-rhinestone shoes Fox was wearing, the red-lined cape, and the inevitable comparisons to Liberace, whom Fox quoted in return to answer criticism that he was "hyping" classical music: "'I cry all the way to the bank,' he says."

But Biggs had been prophetic. In Worth's words, "From the beginning, the move to Gloucester generated one disaster after another. It seemed that every 'improvement' he made angered either the archdiocese or the Gloucester Historical Society—whether these improvements entailed moving the organ console, or purchasing a second organ in order to enlarge the first (reflecting his impossible dream to have an unparalleled large house organ), or redoing a suite for his private living quarters in his inimitable taste (which ranged from pink telephones to pink Cadillacs)." Fox's weird hours also didn't mesh at all well with a museum schedule that admitted guests in the morning; Fox was rousted out of bed by the crowds. And there were mutterings in Gloucester about the "mad organist" and "his kind." Fox occupied the suite that Mrs. Hammond, a painter, had lived in, with an ocean-view porch, but he removed the hand-painted wallpaper decorated with views of the Himalayas and camped out with a bed and clothes on the floor. Snyder's adjoining bedroom was also off-limits to the public, but Torrence, Yaeger, and the rest of the Fox "family" lost all privacy when the doors opened at 11 A.M.

As the archdiocese had found, the castle was a money pit. Fox had tried to control expenses, but he had no idea what they really were. At the housewarming party, 100 people, including close friends, had to contribute $50 a head. "The roof leaks, and it'll be $50,000 just to fix that—that's why we're here tonight," he told them. Only Snyder and Fox's mother, who had flown in from Pasadena to surprise him, got in free.

Fox had spent a fortune on a dance band for the party and on a bubble machine that flooded the indoor reflecting pool with a mass of suds after some of the inebriated guests poured in too much soap.

The first sign of real trouble came only two months after the party. Concerts at the castle and admission fees were falling far short of expenses, the trustees discovered, and so far there was no sign that plans to raise $4 million for an endowment had any chance of success. The trustees took drastic action, with Fox's full support, and forced Richard and Roberta Johnson to resign on July 9, 1975. The Johnsons were "placing less stress on the business end," and their total salaries of $30,000 were more than the museum could afford, two of the trustees explained to the *Gloucester Daily Times* a few days later.

Betrayed a second time by a figure she idolized, Roberta Bailey wrote to Fox on July 11: "Wednesday night was total disaster for me—I honestly couldn't handle it all without breaking down in front of the trustees," she told him. "Virgil, you must get professional counsel regarding the future of the entire program and its funding—none of which can or will come from the present trustees. The budget can never balance, you must have funding and you can get funding, but only if you are convincing that you are doing what you proposed. . . . Dick and I, believe it or not, worked very hard for *you*, Virgil, *and* the Museum . . . too hard."

Five months later, Fox was out too, after accusing the trustees and the new acting director of terminating his "artist-in-residence" status at the castle, "harassing and insulting" him and his friends "in order to force them to abandon the premises," and refusing to pay back over $250,000 he said he had loaned the corporation. Lawsuits and countersuits followed, ultimately leaving Fox with losses and legal fees of about $130,000, he told Roberta Bailey long afterward.

He kept the Harvard organ—though the trustees claimed in their suit that this was a $100,000 breach of promise—and sold his own minicastle in Englewood for $238,000. He paid off the loan from his mother and moved, with Snyder and Merle Webster, their cook, and Fox's 1963 Cadillac Eldorado convertible—white, not pink—to Florida, after buying a Spanish villa called Casa Lagomar, a block from the ocean in Palm Beach.

Then real disaster struck.

In September 1976, Fox and the Royal V went to San Francisco for a series in St. Mary's Cathedral, whose four-keyboard pipe organ combined with the Rodgers instrument in a "Festival of Organ Virtuosos and Illumination" that was a great success for its organizer, Ted Alan Worth. Fox's two "Bach Gamut" performances drew overflow crowds of 5,000 to the cathedral. Between engagements, Fox underwent a physical examination by a friend of Worth's, Dr. William T. Armstrong, a cardiologist and organ buff who performed a prostate examination in his home office up the stairs from the living room of his house. "Surely, I'm wrong, I kept saying to myself!" Dr. Armstrong remembered years later. "Yet, even to a heart doctor, there was no mistaking the bump I felt that hadn't been in him the previous year."

Fox came down the stairs and drove out to "Bud's" ice creamery, where he bought five half-gallons of ice cream, and then went back to Worth's house to spoon it out to his friends and tell them what the doctor had found. A week later, in Florida, a specialist determined that Fox's prostate was cancerous.

This was not Fox's first cancer scare. In 1953, he had had a growth removed between the thumb and index finger of his right hand, but in Europe the following summer, he noticed that it had returned. Roberta Bailey had taken him to a pathologist who called in three assistants and frightened Fox off, in Bailey's recollection, by saying, "Well, we'll have to cut deeper." They had gone to Anne Archbold's office in Rockefeller Plaza and called another doctor who decided that the growth was not malignant, but cut it out the following November.

Fox sounded devastated when he telephoned Worth with the shattering news that he had prostate cancer. "He told me he felt completely unclean. He had never been sick a day in his life, had rarely drunk alcohol, abhorred cigarette smoke, and had always pampered himself. God knows he always got enough sleep! I had never heard Virgil sound so depressed, or heard him sob like that. He told me he felt like walking out the door toward the ocean, wading in, and ending it all."

Fox canceled his concerts for the rest of 1976 and in early December underwent surgery to remove his prostate gland. Assured that the surgeons had gotten it all, he retreated to his villa to recover, with the ministrations of his mother and Snyder, who kept him supplied with the infusions of vegetable and fruit juice Fox thought would help bring him back to health. "I'll have to hurry because it's soon going to be honeydew time," Snyder told a visitor, who thought he meant juice from honeydew melons. "Virgil will soon be getting up and saying, 'Honey do this, Honey do that,'" Snyder said.

Early the next year, Fox was back on the road, but he seemed thinner and paler to Torrence and his friends when they joined him in California at Dr. Robert Schuller's Garden Grove Community Church (the future "Crystal Cathedral"), where Fox was to inaugurate a new five-keyboard pipe organ by the Ruffatti Brothers Organ Co. of Padua, Italy. Fox was impressed with the powerful sound of the organ and set to work practicing monumental works to show off the 117 ranks of pipes, later recreating the concert on two recordings using the new digital technology for a small label called Crystal Clear Records, which issued them as "The Fox Touch"—the last two commercial recordings Fox made.

Torrence and Yaeger, who had arranged the project and overseen the recording, found Fox increasingly impatient and irritable. He fussed about the terms of the recording contract, which paid him no money up front. He also worried about the tuning of the organ, making impossible demands even on Snyder, whom Fox's managers by then thoroughly detested as a meddlesome intruder. Fox was fixated on money problems, although his fees were higher than ever, thousands of dollars a concert.

Dr. Armstrong saw him and was concerned about a recurrence of the cancer. He demanded that Fox undergo another examination, which found that the doctors had not gotten it all. Fox then underwent cobalt treatments in Presbyterian Hospital in San Francisco, where Dr. Armstrong was on the staff. Fox commandeered a refrigerator at the nurse's station for his ice cream, and, wearing the red-lined cape over his hospital smock, he regaled nurses and visitors with stories during a television rerun of "The Joy of Bach," featuring himself and Rosalyn Tureck. "What a lot of nerve she has! But she sure can play!"

The treatments seemed to be working, and in June 1977 Fox and Snyder went to Tokyo for two concerts in the hall of the NHK television network, which had a large German-built Schuke tracker organ. The organ had two consoles, one attached to the pipes from which the performer was mostly invisible to the audience, and a movable one where Fox could show off, which was of course the console he chose for a condensed version of his "Bach Gamut," after insisting that technicians rewire some of the controls to suit his preferences. In the second performance, with the NHK Orchestra playing the Jongen *Symphonie Concertante,* Fox sounded almost as good as ever.

But when Fox stopped in San Francisco on the way home, Dr. Armstrong thought there was something odd about the way Fox was using his hands. "Well, Honey, you don't hear any mistakes, or notice too many split notes, do you?" Fox retorted. However, he submitted to X-rays, which revealed small fractures in the bones. Further examination by a neurologist revealed a tumor growing behind his ear. By then, the cancer had metastasized to his bones. "At this point," Dr. Armstrong noted, "only palliative therapy (but no cure) was possible."

Fox sought consolation with friends, and with the Schullers, who asked him to design the huge pipe organ they planned for the Crystal Cathedral, which was being designed by the noted architect Philip Johnson. Fox sold the church a few Skinner pipes he had, and got the Schullers to buy the Philharmonic Hall organ that he had helped inaugurate a decade and a half earlier—its 5,498 pipes removed as part of Lincoln Center's unending search for an acoustical Holy Grail in the unsatisfactory auditorium that had been renamed Avery Fisher Hall.

Fox tried to persuade Johnson and the Crystal Cathedral leadership to install a rank of sixty-four-foot pipes that would have produced a subaudible earthquake-like rumble to undergird the hymns, but there wasn't room. Fox did succeed in having some of the organ's trumpets installed horizontally. "It'll be a bevy of herald trumpets just like the Queen of England has," he told Johnson, whose reply greatly tickled Fox: "Personally, I've always preferred my organs upright."

Fox came to New York City in January 1978 to play a concert on a small Holtkamp neobaroque organ that had been set up in the Metropolitan Museum's vast entrance hall. His performance of the six delicate "Schübler" chorale-preludes by Bach, Allen Hughes wrote in *The New York Times*, were "for the most part, so splendidly paced and colored, so flowing and so lyrical that one wondered if Mr. Fox had decided to abandon the excesses that have cheapened his playing in the past. Was he now ready to assume at last what should always have been his proper place among the major musical artists of this country?" Fox had nothing but contempt for such condescension, and showed it by insisting on following the Bach with Vierne, Franck, and even Alexandre Guilmant's "*Marche Religieuse*," which Hughes dismissed as "really scraping the bottom of the barrel."

His physical state continued to decline. In July, he told Dr. Armstrong that he was having trouble moving his left hand and fingers and had to cancel a number of concerts. Radiation treatments continued with the aim of fending off the ravages of the disease as long as possible, but by now it was clear how this struggle was going to end.

Fox was becoming ever more dependent on David Snyder, whom he now wanted to adopt as his son and, in a will dated in 1978, named as his heir. Although the state of Florida barred homosexuals from adoptions, Fox and Snyder went through with the process, maintaining that they were legal residents of California, where Bird Fox had long lived in Pasadena. By now, Fox had totally estranged himself from his managers, Torrence and Yaeger, who were continually exasperated by Snyder's interference and finally quit.

Their last official act as managers was to arrange the return of the prodigal son to Riverside Church for a solo recital on May 6, 1979, sponsored by the Virgil Fox Society, an organization set up two years earlier by Marilyn Brennan and other organists who admired his playing. But neither Torrence nor Yaeger attended the concert, so bitter had their relations with Fox become by the time the date arrived.

"I'm going to roll General Grant around in his tomb," Fox boasted, and indeed, the concert at Riverside was a tour de force that demonstrated Fox's prodigious memory, his energy, and his sheer infectious enthusiasm. When "Dr. Virgil Fox" was introduced to the packed auditorium by David Snyder, he clearly savored the moment. "So, shall we say, we are off to a new beginning," he told his assembled followers, who applauded. "I am determined that this shall not be a stuffy occasion," he said, introducing two of the Schübler chorales and then playing them romantically, with shimmering string stops and vibrato, to milk the pieces of every bit of the emotion Fox always insisted on drawing out of them. "Play from the heart, not like a trained bird!" he had always told his students. And on he went, playing Duruflé's difficult *Suite* in its entirety, from memory, after telling the audience how he had been in the composer's apartment high on the Mont-Sainte-Geneviève in Paris one night not long before when Duruflé had opened the louvers to reveal the entire length of Notre Dame Cathedral illuminated in all its glory, an inspiration, Fox thought, for the medieval plainchant spirit that suffused all of Duruflé's work. The program would have exhausted most fit players half Fox's age: a lighthearted *Giga* by Marco Enrico Bossi; the tormented *Litanies* of Jehan Alain, a prayer of the Christian soul, the repetition of faith in the face of despair and unbelief; transcriptions of Debussy's *Clair de Lune,* and the *Liebestod* from Wagner's *Tristan und Isolde,* with the high F sharp that Kirsten Flagstad had seared into his memory; Franz Liszt's huge Fantasy and Fugue on the Chorale *Ad nos, ad salutarem undam,* and the *Toccata* from the Jongen symphony, using the soaring Trompeta Majestatis stop that had been installed in the organ by Anthony A. Bufano, its longtime curator, after Fox had left the church.

The showman in Fox ceded to the church organist for the finale. This was Fox leading those assembled in a full-throated recitation of William Croft's great hymn, "O God, Our Help in Ages Past."

"This is the House of God," Fox intoned as the concert approached its conclusion. "I would like very much for us to make music together before we go." First, the audience had to learn how to take and hold what he called "a singer's breath." Then, he explained how he would modulate from key to key between stanzas. He invited Hazel Gravell, an old friend who had been the soprano soloist at Riverside during his tenure, to come up on stage and sing the fifth stanza solo "if she feels like it." And at the end, after the sixth stanza, all were to join in an "Amen," but, Fox warned, "I would like very much to have none of the mewing, pewing that usually goes on in the congregation during the Amen." And, "If you don't have your glasses and can't read the words, just sing the first verse six times."

Hymn, congregation, and organ accompaniment came together in a spiritual statement that attested as much as Bach or Brahms or Beethoven to the power that music has to uplift the human heart.

> *Time, like an ever-rolling stream,*
> *Bears all its sons away;*

They fly, forgotten, as a dream
Dies at the opening day,

Hazel Gravell sang before the sixth and final verse, and after the soaring three notes of the Amen, as Fox had asked, silence was observed in the great nave.

Incredibly, Fox was able to keep up his concert schedule after this. But when Carlo Curley saw him in London in September of 1979, he could see the decline. Fox had lost weight and energy, the bounce in his step was gone, and his ankles were swollen from water retention. But he could still summon the strength to play, although he was disappointed in his new managers when only 350 people turned out in April 1980 to hear him play a concert in the Marin Civic Center in San Francisco, in an auditorium that seated 2,000. "Kids, you see how they think that just by mentioning my name, there'll be a full house automatically," he complained to Worth.

A dying man, he struggled heroically as if nothing were wrong, through ordeals that would have taxed a man in the prime of life. An outdoor concert in New Jersey on May 31 with the New Jersey Symphony Orchestra was blown out by a thunderstorm as the orchestra began playing the Saint-Saëns *Organ Symphony* and the power failed as the rain blew in.

Fox seemed to be trying to settle the accounts of his life, responding with grateful tears when Worth arranged a reunion in San Francisco with Richard Weagly, who was teaching and playing for a church in San Diego. They met for dinner at a restaurant; Weagly broke out in tears when somebody snickered at Fox's white mink coat, matching pillbox hat, fuchsia silk shirt, white trousers, pink socks, and white shoes. "That is one of the greatest musicians in the world!" he sobbed. "He's dying of cancer, and you dare to laugh?"

Fox kept taking on concert engagements, including a commitment to inaugurate a new Ruffatti organ at St. Paul's Lutheran Church in Orlando, Florida, in November 1980, a date he wanted to keep, for the phenomenal fee of $12,500. But he had to undergo cobalt treatments in the hospital in Palm Beach, where Snyder also persuaded him to submit himself to a faith healer's incantations. "It satisfies David," he apologized. "At this point, I'll try anything." He complained of constant back pain he could not alleviate even with a long bath, and his doctors prescribed morphine.

At the end of September 1980, he dragged himself to Dallas for two performances with Eduardo Mata and the Dallas Symphony, playing both the Poulenc concerto and the Saint-Saëns symphony. "He was determined to start that last season, and to get the ten grand," Fox's friend David Lewis recalled, but "he was completely deaf in his left ear; and his fingers, hands and arms were so weak and sore from bone cancer that he couldn't reach the top rows of the drawknobs."

The first concert, on Friday night, September 26, amounted to a minor miracle. In Lewis's words: "Virgil couldn't possibly play this music—he could barely sit on the bench; and yet he did it." But the next night, Fox, in his dressing room, finally gave in. "I can't do it," he conceded in a weak voice, and Ladd Thomas, an admirer who had come knowing he might have to stand in for the ailing Fox, performed instead.

Fox and Snyder flew back to Florida, where for the next month Fox was in constant pain. Visiting Robert Hebble, who had settled in Palm Beach a year earlier, he tried to play one evening but lacked even the strength to depress the keys. "It is finished," he told his old friend. "You take it and see what you can do with it."

Virgil Fox drew his last breath in Good Samaritan Hospital in West Palm Beach early on Saturday morning, October 25, 1980, at the age of sixty-eight. There was a private funeral service in Fox's villa by the sea three days later, and a public celebration of his life at the Crystal Cathedral on November 9. Robert Schuller's eulogy began: "Well, Honey . . . "

The concluding hymn was, as it had to be, "O God, Our Help in Ages Past," but there was a sad and poignant postlude. Bird Fox died a few months after her son and willed her considerable estate to his brother, Warren. But David Snyder, sole heir to Fox's million-dollar Palm Beach house and everything in it, sued Bird Fox's estate on the grounds that, as Fox's adopted son, he was legally her grand-son and entitled to a share of the inheritance. Like Weagly before him, like Roberta Bailey and Richard Johnson, like Richard Tor-rence, like all who had passed in and out of Fox's penumbra, Sny-der yearned impossibly to share in Fox's brilliance, and this was his way of trying to lay claim to it—so Marc Johnson, Bailey's son, who had worked with Snyder and Fox at the Revelation Lights show at Wolf Trap, explained Snyder's behavior.

Snyder's suit was unsuccessful, and he left for Canada, where he opened a bed-and-breakfast in Southampton-on-the-Lake, Ontario, before disappearing from public view. There, years later, members of the Virgil Fox Society recovered the organ console that had been in the mansion in Englewood, and other items.

A pink granite tombstone stands in memoriam to Virgil Fox in the Pioneer Cemetery in Dover, Illinois, five miles from Princeton, and it remains a place of pilgrimage decades after his death. Mil-lions of people, in America and Europe, heard Fox during his life-time; 1,500 admirers came together at Riverside Church for an organ concert in his memory on the twentieth anniversary of his death, an event organized by the Virgil Fox Society and its still-faith-ful acolytes, who established a scholarship in his name with the American Guild of Organists to encourage young musicians to be-come familiar with the instrument he did so much to make popular.

Few performers on any instrument have ever had a more loyal following so long after they died; Fox's reputation was further at-tested to in 2001 by the publication of *Virgil Fox (The Dish)*, a biogra-phy by Richard Torrence and Marshall Yaeger.

Over all the adulation hung one great regret. "Too many people were offended by a showman when they should have been dazzled by a genius," Torrence wrote. That statement could stand as Virgil Fox's epitaph.

‖ 8 ‖

Back to the Future

I am expecting any day now to hear someone come out for the unequal temperament just as Silbermann did it," Ernest Skinner wrote to *The Diapason* in 1941. If he had lived until 1969, he would have seen the construction of the first large modern American organ in unequal temperament like the system Gottfried Silbermann used in the eighteenth century: a tracker instrument built by John Brombaugh & Co. for the First Lutheran Church of Lorain, Ohio. Brombaugh, an electrical engineer, had been converted to the tracker cause by listening to the recordings of E. Power Biggs, although the organ in Lorain, one of his first instruments, used electric controls for bringing the stops on and off.

Not even that much concession to electricity was made in an organ that C. B. Fisk built in 1985 in Blanche Anderson Moore Hall at the University of Michigan. Its twenty-seven stops are tuned in unequal temperament just like instruments built more than 250 years earlier—if not "just as Silbermann did it," close enough. It even has a historically authentic "klingel," a bell to signal a bellows assistant to start pumping air. This last feature would certainly have caused Skinner to ask from his grave whether the Michigan organ had an electric blower for those organists who do not insist on arriving in a horse-drawn buggy or on using a privy instead of indoor plumbing between practice sessions. (It does.)

Skinner would also have pointed out that of all the features of Silbermann's organs, the temperament, or tuning system, was what Bach liked least. "Silbermann preferred the old untempered scale, which prohibited freedom in modulation and rendered certain keys useless," Skinner said. "He violently opposed Bach's desire for the equal temperament."

That is overstatement, but Bach did write *The Well-Tempered Clavier* to demonstrate that it was possible to make pleasing sound with music written in all twenty-four major and minor keys with a more modern, evenly tempered tuning system. The older unequal temperaments, like the ones Silbermann and his predecessors used, did not divide the octave into equal semitones, the way a modern piano does, spreading the dissonance inherent in certain intervals (a sixth or a second, for instance) over the whole keyboard. The old systems left intervals in some keys sounding purely in tune and others sharply dissonant—acceptable to musicians at the time of the Renaissance, who just avoided those intervals in their compositions, but "barbaric" to Bach's demanding ear. As David Ponsford, an English organist and scholar, pointed out, on Silbermann's great organ in the cathedral at Freiberg, some of the greatest Bach organ works would have been unplayable in Silbermann's original temperament, including even the *Passacaglia in C minor*. Later alterations modified the Freiberg organ's tuning system to make it more friendly to such pieces.

Equal temperament made possible the chromaticism, the modulation from key to key, that was characteristic of romantic composers such as Franck, Wagner, and Rachmaninoff, and of twelve-tone composers such as Schoenberg and Stravinsky. Music as we know it today would be almost unthinkable without it.

But in mid-twentieth-century America, while urban designers were tearing down the nineteenth- and early-twentieth-century architectural equivalents of romantic organs, masterpieces like New York City's Pennsylvania Station, and replacing them with modern construction, organbuilders were replacing romantic organs with instruments that purported to be from an earlier age but just as often were the equivalent of postmodern architecture, thin and sterile.

In the world of the American pipe organ, progress meant going back to the past—far back. Scholars dug into the organ's historical roots in what seemed to the general public like arcane exoticism. Some students were encouraged to learn to play the pedals with toes only, never using legato, because that was the way organists had done it 200 years earlier. Early and mid-twentieth-century organs were rejected and reviled as corruptions of "true" organbuilding principles. All this put the world of organ music and organists into a kind of reverse time warp. The organ, once at the center of American musical life, now began to be seen as intimidating, austere, and removed from the real world.

That result was not what people like Brombaugh and Fisk had intended when they built pipe organs influenced by historical research and scholarship. Places like the University of Michigan School of Music wanted such instruments as teaching tools. The Fisk company built the Silbermann-style organ there because the school wanted American students who might never get to the remote reaches of Saxony to be able to hear what the music of Bach sounded like on the organs he wrote for—what had been in Bach's head when he composed for the organ, an unimpeachable pedagogical goal. The Fisk organ, with two keyboards, was not a copy of any organ Gottfried Silbermann built, although it closely resembled the two-manual, twenty-three-stop organ made between 1718 and 1721 for the St. Georgenkirche in Rötha, in eastern Germany.

In their enthusiasm for rediscovering the genius that had made the baroque organ the king of instruments, many in American academic musical circles from the 1960s to the 1980s rejected the all-purpose eclectic organs the previous generation had known. Baroque tone, tracker action, the "chiff" that preceded the speech of baroque pipes—these and all the other accoutrements that E. Power Biggs found so essential were now in demand, although Biggs had never insisted on reinstating unequal temperament. As for Fox and his electronic-organ concerts, they belonged in another world of monumentally bad taste.

For companies like Aeolian-Skinner, which had tried to go on building all-purpose electropneumatic organs, the new dogmaticism spelled disaster. The revolution begun in the 1930s by Harrison and Walter Holtkamp had progressed so far by the 1980s that it was destroying Harrison's legacy. The Aeolian-Skinner Organ Co. began a long and steady decline after his death in 1956, with many complications before its demise. The first was strictly mechanical. The leather in the little pouches that worked the electropneumatic pipe valves had held up well enough in the first half of the twentieth century, when good leather was available. But after World War II, air pollution and the difficulty of obtaining high-quality leather led to rapid deterioration. An organ that once might have needed releathering every fifty years or so would begin to suffer dead notes or ciphers in as little as a decade after the organ was built. Harrison's last organ, the one completed at St. Thomas Church in New York City in 1956, apparently already needed complete releathering in 1964. Told that it would cost $30,000 to $40,000 and that the work would have to be done again in another eight years, the organist and the vestry decided to replace the Aeolian-Skinner action with a hybrid system that used electricity but put the pipes on the kind of windchests tracker organs had. This and subsequent changes by the rebuilder, Gilbert F. Adams, modified Harrison's tonal design so much by 1968 that Aeolian-Skinner asked that the Harrison nameplate be removed from the console.

"Releathering" became the curse of the large urban electric-action organ. Aeolian-Skinner tried leather substitutes, with disastrous complications in a renovation of the E. M. Skinner organ in Trinity Church, Wall Street. The company had other problems as well. The building of Boston's Southeast Expressway had taken half the factory in 1957, forcing the relocation of some of the operations to a workshop in South Boston that had originally been built for the Perkins Institute for the Blind. The inflation that set in with the 1960s and intensified during the Vietnam War also put the company in a financial squeeze. The pressure was particularly acute in the organ business, which required large capital expenditures on costly pipe metals, wooden materials, and intensive labor starting years before the product could be delivered and payment in full demanded. Costs were spiraling, and the company was charging more than $2,200 a stop; by 1966, however, orders had stopped piling in. "Organs are being sold and it's time we found out why not ours," management pleaded with the sales staff in 1968. Red ink began to flow. Joe Whiteford, who had withdrawn to Arizona a few years earlier to alleviate the symptoms of arthritis, resigned from Aeolian-Skinner that April. Although the organs the company built under his direction included some notable successes, under his leadership Aeolian-Skinner too often tried to meet the neobaroque trend halfway and fell between two stools. Organists found many of these instruments anemic and shrill, with thinned-out fundamental tones overwhelmed by high-treble mixtures and mutations.

When Aeolian-Skinner couldn't beat the neobaroque competition, it tried to join it. There were discussions in 1968 about a merger between the company and Fritz Noack, a German-American builder of tracker organs whose factory, the Noack Organ Company, was in Andover, Massachusetts. Noack thought it over but decided that each company would do better to stick with what it did best, and stayed independent. Aeolian-Skinner then acquired another mechanical-action builder, the Robert L. Sipe Company of Dallas, in 1969, but philosophically it was never a very happy marriage. Among the last Aeolian-Skinner instruments were the only two all-mechanical-action organs ever built in its Boston shops, numbered 1525 and 1527, for the Church of the Transfiguration in Dallas and for Old North Church in Marblehead, Massachusetts.

John J. Tyrell, Aeolian-Skinner's chairman of the board, resigned in October to go to work for one of its chief electronic nemeses, the Allen Organ Company. A new investor, E. David Knutson, bought into Aeolian-Skinner when it moved to a new factory in Randolph, Massachusetts in 1969, but in 1971, struggling with the expenses and other difficulties of renovating the huge organ in St. Bartholomew's Church in New York City, the company was forced into Chapter 11 bankruptcy. Aeolian-Skinner limped through the work at St. Bartholomew's, completed an organ in the concert hall at the Kennedy Center in Washington, and made one last attempt to merge, this time with Austin Organs of Hartford, Connecticut, in

1971. But after finding out just how bankrupt Aeolian-Skinner was, Austin backed out of the talks that November.

So, in 1973, the great company that Ernest M. Skinner and G. Donald Harrison had made the Cadillac of its field wrapped up its few remaining contracts and stopped making organs for good. As Michael Harrison had written to his father many years earlier, "Organ building is always much of a one man show since so much depends upon the tonal discrimination of the organ builder himself. They are not machines that can be produced to a set of hard and fast (and permanent) rules as one can see by looking through lists of old firms. The master starts a company and builds a fine organization on his artistic ability; when he dies the firm continues to exist on his name for a generation using an 'ordinary' organ builder to carry on. Finally the public wakes up and the firm closes down."

Unthinkable as it had seemed, the smaller tracker-action organ-builders had nibbled Aeolian-Skinner to death. With Biggs's Harvard Flentrop organ fresh on their minds, American churches imported 200 tracker-action organs by European builders in the 1960s. But by the end of the decade there were twenty-seven American builders like Noack, Fisk, and Schlicker producing tracker instruments—166 of them—over the same period.

"Tracker enthusiasts cheered for the young organists studying in Europe on Fulbright grants, and absorbing the 'truth' about organ style," the organ historian Orpha Ochse wrote. "They cheered even more for the young organ builders beginning to find a market for their skills . . . David defying Goliath. Established organ companies were pictured by the most extreme tracker backers as insensitive factories that built look-alike machines loaded with unnecessary accessories that only served to distract the performer and divert attention from the music itself. It was difficult in the 1960s to find a moderate viewpoint about anything."

If, as Biggs had concluded about Harrison's experimental "baroque" organ in 1937, the first American experiments in authenticity had not gone far enough for aficionados, by the 1970s and 1980s the "purists" Virgil Fox detested were going too far for

the general concertgoing public. People had flocked fifty years earlier to hear organists play romantic symphonic transcriptions on big
orchestral organs that were now scorned as distortions of the
baroque ideal. The terms of organbuilding contracts were being
dictated by scholars, teachers, musicologists, and organists who
wanted to understand the spirit of old French, German, Dutch, and
Iberian music, not by entertainers like Edwin Lemare and Fox who
wanted to attract the masses. Now organbuilders were producing es-
oteric organs with unequal temperament, no swellboxes, astrin-
gently "authentic" baroque tones, and the flat, straight pedalboards
that had disappeared half a century earlier in favor of concave, radiating ones.

As research developed, the vision of what was "authentic"
changed, both in playing and in building. In 1958 or even in 1976,
a Flentrop organ had been considered "authentic" if it had mechanical action and pipes voiced more or less the way pipes had been
voiced 200 years earlier. Flentrop used modern tuning in the Busch-
Reisinger organ and in the large baroque-style organ he installed
over the entrance of Duke University Chapel in 1976. Fenner Douglass, the university organist, observed approvingly, "The instrument
was freed from virtually all corruptive influences deriving from periods later than the early eighteenth century. Thus, a musician will
not expect to change stops electrically, to set pistons before playing,
to couple the manuals without a commensurate response in the key
action, to open or close Venetian swells, to operate distant antiphonal divisions, or to find console measurements in conformity
to the latest standards of the American Guild of Organists."

But the tuning of the Duke organ was modern, leaving it capable
of playing music in any key. This was not the case with all such instruments—for example, a Fisk organ built for Houghton Chapel at
Wellesley College in Wellesley, Massachusetts, in 1981. This instrument has two keyboards of fifty-one notes each, with the pipes
voiced as much as possible the way Gottfried Fritzsche, an early seventeenth-century North German predecessor of Schnitger, might
have done them, and tuned authentically in a particularly unequal

temperament. But the front part of some flat and sharp keys is separate from the back, so that one key can play separate pipes, flat or sharp, depending on the musical scale in which a piece is written.

The right kind of music—Scheidt or Scheidemann, for example—can speak as a revelation on an organ like this. Most romantic organ music would sound perfectly awful on it; the point of the instrument was to demonstrate how perfectly wonderful early music could sound. Fisk and Wellesley didn't pretend that the new organ could do everything equally well, so they left undisturbed the main service instrument in the chapel, a modified G. Donald Harrison all-purpose Aeolian-Skinner from 1936. Duke University did the same in its chapel, not modifying a 122-stop Aeolian organ that had been installed in 1932. Although its pipes were in chambers, it was considered one of the all-time great romantic American organs. Duke added a third organ in 1997, a small Italian-baroque instrument tuned in mean-tone temperament that, as the builder, John Brombaugh, acknowledged, permitted pre-Bach music to be played only in a "limited constellation of keys (corresponding to those commonly used in the repertoire at the time)."

Academic specialists and many of the organists understood this new (old) tonal language and communicated it well among themselves. But to the uninitiated, the point of many organ recitals became "stay home; this isn't for you." How far organbuilders and organists had come from Biggs's and Harrison's day, they would congratulate themselves—but how far also from the world that Biggs had described to Columbia Artists in 1950, when 30 million people went to classical music concerts and only 16 million to baseball games, and when his own records were bestsellers. By the turn of the twenty-first century, organ recordings and classical music recordings of all kinds were available in unprecedented profusion in record stores, but they were not selling. The giant entertainment conglomerates that had gotten rich on Madonna and Britney Spears and the like were looking for ways to dump contracts with symphony orchestras and opera companies. Yet, in the twenty years leading up to this calamitous state, many organbuilders had been acting as if popular appeal didn't matter, although some of them may have had second thoughts. "I think . . . that this whole organ is, in a way, an educational toy," Charles Fisk said of his Wellesley organ at a conference at Greensboro College in Greensboro, North Carolina, in 1980.

Apart from the small numbers of early-music devotees of authentic performances, the public mostly stayed away in droves from organ recitals that were so often limited to early and baroque music. The situation was hardly better in some churches whose organists had persuaded clergy and lay leadership to buy instruments that were too specialized for broad tastes. "An instrument that is a work of art in the North German Baroque style may, in its first year, be an attractive novelty in a mainstream Presbyterian church, but over time may prove to be of limited usefulness," one organbuilder, Jack M. Bethards, of Schoenstein & Co. in San Francisco, observed. As organists specialized, churches became more diversified, and some of the most successful "megachurches" attracted large congregations with nontraditional liturgy and popular, not classical music. By the end of the 1990s, Hellmuth Wolff, a Canadian organbuilder, observed that companies like his were "engaged in producing instruments that apparently interest fewer and fewer people," even in churches. "The denominations currently gaining ground in North America seem to be those in which classical organ music is marginal or simply not relevant," he said.

Fortunately, not even organbuilders and organists could drive the organ to extinction. Inevitably, the pendulum began to swing back from the excesses of the mid-1970s, and it has been swinging back steadily since.

There is no better illustration of the trajectory—although it is hardly a simple parabola—than the work of C. B. Fisk, Inc. over its first forty years. Less than twenty years after Virgil Fox denounced Fisk and his ilk as the antithesis of everything he stood for, the firm Fisk founded was making organs that even Fox might have been amazed and delighted to play.

Charles Brenton Fisk was a scholarly, gentle, physically frail man of science who became fascinated by the organ as a choirboy in

Christ Church in Cambridge, Massachusetts, while E. Power Biggs was organist and choirmaster. With his clear-framed glasses, tousled blond hair, and plaid shirts, Fisk looked like a university teaching assistant in physics who had somehow wandered onto the organ shop floor. No dictatorial factory foreman, he was a quiet, Socratic teacher whose manner endeared him to his employees despite the paltry paychecks he gave them. He collected a staff of people like himself—bright minds with a burning sense of curiosity about how a mechanical instrument could be brought to sound like a living, breathing organism, and about why European organs hundreds of years old come so vividly alive in performance. Organs, Fisk told the members of his staff, were like children: "One loves each one and hates each one just about the way one loves and hates one's children."

Fisk was born in Washington, D.C., in 1925 and grew up in Cambridge, where in high school he was an electronics and physics prodigy. With World War II drawing to a close, he was accepted by Harvard College, but military service called and the army assigned him to Chicago, putting him to work as an electronics technician in the Manhattan Project. Later he was transferred to the bomb physics division of the national laboratories in Los Alamos, where he worked briefly on the detonation device for the atomic bomb.

He finally enrolled at Harvard in the fall of 1945, after his discharge from military service, and there he studied physics and engineering. But he had not lost his powerful interest in music. He sang in the Harvard Memorial Church choir under G. Wallace Woodworth, and he took organ instruction at the Longy School from Melville Smith, who championed French organs of the seventeenth- and eighteenth-century classical period and the lively music that composers such as Louis Nicolas Clérambault and Louis-Claude Daquin had written for them.

After getting his A.B. degree in physics from Harvard in 1949, Fisk briefly did cosmic ray research work at Brookhaven National Laboratories. He arrived at Stanford University in 1950 intending to start work on a Ph.D. in nuclear physics, but after only a few weeks, he abandoned the field, despairing that high-energy physics would have only military uses and not wanting to be a part of it if that was the case.

He transferred to the Graduate School of Music, taking classes in theory and composition and studying organ with Professor Herbert Nanney, the university organist. Fisk was modest later about how well he had learned to play but said, "One thing I did learn was that American organs were totally unsuited to playing the music of J. S. Bach." That was clearly hyperbole, though perhaps not when applied to the 1901 organ in the gallery of Stanford Memorial Church, built by the same company that designed what became the Wanamaker organ in Philadelphia.

Fisk decided that his future was in building organs rather than playing them, a field that would enable him to combine his interest in music and his background in physics. Professor Nanney put him in touch with John Swinford, the builder who maintained the Memorial Church organ. Fisk joined Swinford's firm as an apprentice, to learn the art of organ building, and three years later moved to Cleveland to learn from Walter Holtkamp Sr., whose exploration of neobaroque organ principles made him what Fisk considered "the most avant-garde American organ builder of the time."

But Fisk and Holtkamp did not see eye to eye, and Fisk soon began looking for other opportunities. He found one in 1955 in an advertisement from the Andover Organ Company, which had been spawned by an institute led by Arthur Howes that was devoted to studying historic American organs and bringing traditional organ-building principles back to the craft in modern times.

In 1958, Andover's founder and owner, Thomas Byers, sold the company to Fisk. Under Fisk's leadership, the firm began trying to build instruments the old way, with mechanical instead of electro-pneumatic action, with notable success in Baltimore, in an instrument built for Mount Calvary Church. Arthur Howes, the organist of the church and a teacher at Peabody Conservatory in Baltimore, had introduced Fisk to Dirk Flentrop. Flentrop's ideas inspired Fisk to design the organ along Dutch classical lines, right down to the Dutch names he gave to its stops. In fact, the nameplate on this organ, completed in 1961, reads "Andover-Flentrop." Fisk was pleased with his work. "I think I can safely say that this organ *is* a work of art," he said.

By then, Fisk had made the first of a series of research trips to Europe to discover European classical organs for himself. On one of Arthur Howes's European organ tours, in 1959, Fisk was captivated by the clear, bright sounds of the early-eighteenth-century instruments built by Andreas Silbermann, Gottfried Silbermann's brother, in Marmoutier and Ebersmunster in Alsace. He had heard them from recordings that Melville Smith had made on them, but now he wanted to climb up to the galleries, open up the casework, and measure the pipes to see how Silbermann had made them and to inspect the mechanical workings of the action.

While enjoying the excitement of discovery, Fisk suffered during the trip from debilitating liver problems. He had never fully recovered from an operation a few years earlier for a defective bile duct. The weakness in his liver brought on bouts of jaundice and nausea, and it worsened with the years.

Still, in 1961, Fisk struck off anew. He parted ways with the Andover Organ Company and set up a new shop not far away in the fishing port of Gloucester, Massachusetts, near Rockport, where he had spent the summer vacations of his childhood. His new company opened for business as C. B. Fisk, Inc., in a ropewalk on the waterfront, a barnlike building in which rope had been laid in the old sailing days. There was room enough for Fisk and the new team of craftsmen, artists, and researchers he was putting together to assemble large organs.

Fisk demanded much of his employees, putting most of what little money the company earned back into the business and into the research that went into producing new instruments. Some of them came to see him more as a respected teacher than as a demanding boss, and he taught with the Socratic method, asking questions that led his coworkers to their own discoveries of better ways to do things rather than imposing his own methods on them. He thought of organs as living beings that interacted through the centuries with composers and performers alike. "The more like an animate object the organ can be made, the better it is," Fisk said. He wanted to build instruments that let performers hear and feel the music in their hearts and ears in just the way the composers of that music had heard and felt it. In particular, he wanted to build American organs that could bring out the best in Bach's works.

The three-keyboard organ that Fisk completed in the historic King's Chapel in Boston in 1964 was then the largest mechanical-action instrument built in the United States in modern times. It replaced an early Skinner organ from 1909, although Fisk did reuse some of the Skinner pipes and tried to compensate for the dry acoustics in the sanctuary, which was devoid of reverberation. Tonally and visually, the organ was designed along classical English lines, like the eighteenth-century church in which it stood, and like many English organs after about 1712, it had a "swell" division whose pipes were enclosed in a case with louvered doors that could be open and shut to "swell" the notes. It fulfilled every hope that Daniel Pinkham, the church's organist and resident composer, another Biggs disciple, had for it. It also pleasantly surprised the donor, Amelia Peabody, who had anticipated a more standard Aeolian-Skinner when she endowed a new organ for the church. King's Chapel needed an organ whose essence matched its surroundings, Fisk insisted, and he persuaded her that a mechanical-action instrument would work well in the building.

With Pinkham, Melville Smith, and Biggs now all in his corner, Fisk continued to build mechanical-action organs whose musical style was usually not limited to one particular period. Before Smith died unexpectedly in 1962, he and John Ferris, the university organist at Harvard from 1958 to 1990, had begun working to persuade the authorities of the university to commission an organ by Fisk to replace the 1932 Aeolian-Skinner in the Memorial Church. With help from Biggs and others, Ferris finally got the approval he wanted.

For the organbuilder, the challenge was considerable. The sanctuary was acoustically unreverberant, and Ferris wanted an organ that could accompany congregational singing in the main part of the sanctuary, yet not drown out the choir in the chancel. At the end of the chapel was where Fisk decided the new organ should go, standing on the central axis and facing into the chancel (the Appleton Chapel).

In 1967, the Fisk instrument, even larger than the Kings Chapel organ, with four keyboards and, again, mechanical key action, opened in the Memorial Church. With forty-nine stops, it was a modern instrument, despite the Italian-baroque positive division and the enclosed swell division with a romantic voix céleste. The organ case was highly ornamented, with rich, gilded carvings of sea life. It was a work of stunning visual beauty, and when Biggs played one of the opening recitals, he included a work fittingly called *A Prophecy* written for the occasion by Daniel Pinkham.

But the builder's feelings were complex. The Harvard organ, Fisk said, lifted him to greater heights and consigned him to "the depths only an organ builder can know" more than any of his others. "An acoustically merciless building encloses this organ, and, as if to compensate, the organ sometimes behaves like a caged animal. It can seem to fret, squabble and throw tantrums at times; it can also soothe, cheer and thrill beyond measure." Like a living organism, the organ was completely responsive to its surroundings and to those who played it, capable of showing either empathy or antipathy. It faked nothing, covered up nothing. "It is by far the most sensitive, responsive, high-strung organ we have ever built," Fisk said, and it put what he called a unique "burden of proof" on the player. "One cannot say of this organ that it is beautiful, because it becomes beautiful only in the hands of a tasteful performer with the God-given gift of touch," he concluded.

What Fisk's tracker-action Harvard organ had that so many neo-baroque electropneumatic experiments of Aeolian-Skinner, Möller, and others did not was a solid, full-voiced ensemble of powerful foundation stops, with wide pipes that sang out in powerful unison tone. If the foundation of an organ sounds too timid or thin-toned, high-pitched stops that are designed to reinforce the treble overtones of those foundation stops make the ensemble sound strident and screechy, a quality Aeolian-Skinner's detractors found and intensely disliked in its post-Harrison attempts to imitate baroque clarity.

Fisk kept listening, hard, to recordings of other historic instruments in Europe whose sounds he wanted to bring to America in his own instruments. Then he would work in the shop, trying out different pipes and looking at variations in the shape of the mouth, the size of the toe-hole that admitted air, any detail that might give some desirable new accent to the musical speech of an instrument, involving his employees in discussions to figure out how to build better organs. "Brainstorming," they called it, and Fisk said he had learned it from the scientists at the Manhattan Project.

In 1971, Fisk built an organ for Old West Church in Boston that, in his mind and ear, was a tribute to his late mentor, Melville Smith. When he built an organ, Fisk said, he had often imagined how it would sound under Smith's exquisitely sensitive touch. The conception of the Old West Church organ, Fisk wrote, "is essentially Alsatian and is most closely related to the single Andreas Silbermann organ that Melville Smith loved above all others: Marmoutier." The voicing of the stops, the pipes themselves, he noted, "all are, as it were, appointed to please our deceased friend."

Yet the organ, Fisk's Opus 55, did not look particularly Alsatian. Part of its handsome mahogany case was salvaged from another organ, the work of Thomas Appleton, a Boston builder whose shop in the 1830s had been located a block from Old West, and the case had a distinctly English look. But Fisk gave the ensemble the typically reedy, nasal tones found in French instruments of the 17th-century classical period, and in the organs that Andreas Silbermann, inspired by both French classical and German baroque instruments, built 100 years later. The lovely eighteenth-century riffs on French Noëls by Daquin, Jean-François Dandrieu, and Claude Balbastre that Melville Smith had recorded so memorably, to Fisk's ears, at Marmoutier sounded equally at home on the Old West organ. It represented something uniquely American, a blend of old world and new, of French and English tradition combined in a way no French or English builder would think of doing.

Fisk had the ambition of reaching a wider audience with his instruments. A few years later, an opportunity arose with the contract for a large organ in the House of Hope Presbyterian Church in St. Paul, Minnesota. On his 1959 trip, Fisk had studied not only eighteenth-century German and Dutch organs but also nineteenth-century romantic and symphonic instruments built by Cavaillé-Coll. He returned to Europe in 1974 and 1977 to visit more organs built by the Silbermanns. "Recent trips to France and Germany have let me see more clearly how we might synthesize a design that really will accomplish the 'unattainable' ideal of playing all literature well," he wrote in February 1977 of the House of Hope project.

For one of the leading figures in the authentic-organ movement, this was a major departure. What Fisk was saying amounted to recognition that G. Donald Harrison and other American organbuilders who had tried to design and construct eclectic organs that could play all the organ literature well had not been hopelessly deluded, as authentic-performance conventional wisdom insisted. For Fisk, who enjoyed the emotional power of Gustav Mahler's romantic music as much as the contrapuntal precision in J. S. Bach's, *trying* to build organs that could play any kind of music well was an artistically valid goal.

Fisk pursued that goal in pipes and pedals and stops and keyboards in the House of Hope organ, Opus 78. It would be his lifetime magnum opus, Fisk began to sense, for his liver problems were worsening. "He was still well, but I think he had an inkling that his health problems were not going to give him a long lifetime," his collaborator Charles Nazarian recalled.

The House of Hope instrument, completed in 1979, was the largest organ that Fisk himself ever saw through to completion. It was not a recreation of a specific historical style but a synthesis of many different ones—a more scientific and historically authentic realization of what Harrison and others had tried to do in previous decades. It was mechanical-action, of course, but it combined

Charles Fisk voicing pipes in the organ at North Carolina School of the Arts in Winston-Salem in 1977

French romantic stops like the haunting flûte harmonique and the shimmering voix céleste so necessary for Franck and Vierne with reedy German baroque sounds like the schalmey and the trechter-regal, which sound like bees in a bottle, and plaintive French classic sounds like the cromorne, a precursor of the clarinet. The heart of the instrument was full-voiced foundation stops that were as rich and powerful in tone as any in the romantic orchestral instruments Cavaillé-Coll built in nineteenth-century France. But there was also a baroque-inspired rückpositiv at the player's back, in a case separate from the rest of the organ. The fourth manual played a brustwerk, with gentle-speaking stops at the height of the player's chest, that Fisk said was inspired by the one in an eighteenth-century North German organ in Lübeck.

There were nearly sixty stops in all, tuned in slightly unequal temperament to allow for slightly purer fifths and thirds in the most often used keys, while still permitting the chromatic modulation so characteristic of composers like Franck and Vierne. In the church itself, Fisk insisted on the removal of echo-deadening insulation and other materials to improve the acoustics. Again like Cavaillé-Coll, Fisk was ready to spend his own money, up to $100,000 beyond the original contract, to get it right even if it meant bankruptcy for the company. Finally, a generous donor gave the church the necessary additional funds.

By this time, Fisk's health was failing steadily. Having built a landmark organ for Harvard, he jumped at the chance to bid for a major project at Stanford, his second university, when it announced that it wanted a new, historically authentic neobaroque instrument in the Memorial Church. Fisk won the contract with a design combining features of East German, North German, and French organs of the seventeenth and eighteenth centuries, with one entire keyboard's pipes in a temperament suited to early seventeenth-century music and the other three keyboard divisions able to play in either well-tempered tuning or the older mean-tone system. This was made possible by a special lever the organist could throw to switch from one tuning system to the other, since on three of the four keyboards there were two pipes for each "black" key in every octave, one tuned for the old uneven temperament and one for the "well temperament" that Bach favored. It took Fisk's team many brainstorming sessions to figure out how to do this. "Our purpose in building this organ," Fisk wrote, "has been to provide a large instrument which can play everything from Praetorius to Bach with all possible authority."

But Fisk never heard his organ played in Stanford. While it was under construction in Gloucester, he had a severe liver attack that sent him to Massachusetts General Hospital in Boston for a month at the beginning of 1983. He summoned Steven A. Dieck, his project manager, to his bedside and told him, "I'm on my last days." He said he knew he had paid his workers less than he might have and apologized for spending the money instead on research and experimentation. "What would really distress me," he told Dieck, "would be if this wonderful group of people I've collected around me were to disband because of my death." He implored Dieck to see to it that the company would carry on if he died, and told him, "You're the one to make sure the team stays together." The business was by then thriving and had moved from the ropewalk to an industrial park on the outskirts of Gloucester.

Fisk returned home, but was never again able to come to the shop, leaving the details of the work to the team he had so painstakingly assembled, often by asking prospective hires less about what they knew of organs than about whether they had ever taken a car apart. His second wife, Virginia Lee Fisk, and Dieck took over the Stanford project, as Fisk reached out at a few other last opportunities to leave his mark.

Like Harrison and Skinner and so many other American builders, Fisk wanted to bring great music to as many people as possible, not just to those who already knew what organ music was. When San Francisco invited bids for a new instrument at Davies Hall in the late 1970s, Fisk had submitted a proposal, but he had lost out on that one to Ruffatti. "You wouldn't want to build an organ in a concert hall," Dieck told him then, reflecting the reality of the times in concert halls in Boston, New York, and Philadelphia where organs were seldom heard—"It would just sit there for a hundred years and never get played."

But in 1979, the city of Dallas decided to build a new home for the Dallas Symphony Orchestra, to be designed architecturally by I. M. Pei and acoustically by Russell Johnson of Artec Consultants, Inc. Dallas was determined to have a first-class organ in the new complex, the Morton H. Meyerson Symphony Center. Eugene Bonelli, then dean of Meadows School of the Arts at Southern Methodist University, was the chairman of the committee that was to select the organbuilder, and he wrote Fisk asking for a proposal.

At first Fisk was disinclined to reply, but Bonelli and the others involved in the Dallas project persisted and finally persuaded Fisk that this concert hall organ was going to be used plenty, not only in concerts but also in a new and highly remunerative international organ competition to encourage young organ performers. When a donation from the Lay family of Dallas—Lay as in Frito-Lay—assured that there would be virtually no limit on the size of the organ, Fisk started his brainstorming in earnest in mid-1982. Among the experts he consulted was Calvin Hampton, an organist and composer in New York City who had just published an article in *The Diapason* on what concert hall organs needed. That was, he told Fisk, a big enough sound to enable the organ not just to hold its own with the orchestra but to soar over it in a climax, with a "heavy wall of sound." "Take one of your standard organs and put a high-pressure division on it," Hampton said.

E. Power Biggs had also given Fisk advice that ran against the grain of neobaroque orthodoxy. An organ designed to play with the orchestra, Biggs had told Fisk in 1976, should have a powerful voice capable of holding its own with combined brasses, flutes, strings, and percussion—for moments like the final movement of the Saint-Saëns symphony—as well as the soft, shimmering stops that come in during the quiet moments of works like the Poulenc concerto. It also needed electric-action combination pistons that would allow the organist to change registration quickly to comply with the conductor's dynamic commands, and other such practical devices as a crescendo pedal (a swell pedal that moved no swell shades, but instead added stops as it was depressed). A concert hall organ did not need imitative orchestral stops, for the orchestra, after all, was right there, Biggs pointed out. But to be usable in solo recitals, it also needed the full panoply of distinctive organ sounds.

Fisk began working out a stoplist and discussing the matter with associates, at home after he was no longer able to come to the shop. When the voicers began working on the pipes at Stanford, he desperately wanted to go himself to hear the instrument taking shape, but his illness made travel impossible.

His liver finally failed in 1983, and on December 16, Charles Fisk died. The following month, on January 21, many of the same people who had gathered only a few years earlier for the funeral of E. Power Biggs came together again in Harvard's Memorial Church to pay tribute to Fisk's life and works and to hear music performed on

The author playing a landmark concert-hall instrument,
The Lay Family Concert Organ installed in 1992 by C. B. Fisk, Inc.
in the Meyerson Symphony Center, Dallas

one of his most important creations. At Fisk's request, Thomas Murray played the organ.

The Fisk company's design work on the Dallas organ went on. Led by his widow, who became president of the company, and by Dieck, Robert Cornell, Charles Nazarian, and the other thirty-two members of the Fisk team—many now shareholders in the company—collaborated with the architect and the acoustician to produce a revolutionary design for the organ of sixty-five stops, Fisk's Opus 100. Completed in 1992, with 4,535 pipes fronted by the shining tin tubes of the Prestant stop towering thirty-two feet over the orchestra in a colossal cherrywood case, this, the Herman W. and Amelia H. Lay Family Concert Organ, cost $2 million. It brought American thinking about concert hall organs back to what it had been with Biggs and Harrison at Symphony Hall in Boston. The Fisk organ, in one sense, was a new kind of American Classic, an eclectic organ that drew on three separate European traditions to produce a uniquely American blend.

The backbone of the Dallas organ is a great division with classic German specifications, alongside a positiv with a bright German baroque character. The swell, however, is completely French romantic in its sounds and its stop names, from viole de gambe to trompette and hautbois. On the fourth keyboard, at the top of the console, is an English concert-hall tuba division, with both tuba and royal trumpet on high wind pressure for extra tonal strength, operating on the electropneumatic action that high pressure requires.

The glory of the instrument is an entirely independent ensemble section, the résonance division. This consists of pipes of French tonal inspiration that are a powerful treble extension of the pedal organ, playable by both hands and feet and capable of producing a massive sound. Together, the résonance and tuba divisions can soar out over the full orchestra with an "iron-willed sound of riveting impact," as Fisk's head voicer David Pike described it in *The American Organist.*

Like the large Cavaillé-Coll organs in France, apart from the tuba division, the organ's key action is largely mechanical, but with a revolutionary servopneumatic device of the company's own design, perfected by Stephen P. Kowalyshyn. This is an updated version of the old "Barker lever" that Cavaillé-Coll, Willis, and American organbuilders used a century and a half earlier to lighten the finger pressure needed to play the entire organ when all stops were drawn and all keyboards were coupled together. It did what Charles Fisk had always said he was trying to do; it made the organ not a machine but almost a living organism, an instrument that was subtly responsive to the player's every nuance of touch. Jean Guillou, a virtuoso French organist and composer, paid this new Fisk "servo-mechanism" the ultimate tribute with a Gallic pun: It was a "cerveau-mécanisme," a "brain-mechanism," he said, that brilliantly and precisely transmitted the organist's thought to the valves and the pipes that express it. Registration was modern: the organist could change stops instantaneously with a complete array of electrically operated combination pistons.

Any organ's effectiveness depends heavily on the acoustics of the room it stands in. Even the Cavaillé-Coll organ in Saint-Sulpice would be an overwhelming disappointment in an acoustically dead hall. The acoustics that Russell Johnson of Artec Consultants designed in Dallas can be made to seem as reverberant as a cathedral or as intimate as a salon. A forty-two-ton acoustical canopy can be raised or lowered, and giant reverberation chambers above the ceiling can be opened (for, say, the Mahler *Resurrection Symphony*) or closed (for the Beethoven string quartets). In this hall, the Fisk instrument can sound majestic or intimate, as the music requires. With the support of the Dallas Symphony Orchestra's conductors, Eduardo Mata and his successor, Andrew Litton, the organ can be as integral a part of the musical life of the Meyerson Center as Fisk had been assured it would be.

The Dallas organ was a stunning achievement, one that set a new standard for concert halls all over America and the world. Guillou, who had been calling on French and other European builders to produce instruments responsive to musicians and music rather than slavishly imitative of historical precedent, wrote, "Fisk organs herald a movement which, without a doubt, will lead gradually to an original American organ in the same way as the instruments Skinner created in times past."

In the House of Hope organ, and in his thinking about the Dallas organ, Fisk was following in Harrison's footsteps, or rather tracing a new path beside Harrison's. "His results were artistic," Fisk observed in 1980. "Indeed, the American Classic Organ as conceived by G. Donald Harrison during the late thirties still commands our respect, even though it falters in its original purpose of imparting authenticity to performances of serious organ music. . . . In his organs, Harrison achieved beauty, and American organ builders are going right on with his dream, his quest for the all-purpose organ, knowing that such a thing may not really exist, but that results of great beauty are possible along the path. . . . Knowing that an all-purpose organ *cannot* exist, we can still strive for excellence in a *multi*-purpose organ."

By the end of the 1990s, the Fisk company had produced numerous recital- and concert-hall organs in the United States and Japan that were not pure recreations of earlier historical styles but eclectic combinations capable of bringing popularly pleasing music to a wider audience. As Jonathan Ambrosino has pointed out, the Fisk company and mechanical-action builders like it had also turned the tables in the long-running American debate that had started with champions of baroque tracker organs denouncing the romantic excesses of electropneumatic instruments. "The beefy, decibel-rich sound was now coming from the 'stick' organs," Ambrosino wrote in 1998. "While a certain few clung to the old Classic-Romantic notion, the organs that were supposed to be Classic no longer fit the mold, while the organs that were supposed to be Romantic rarely were, aside from the possibility of a few good celestes."

It could be argued, as Ambrosino does, that the later neoromantic Fisk organs like the one in Dallas were no more truly romantic in character than the early neoclassic Fisk organs were truly classical. What seems clear is that many organists and organbuilders have regained an appreciation of the romantic sounds of nineteenth- and early twentieth-century organs whose excesses had so repelled them half a century earlier. In 1995, the Fisk firm assumed the contract from Rosales to build a seventy-five-stop organ combining French classical and romantic sounds, much as Cavaillé-Coll had done at Saint-Sulpice, for Rice University's Shepherd School of Music in Houston. Rosales remained involved as collaborator and co-voicer, and when it was completed in 1997, this organ, like the one in Dallas, had a servopneumatic device that helped the player push down the keys without dulling the sensitive "feel" of the touch when keyboards were coupled together. The amphitheater-style console with its curving stopknob terrace looked like those Cavaillé-Coll built for Saint-Sulpice and Notre Dame, and the sound of full organ was designed to be equally fiery and powerful in tone.

Four years later, the Fisk company produced another mechanical-action instrument in Cavaillé-Coll's symphonic style, for the Finney Chapel at Oberlin College. Built with the teaching needs of

Oberlin's prestigious conservatory of music in mind, and as a complement to the Flentrop in the Warner Concert Hall where Biggs had received his honorary doctorate a quarter century earlier, the Finney Chapel Fisk was, in the words of the builders, not a copy of a Cavaillé-Coll organ "but rather one that Cavaillé-Coll might have built," with 4,000 pipes. It was based on extensive research into Cavaillé-Coll's building methods and voicing techniques carried out in the Rice University project, and designed with the full range of bombarde, trompette, clairon, flûte harmonique, and voix céleste stops typical of his nineteenth-century French instruments. And it opened, appropriately, with performances of the Saint-Saëns *Organ Symphony* and the Jongen *Symphonie Concertante.*

In early 2002, the Fisk workshops in Gloucester were bristling with metal pipes and filled with wooden cabinetwork for their largest instrument, a 100-stop organ with five keyboards for the Cathedral in Lausanne, Switzerland, the biggest American installation yet in Europe. Paradoxically, here were American organ-builders who had taken traditional European methods and created something so new and original out of them that Europeans wanted to import it. "We were convinced not only by the quality of Fisk's organs, but also by the scientific spirit of the enterprise. They know everything about Europe, even better than the big German builders do," one of the officials involved in the selection told the Lausanne newspaper *24 Heures,* which had reported that the word at Fisk's biggest Swiss competitor was that the cathedral instrument would have "the flavor of hamburger." But it was only sour grapes, backhanded recognition that the American organ had—once more—truly come into its own.

Reborn

So, forty years after it began, the American historical organ movement could be said to have come full circle. At the start of the
twenty-first century, as a hundred years and more earlier, a mechanical-action pipe organ did not have to be built to exclusively
baroque specifications. Money and care were again being lavished
on nineteenth-century American orchestral organs that prevailing
opinion in the 1970s might have favored junking. Even more re-
markably, the unthinkable came back into fashion: electropneumatic organs built by Skinner, Aeolian-Skinner, Austin, and others
were judged worthy of preservation and restoration.

Although Charles Fisk never paid Ernest M. Skinner the kind of
tribute he gave G. Donald Harrison, he wrote in 1980 a sentence
that perfectly described Skinner: "America is a land of problem-
solvers, of tinkerers, of people who are given to making adjustments
to the culture they borrow from abroad." It was not until the 1980s
that Skinner's homegrown ingenuity regained respect from the
mainstream of American organ aficionados. Gradually, Skinner and
the few Skinner organs that had survived more or less intact began
to emerge from opprobrium.

As former Yale University organist Charles Krigbaum has written,
when he arrived in New Haven to teach in 1958 most of the organ
students tended to avoid the huge Newberry Memorial organ in
Woolsey Hall—the one Skinner and G. Donald Harrison had transformed in 1928 and 1929 into one of the largest and finest American orchestral organs ever built. Most of the students in the late

The Newberry Memorial Organ, Woolsey Hall, Yale University

1950s tended to favor the Holtkamp organ in Battell Chapel for their recitals.

But even if Yale had wanted to yank the Woolsey Hall organ out and replace it, the university's shaky finances through the 1970s and 1980s would have ruled out such expensive and drastic change. By 2001, Krigbaum wrote, "the aesthetic preferences of many stu-

dents seem to have shifted. Some are drawn to Yale precisely because of the Woolsey Hall organ and the chance to study appropriate music on it with a renowned master," Krigbaum's successor,
Thomas Murray. By that time, Ernest M. Skinner had once more
come to be appreciated as the genius he was, and the Woolsey Hall
organ as he and Harrison left it could be seen not as an orchestral
distortion of a baroque organ ideal, but as a great work of art on its
own terms.

Its curators, the A. Thompson-Allen Company of New Haven,
had protected the big instrument through the decades. With steady
maintenance of the electropneumatic playing action and gradual,
periodic replacement of leather parts with properly treated leather
when they wore out, the old organ was still playing reliably a century after the first part of it was built, even though no complete
overhaul had been done since Skinner finished it in 1929.

Similarly careful restoration, sixty years after it was completed in
1931, preserved Skinner's Opus 820, a sixty-stop organ that is in
nearly original condition in the Cathedral of Our Lady Queen of
the Most Holy Rosary in Toledo, Ohio. The result, in Jonathan Ambrosino's estimation, is "one of the very, very few Skinner organs
handed down to succeeding generations that the builder himself
would recognize in its entirety." And without the overlay of neoclas-
sical dogma that prevailed thirty or forty years ago, it is easier for today's generations to recognize the Skinner's artistic qualities.

Rescuing some of these old organs is like retrieving an artifact
from a time capsule, like the Skinner organ built between 1929 and
1931 for the Cleveland Orchestra in Severance Hall. Schantz, the
Orrville, Ohio, company for which Skinner had worked briefly as a
consultant in the late 1940s, rescued the 6,000 pipes from a ceiling
chamber above the stage shell that the Cleveland's great conductor
George Szell had built in 1958 to improve the acoustics for the orchestra. The shell had effectively entombed the organ, which had
not been played since 1976, but the orchestra rediscovered the instrument when it decided to expand and refurbish the hall in the
late 1990s. It was, as Gary Hanson, the Cleveland Orchestra's associ-

ate executive director, told Associated Press, "like finding a 1929 Cadillac in your aunt's garage with 1,100 miles on it." Schantz dismantled the organ, took it away through a hole cut in the back of the stage, cleaned it, restored it to original condition, and then replaced it in a new position behind the orchestra onstage. The restoration left Skinner's list of stops and his original electropneumatic playing mechanism unchanged. This, the Norton Memorial Organ, was heard again on January 6, 2001, with the British organist Thomas Trotter and a program of music by Bach, Dupré, and Liszt for organ, percussion and brass, and the restoration was acclaimed as a resounding success.

"Twenty-five years ago, no one would have given the time of day to these venerable instruments," the critic Scott Cantrell, himself an organist, wrote in 2001. By that time, the Organ Historical Society, which had been founded in 1956 to preserve old tracker-action instruments from destruction, had begun to recognize the historic value of the original electropneumatic mechanisms developed by Skinner and others. "Certain 20th century organs," the society's "Guidelines for Conservation and Restoration" specified, were to be regarded as historic, "especially if they represent important periods in a given builder's work, or milestones in the development of a particular style."

This newfound interest in preserving early-twentieth-century organs has led to bold restoration projects. After the Art Deco rotunda of the Cincinnati Union Terminal, built in the Great Depression but allowed to fall into disrepair after the 1950s, was renovated and reopened as the Cincinnati Museum Center in 1990, the reverberant space seemed to cry out for a pipe organ. Under the guidance of an organ expert, Harley Piltingsrud, the Museum Center bought the 1929 Skinner organ of the Church of the Immaculate Conception in Philadelphia and installed the pipes in chambers behind the station's old ticket counters, newsstand, and snack bar under the rotunda, letting the organ speak into a resonant room that is 170 feet wide, ninety-five feet high, and has a reverberation time of five seconds. Later, the museum acquired another 1929 Skinner, complete with automatic player mechanism, from what had been the home of a local industrialist, Powel Crosley Jr., planning to make its pipes an antiphonal division in the rotunda. The organ is heard in periodic concerts and used daily in educational programs, the rumble of two thirty-two-foot pedal stops mixing with that of occasional Amtrak and Norfolk Southern trains.

Another impressive restoration is under way at the California Palace of the Legion of Honor art museum in San Francisco, where Edward Millington Stout III and Richard Taylor cleaned the 4,526 pipes of a 1924 Skinner organ, returning to playing condition stops that had long fallen silent, along with the tambourine, the snare drums, the gong, and the celesta, actually a replacement part from a Wurlitzer. Its working parts had been played every weekend since the 1920s, but, Stout said in early 2002, "the Legion organ did not come back into favor until the mid-'80s. Now the museum thinks of it as a tremendous asset. They rent the organ out for reception concerts and play dance music on it!" The restoration was made possible by a grant from the charitable foundation of Joseph G. Bradley Jr., a theater organ enthusiast.

As they had done in the nineteenth and early twentieth centuries, Americans also began demanding and appreciating large pipe organs in halls built for orchestras. "Concert halls bring people who would never be caught dead in church—or who would only be caught dead in church—into contact with organ music," Steven Dieck of Fisk said. A decade after the Dallas organ was completed in 1992, new concert hall organs were being planned for Disney Hall in Los Angeles, with Frank Gehry's design for a display of pipes wildly splayed as if already struck by an earthquake, and for Verizon Hall in the Kimmel Center, the new home of the Philadelphia Orchestra, in acoustical collaboration with Russell Johnson of Artec. The Verizon Hall organ, by Rosales and Dobson Pipe Organ Builders, Ltd., of Lake City, Iowa, will be a 6,000-pipe instrument costing $4.3 million. New or restored instruments were also in the works in the Performing Arts Center of Greater Miami, in the Meyerhoff Symphony Hall in Baltimore, and in the Orange County

Performing Arts Center in Costa Mesa, California. Orchestra Hall in Chicago, remade into Symphony Center, replaced its organ in 1998, recycling some of the pipes into a sixty-rank instrument built by Casavant and specially designed by Jeff Weiler with high wind pressures for extra oomph. "It rocks," as William Eddins, the Chicago Symphony's resident conductor, put it. In Seattle, Fisk built a concert organ in 2000 for Benaroya Hall, home of the Seattle Symphony, and the orchestra commissioned new works for its dedication. In Florida, Quimby Pipe Organs, Inc., of Warrensburg, Missouri, rejuvenated a 1914 Casavant organ from New York State and gave it a new home for the Jacksonville Symphony Orchestra. And in Boston, where the Symphony Hall organ that G. Donald Harrison and E. Power Biggs had designed in 1949 had fallen into disuse, the Boston Symphony Orchestra signed a contract in 2002 for a $3 million rebuilding project.

In Boston, Philadelphia, Chicago, Dallas, San Francisco, Seattle, and other cities, concert halls were once again being considered incomplete if they did not have the biggest of all instruments. As Henry Fogel, the Chicago Symphony's president, said, "It is crucial to a major symphony orchestra and a major concert hall to have at its disposal an organ of world-class quality."

In New York City, Kurt Masur, finishing his eleven years as director of the New York Philharmonic, confessed in mid-2002 that he was leaving with at least one disappointment: "I was promised that the new hall will get a new pipe organ," he told James R. Oestreich of *The New York Times;* "there are more than 200 pieces we cannot play because of the lack of an organ." Three decades after the renovation that had thrown out the organ that Biggs, Fox, and Catharine Crozier had dedicated in 1962 when it was still Philharmonic Hall, Avery Fisher Hall was still pipeless, even though a donor had left the orchestra with a million dollars for a new instrument.

Plans to tear Avery Fisher Hall apart yet again or replace it altogether included provision for a new pipe organ in either case, Zarin Mehta, the Philharmonic's executive director, assured me in late 2002. But with the boom of the 1990s a fading memory, renovation of the Lincoln Center complex was relegated to the distant future. As for Carnegie Hall, it had lost even the Rodgers electronic organ that Virgil Fox had inaugurated in 1974—the instrument has gone to Oregon, to the Portland Center for the Performing Arts. So in the two premier concert venues in New York City, orchestral pieces with parts written for organ, from the Saint-Saëns symphony to *Also Sprach Zarathustra*, Mahler's *Resurrection Symphony* and his *Symphony of a Thousand*, Respighi's *Pines of Rome*, Scriabin's *Poem of Ecstasy* and his *Poem of Fire*, either cannot be played at all or have to be played on substitutes for the real thing. "No doubt electronic organs have their place," *The New York Times*'s critic John Rockwell wrote. "But that place is not with a major orchestra in a major hall; the aural intrusion can be downright painful, with a slick, glossy artificiality replacing the honest aural textures of a true pipe organ."

In many American cities, as Steven Dieck observed, pipe organs have regained the status of objects of civic pride. When I was a teenager, the main use of the pipe organ in the Mechanics Hall auditorium on Main Street in Worcester, Massachusetts, was seating for kids who climbed up on it for a better view of wrestling matches featuring characters like Haystack Calhoun and Killer Kowalski. It had been built in 1864 by E. & G. G. Hook, of Boston, and 100 years later, the 3,504 pipes were still there, but they were badly out of tune and the four keyboards were barely playable. But two decades later, in 1982, Worcester beautifully restored the hall and Noack restored the instrument, the oldest unaltered organ of its age and size in the Western Hemisphere, and frequently showcases it in concerts. In Boston, another priceless Hook in the Italian-baroque Church of the Immaculate Conception in the South End was saved from possible demolition in 1986 by protests from architectural groups and the Organ Historical Society. Today, with a new mission and a revitalized inner-city core, the authorities of what is now called the Jesuit Urban Center rightly regard the organ, built in 1863 and enlarged in 1902, as one of the city's finest musical treasures.

In San Diego, the outdoor organ in Balboa Park, Austin's Opus 453, is still attracting weekly concert audiences as it approaches ninety years of age, and its near-twin in Maine, the Kotzschmar organ in the City Hall in Portland, has been basking in resurgent public enthusiasm since its restoration in 1997. "Whenever I play in San Diego or in Portland, the audiences are eager and responsive," the organ virtuoso John Weaver told me. "The people of the City of Portland own that organ, and having contributed to the restoration through the Friends of the Kotzschmar Organ, they really feel as if it's their thing. And at every concert, there seems to be at least one person for whom the organ and the music come as a revelation—people come up with tears in their eyes and say they had no idea it could be so beautiful."

In San Francisco, a committee is laying plans to build an outdoor pavilion near Fisherman's Wharf to house Austin Opus 500, the huge municipal organ built for the 1915 Panama-Pacific International Exposition and relocated to the San Francisco Civic Auditorium. Acoustic redesign of the hall had already dealt a severe blow to the organ before the Loma Prieta earthquake of 1989 made it unplayable. With the help of Federal and city disaster relief money, the forty-ton organ was loaded into trucks in 1991 and shipped back to Austin Organs, Inc., in Hartford, Connecticut, for overhaul and repair, but the city withdrew funding for the project shortly after work started, and the organ, in pieces, went back into storage on the West Coast. At the end of the 1990s, James W. Haas, a lawyer who had led efforts to restore the waterfront Embarcadero to civic use after the earthquake, proposed a Music Concourse and an outdoor Organ Pavilion near the Ferry Building. Modeled on the Spreckels Pavilion in Balboa Park in San Diego, the pavilion would be, Haas said, an attraction for lunchtime and weekend visitors to the waterfront, and in the summer of 2001 the project got $100,000 in state funds for engineering studies.

This project would cost about $1 million, on top of the $5 million it would take to build the pavilion and another $5 million to endow the program, Haas said in early 2002, but he was confident of obtaining the necessary private funds and hopeful that the organ would be up and playing for people by 2004. Not an organ buff himself, Haas said, he was surprised by the extent of public enthusiasm for bringing back the old Austin. "People I'd never expect to be interested come up to me and say 'My grandfather used to have an organ in his house,' or 'I used to hear this organ all the time,'" he said.

Nostalgia for the seemingly simpler, more optimistic days when these organs were built—as symbols of American ingenuity, industrial prowess, and technological achievement—explains some of this new enthusiasm. Some might have dismissed these great machines in the 1960s, when their newness had faded and the idea of "progress" that had inspired them seemed to be discredited. But by 2000 there was tolerance, even pride. "After years of neglect, destruction, disfigurement and ridicule, instruments in this aesthetic have found a new generation of admirers once more," Jonathan Ambrosino wrote. "Restoration, and not rebuilding, is the outcome of a welcome cultural phenomenon: a growing respect for all styles of organ building, rather than a desire to transform instruments into something they were never meant to be." Organizations like the American Guild of Organists, the Organ Historical Society, and the Organ Clearing House gladly offer advice to churches and municipalities wondering whether old organs are worth saving, or can help find new homes for them if necessary. "I do not believe that our opinions should keep us from appreciating the great qualities of those instruments we do not prefer," John Bishop, head of the Organ Clearing House, wrote in 2002.

Dirk A. Flentrop himself had told Margaret Mueller, the organist of St. Paul's Episcopal Church in Winston-Salem, North Carolina, in the 1960s that the 1929 E. M. Skinner there would not be improved by adding a baroque-style mixture to its romantic textures. "You must leave it just as it is," Flentrop told her. "It is a perfect example of an American organ of the 1920s: an entity in itself."

St. Luke's Church in Evanston, Illinois, has an even more perfectly preserved Skinner, installed in 1922. Underneath the dust of decades, the organ's fifty-six stops and 4,336 pipes retained their own distinctive musical character and personality. Friends of the instrument started calling it "Lucy," as in *I Love Lucy*, Lucille Ball's 1950s television show. "It soon became clear," Richard Webster, the church's organist, explained, "that this instrument's stature called for a grander name," and the organ was dubbed "Lucille." By 1993, when the church was ready to start restoration, it had decided not to change the organ but to restore it as much as possible to its original condition, a task that took five years. "Here," wrote Joseph F. Dzeda of the A. Thompson-Allen company, which did the restoration, "is an organ at which one can sit and play, hearing and feeling the entirety of Mr. Skinner's justly famous creation." The restoration incorporated two stops that had been added in the 1950s, replications of some that had been lost. A few Skinner pipes that had been removed and stored away were put back in their places, and the resulting reborn organ, as Webster put it, "wraps its arms around you when you walk in the door."

G. Donald Harrison's creations, like Skinner's, are again being treated with new respect as musical achievements in their own right, although, as with Skinner's, there are few left just as he built them. The Harrison organs at All Saints in Worcester and the Church of the Advent in Boston are still recognizable as Aeolian-Skinner products, although they have been greatly changed with additions and tonal modifications. In New York City, the great Riverside Church organ was much enlarged and revised in 1967 by Gilbert F. Adams and kept in excellent condition over thirty-one years by its curator, Anthony Bufano. In 1995, the nave ceiling tiles finally got the acoustical sealant Harrison had wanted to improve reverberation. The 1932 organ Harrison built and later greatly altered and enlarged in the Church of St. Mary the Virgin on West Forty-sixth Street was rebuilt and further altered by the firm of Mann & Trupiano between 1988 and 1994. These organs can be heard in all their glory in services and recitals. The great organ in the vast Episcopal Cathedral Church of St. John the Divine—an organ originally built by Skinner and enlarged to 118 stops by Harrison between 1950 and 1954—was temporarily silenced in December 2001 after a fire that destroyed the cathedral's gift shop and filled the church with soot. A project of restoration and repair aims to bring this organ back to life.

The great organ in the Mormon Tabernacle whose sound so greatly thrilled Harrison in 1949 was faithfully restored by its curators forty years later. Schoenstein & Co. made several additions and rebuilt the console. A decade later, they completed an organ of 130 ranks in a new Conference Center next door. The largest organ Harrison ever worked on—the 13,000-pipe instrument of the First Church of Christ, Scientist (the "Mother Church") in Boston, designed by Lawrence Phelps and completed in the early 1950s—was extensively restored between 1995 and 1999 by Foley-Baker Inc. of Tolland, Connecticut, under Phelps's direction. After he died, his widow, the organist Dame Gillian Weir, made a recording on it to his memory.

Churches and Reform synagogues across the country are investing millions of dollars in instruments capable of raising a joyful noise. To take just a few examples from New York City alone, the Roman Catholic Church of St. Ignatius Loyola installed a $1.25 million mechanical-action organ made by Mander in 1993, an instrument of fifty-eight stops and 5,000 pipes that weighs forty tons and sounds as good with Bach as it does with Franck and Vierne. When it was finished, Kent Tritle, the Iowan organist of the church, declared, "I'm in hog heaven." A decade later, in October 2002, people filled the Dominican church of St. Vincent Ferrer, a few blocks away, for Dr. Mark Bani's dedicatory recital on a new sixty-eight-rank, million-dollar gallery organ made by Schantz. Earlier that year, Central Synagogue, a Reform congregation whose nineteenth-century Moorish temple had been nearly destroyed in a fire, dedicated a Casavant organ with two separate sections—4,345 pipes and fifty-five stops including a Trompette Shofar, bringing to mind the Shofar that Ernest Skinner had installed in Temple Emanu-El in San Francisco in 1924, and a real first: a Klezmer Clarinette.

Where I live, in Brooklyn, the parishioners of Grace Church in Brooklyn Heights raised $1 million for a new organ by Austin Organs, Inc. preserving a few pipes originally made and voiced by the

Roosevelt brothers. The organ has electropneumatic action because the console is situated across the chancel from the pipes, and because the organ had an antiphonal division 100 feet away at the opposite end of the church. A mechanical-action organ would have required the console to be placed beneath the pipes. But in this organ, unlike most of Austin's, the pipes stand on windchests built the way they were in the pre-electricity days—"slider" chests that allow the pipes to speak unforced, more directly and naturally, as Paul Olson, the church's organist, put it. "There grew up a fashion in the 1960s that seems in retrospect to have tried to separate or relieve the organ from its liturgical duties," Bruce Buchanan, Austin's tonal director at the time, wrote in the Grace Church dedication program in 2001. "Organ music broke out from the yoke of the liturgy and organs tried to serve the repertoire of pure organ music instead. The labor of congregational accompaniment gave way to the cerebral delights of contrapuntal clarity. For some churches and some liturgies this may well have been an improvement, but in the Episcopal church there was an awkward if not horrid mismatch between the music and its accompaniment." So the Grace Church organ, like many others, has undulating soft stops, French romantic foundation stops and reeds, and English-style trumpets, a return to the eclecticism that many churches have rediscovered since the 1960s.

These musical witnesses to history are all around. Just in one corner of Brooklyn, an 1880 three-manual J. H. & C. S. Odell & Company organ, in need of restoration, still manages to peal out every Sunday in the Roman Catholic Church of St. Charles Borromeo, just down the street from its contemporary, the Brooklyn Bridge. A superb organ built by Ernest M. Skinner in 1925 in the flamboyant Gothic church now called St. Ann and the Holy Trinity, an instrument nearly the contemporary of the Empire State Building, is gradually being repaired and restored, and it is played in regular Wednesday lunchtime concerts by the church organist, Gregory Eaton. And a G. Donald Harrison Aeolian-Skinner completed in 1937 in Plymouth Church of the Pilgrims, where Henry Ward

Beecher preached against slavery, was restored and got a new console in the 1990s. There is even a "Mighty Wurlitzer" down the street in the Brooklyn Paramount, where it was installed in 1928, now the athletic center for Long Island University's Brooklyn campus.

Everywhere, there is renewed interest in pipe organs. Michael Barone, organist and broadcaster with Minnesota Public Radio, has more than 250,000 listeners for his weekly *Pipedreams* broadcasts on Public Radio. *Pipedreams* celebrated its twentieth anniversary in January 2002, marking two decades of successfully mixing counterpoint, romantic orchestral transcriptions, and church music played on organs around the country and around the world. His intention, Barone said, was to get people "to set their religious prejudices aside, along with their musical ones, and to search out the organ for what it can do as an emotional and spiritual engine." On television, niche programs like Diane Bish's *The Joy of Music* explore organs around the world, with her performances taped on location.

Concert halls and universities have also begun encouraging performers to play a broad repertory. The Dallas Symphony Orchestra always includes the Fisk organ and the orchestra's organist, Mary Preston, in concerts for 42,000 schoolchildren every year, and Preston gives monthly organ demonstrations. The Dallas International Organ Competition, held every three years, attracts first-rate young performers from all over the world with $50,000 in prizes (including a $30,000 first prize) and a chance to perform with the orchestra, and the Dallas Symphony Association commissions new works for them to play. The competition finals attract a large and enthusiastic audience, and the event is regarded as one of the most significant in the world of the organ.

Fine performers are also drawn to the quadrennial Calgary International Organ Competition, which in 2002 attracted forty-five finalists from twenty-nine countries to compete for $100,000 (Canadian) in prizes, including three gold medal prizes of $25,000, each sponsored by the TriumphEnt Foundation. The Jack Singer concert hall in the Calgary Centre for Performing Arts has a four-manual, 6,000-pipe Casavant organ that was built in 1987. Lunchtime organ concerts, youth encounters, and related activities, including silent-movie evenings with organ at a movie theater downtown, draw appreciative crowds.

Electronic innovation has led to digital versions of the automatic player mechanism developed by Skinner and Aeolian a century ago. With the new technology, organists can prerecord pieces to a computer disc and, if they like, sit back and let the organ replay them all by itself. Innovations like MIDI permit digital interfacing between organs and electronic instruments and have further broadened the horizons of the possible. Some builders have also developed ways to combine pipes and electronically generated sounds in hybrid instruments that can, for example, bring the unique vibrations of a thirty-two-foot organ stop to a church or concert hall whose finances might crumble under the expense of buying the bottom twelve pipes, each as big as the trunk of an oak tree. This particular electronic application had a long history, and even Aeolian-Skinner had occasionally made use of it in the 1940s, experimenting as well with electronic systems to improve reverberation in acoustically suffocating auditoriums and churches.

But builders of pipe organs and builders of electronic organs have never coexisted easily. "If it Doesn't have PIPES It's NOT an Organ," the Associated Pipe Organ Builders of America, the industry's leading trade group, has said since 1998, when its members agreed that real organs should make most of their sound with pipes, not speakers. "APOBA does not welcome membership of firms that build electronic organs or combination electronic/pipe organs," the group decided, excluding some of the oldest and largest American companies, among them Austin, Wicks Organ Company of Highland, Illinois, the Reuter Organ Company of Lawrence, Kansas, and Cornel Zimmer Organ Builders of Denver, North Carolina.

"Finding organ pipes in an electronic organ factory is like finding birdshit in a cuckoo clock," Virgil Fox once said. Acoustics experts concede that no electronic organ would sound exactly like a pipe organ of the same size unless it had as many separate speakers as the organ had pipes—many hundreds or thousands of them. Even if a full-organ ensemble falls short of the real thing, nowadays, through such techniques as digital sampling, some *individual* stops on the best modern electronic organs can indeed sound surprisingly akin to those on pipe organs. And since a rank of sixty-one pipes costs $10,000 to $30,000 and a good electronic equivalent only $2,000 to $3,000, it is no wonder that electronic organs dominate a mass market in which pipe organs are simply beyond reach.

Better to marry than to burn, in St. Paul's words; better a good electronic organ than no organ at all, except in cathedrals and concert halls and churches that can afford the real thing. One might compare electronic organs to power boats and pipe organs to yachts under sail, with large electronic organs going for $100,000 and up and large pipe organs for $1,000,000 and more. (Incidentally, there are still organbuilders making instruments for yachts; Stefan Maier of Athol, Massachusetts, made a salt-resistant one-manual mechanical-action organ for the 128-foot sloop *Antonisa,* built in Maine for an Italian industrialist at the end of the 1990s.)

Most organbuilders, if not all organists, have stopped being intolerant of eclecticism. Charles Fisk himself had said, in 1981, "I feel sure that we North Americans will never be able to abandon eclecticism entirely. It's such a fascinating game to try to make an organ do more than anybody thought it would. And I have to confess that in my recent studies and imitatings . . . I have never given up the notion that I might be led to a better understanding of how better eclectic organs might be built." Twenty years later, some of the same builders who were designing authentic baroque reproduction organs for those who wanted them were also designing mechanical-action Romantic symphonic organs, and nobody seemed to be scandalized, for the organs were all built with esthetic integrity. As Jack Bethards of Schoenstein & Co. has put it, the stage was set for what he called "the greatest period in the organ's history, a time when symphonic organs will flourish along with organs dedicated to interpretation of specific solo repertoire. . . . It is even possible that the days of academic judgment of organs and organists based on style will change to that based on musicianship and quality." Orchestral pipe organs like those on which virtuoso players such as Alexandre Guilmant, Pierre Cochereau, Edwin Lemare, E. Power Biggs, and Virgil Fox enthralled millions of Americans still exist, or are being built again to standards of craftsmanship never attained in the past, all over the United States, alongside pipe organs none of these artists ever imagined they would see in the United States.

So organbuilders are doing their best to satisfy public demand for the instrument. But whether the organ ever again attains the popular recognition that it had a century ago is something that depends on organists. "It's quite simple," Bethards said—"organists simply have to deliver the same level of performance as good violinists, pianists, cellists, and singers. They should limit their repertoire so that they can achieve perfection. They have to discipline themselves to accept only engagements where they can rehearse for several days in advance to master each different instrument. They have to be so much in love with the music they're playing that they can transmit that conviction to their audiences. A performance reaches the level of art when it seems to the listener at the time to be the only possible way that music could be played."

A few months after Fox died in 1980, *The New York Times* critic Allan Kozinn interviewed Leonard Raver, then the organist of the New York Philharmonic—organist, that is, on a three-keyboard Allen electronic instrument the hall bought after selling its Aeolian-Skinner—and Raver made a confession. "In a sense, we organists live in a specialist world, segregated from pianists, violinists and other people who give concerts," he said. "Too many of my colleagues have musical blinders on: They like organs, choirs, and the liturgy; they like the music of 100 years before Bach and up through Messiaen, if they're that adventurous. But they are cut off from the mainstream. They don't go to symphony concerts, chamber music, or the opera. And they have a very low tolerance for the music of the last 25 or 30 years. So yes, the organ world is facing lots of problems right now, some having to do with instruments and concert halls, but many having to do with organists' attitudes."

Little had changed two decades later. In a review of the memorial concert played on the twentieth anniversary of Fox's death in Riverside Church, the organist Haig Mardirosian wrote, "If we lack a contemporary Virgil Fox, perhaps it owes to societal, economic, and cultural differences as certainly as the lack of an artist holding a particular admixture of talent and personality."

The long preoccupation in the insular organ world with musical scholarship and historically authentic playing style, and the organ's long association with the church, created the impression that entertainment or fun were somehow incompatible with the instrument. Gaylord B. Carter, one of the greatest theater organists of the twentieth century, recalled taking an organ study tour led by Melville Smith through Europe in 1957 and feeling somewhat patronized by the church organists who made up most of the group. In the church in Zwolle, Holland, where Biggs later recorded Bach, Carter was invited by the (apparently) Dutch tour guide up to the bench, where, he said, he "improvised a little gavotte, which was light in quality but not necessarily irreverent. Well, this guy said, 'There'll be no jazz played on this organ,' and he got on the bench and all but shoved me off. I almost landed on my rear on the floor, and I was so furious."

But in Martin Luther's words, why should the devil have all the good tunes? Church organists who take the enjoyment of music-making by their congregations half as seriously as some of them take themselves and the mutually exclusive factional causes they serve will also have more success in drawing people in. Music written by such organists as Calvin Hampton, Dan Locklair, David Hurd, and John Weaver has found its way into hymnbooks, but there is comparatively little new music by American composers who are not organists or church musicians that is now being written for secular organ performance.

Improvisation, an art hardly practiced by most other classical musicians, attracted German audiences 300 years ago to hear Bach conjure musical magic out of thin air, and American audiences to hear Guilmant, Dupré, and Cochereau compose organ symphonies on themes submitted to them on the spot. Gifted improvisers can still draw crowds, whether playing accompaniment for revivals of silent movies or jazz, as Dorothy Papadakos, the organist of the Cathedral Church of St. John the Divine in New York City, sometimes does in recital programs. "Organists should be exposed to, and taught how to play, the musical vernacular they live in. I don't play 'organ recitals,'" she told me. "I do silent movie programs, I do the *Nutcracker Suite,* I do improvisations on the songs of humpback whales, I do Sinatra and Glen Miller stuff, and I improvise, all instead of doing pieces from the organ literature that audiences have heard too often."

Most American music schools have improvisation courses for organ students, and organists in large churches can improvise inspiring accompaniments to hymns and liturgical moments. Gerre Hancock, the organist of St. Thomas in New York City, is an acclaimed master of it. Why not revive the art as an attraction for popular audiences in the concert hall? If composers and organists respond to the renaissance of organbuilding in great American concert halls with music and concert programs that serve the audience, the organ and music written for the organ might again stand a chance of moving back into the musical mainstream. "How often is it," David D. First, a composer in Pennsylvania, wrote to *The American Organist* in February 2002, "that organists perform the variety of great music that might receive acclaim in the concert hall? I admonish all those who have the musical exuberance and the talent to get out there and take their instrument to the heights. It's there! Go for it."

Good organs have always had, in their way, as much dynamic range and variety of tone color as orchestras, yet often organists hesitate to exploit these qualities in performance. "Too many organists think in terms of mathematics or rules," Dr. Charles Callahan, a leading interpreter of the romantic literature and a composer who has written works for organ and orchestra, said. "They don't think in terms of shaping phrases, the way most orchestral musicians do." Kent Tritle, whose performance style is hardly similar to Callahan's, put it this way: "I don't think the art of rhetoric in organ performance—the art of really saying something personal—is taught well. You can have all the notes right and phrase the music beautifully, but for a really convincing performance, the important element is 'What am I saying that no one else has said?'"

John Weaver recalled finding a rarity—an organ selection on a classical music program—on a radio station in Vermont and then being shocked by a rendition of the Bach *Passacaglia and Fugue* by a famous authentic-performance French organist that started out with the full-organ ensemble and never relented, fortissimo through all the variations, for the eighteen minutes the piece lasted. "I thought it was a great shame," Weaver said. "Here was an opportunity to introduce many listeners to one of the most glorious pieces in all the literature, but I'll bet sets all over the state of Vermont were turned off within minutes."

Ken Cowan, an organ virtuoso who was just a boy when E. Power Biggs died, said, "How can any human being sustain interest through fifteen minutes of *organo pleno* sound? There may have been a time, 300 years ago, before people had heard synthesizers, marching bands, radio, television, and rock concerts, when audiences might have been captivated by a loud, commanding sound a bit longer than they are today. But I don't think variations only in touch and rhythm can compensate for some kind of dynamic control. Just because it might have been done that way in the past doesn't mean it's the only way it can be done today."

The organ is a complicated beast and taming it is a challenge. "Only an artist of great technical ability and depth of understanding can bring out the full expressive capabilities of the organ," Bethards pointed out, but a great artist makes audiences hear music in a new way. "The only point to transcriptions in this day and age," Bethards observed, "is to create an artistic result that is in the same league as the organ's own repertoire."

Bach did that, after all, by transcribing Vivaldi violin concerti for the baroque organ of his day. A performance with verve, imagination, and control on a fine orchestral organ, by a master like

Thomas Murray, can infuse even familiar pieces for orchestra with new vitality. Yet, Professor Murray said, it is still fashionable in some academic organ circles to heap scorn on players and organs capable of doing this. "It will not do for us to think that an instrument as costly as ours needs no further development or [has] little need for new literature or that it can survive on the periphery of musical life, where I assert we see it today," he warned.

That is not to say that organs without orchestral "expression," or classical, polyphonic organ music never intended to imitate the orchestra, cannot be exciting to hear. Bach, Buxtehude, and Couperin, for example, performed expertly and sensitively on historically "authentic" organs, can be thrilling if the performer is actually trying to make the music thrill the audience, as James David Christie often succeeds in doing with such music. "At the height of the organ's popularity, there was little radio, no television, and no rock music, and audiences had a level of musical education that the public in general no longer has today," Christie told me. "We have to deal with the taste of the people who come to concerts and choose pieces that will make people want to come back. Tonal color and the idea of projection, of getting the music across as a performer, are essential, as they always have been throughout history. The artistry of touch and good taste have a lot to do with it." Christie, too, has put transcriptions on his concert programs—organ transcriptions of Vivaldi that he made himself, just as Bach did.

The mechanical sensitivity and responsiveness and the tonal eloquence of many modern American mechanical-action instruments made by builders whose work is shaped by knowledge of historical techniques are admired by many performers. Among those Christie singled out are John Brombaugh, of John Brombaugh and Associates in Eugene, Oregon, who apprenticed with Fisk and Fritz Noack; two former partners of Brombaugh's, George Taylor and John Boody, now incorporated as Taylor & Boody Organbuilders in Staunton, Virginia; Paul Fritts, of Tacoma, Washington; Richards, Fowkes & Co. of Ooltewah, Tennessee; Dan Jaeckel, of Duluth, Minnesota, and Bedient Organs of Lincoln, Nebraska. "That is not to say that every organ produced by these builders is perfect," Christie said. "No builder is ever guaranteed of success on every job."

Barbara Owen, who over the course of her career has become the virtual personification of the historical organ movement in America, said, "It is simplistic to think that there is only ONE kind of organ and ONE kind of playing that will attract audiences. There is more than one kind of good organ and more than one kind of good playing, and the whole organ world is rather pluralistic at this point. . . . But sociologically, we don't live in the same world that existed in the late nineteenth century or the era before World War II. There are a lot more options for live music, and a wider range of tastes. Early acoustic gramophone records of organ music were no competition for a live recital, but good CDs played over good equipment are. I think people forget that the audience at a live concert is only part of the audience today. The other part is listening at home, in the car, or on an airplane with a Discman. That's something Biggs caught on to early in the game, and one reason he made so many recordings."

"I think the next couple of decades are going to be interesting," Owen predicted. "There are so many good organs being built (of all styles) and so many good young players coming out of the conservatories (of all stripes). Quality can create an audience. But people have to know about it."

Like Virgil Fox, other organists have discovered that audiences like to see who is playing and sometimes appreciate a brief explanation of what they are hearing. "It's important to hear the person playing and understand his personality," Peter Stoltzfus said. "I explain things about the music, pointing out, for example, pieces where the pedals play the melody instead of the usual base notes, and sometimes I show the audience the pipes that make different sounds. It adds to their enjoyment, and it's no more distracting than libretto subtitles at the opera."

The organ might stand a chance of moving back toward the center of American musical life if more American organists stopped thinking of themselves as members of a closed elite and started thinking of themselves as artists who can educate audiences if they are also willing to embrace and entertain them. And if organists do their jobs well, the churches and other institutions that employ them should pay them salaries commensurate with their professionalism. You get what you pay for, in organ performance as in everything else. When you hear original and lively organ playing in a church, that usually means that the church is paying the organist a decent salary (although the average level of professional organists' salaries is still far below what it should be). Poor playing would be far less prevalent in smaller churches if music committees stopped thinking that they don't really need to pay the organist much because nobody in the pews gets paid for singing hymns.

Never have American music schools done a better job of providing organists with the technical skills, historical knowledge, and education in musical integrity that are necessary for a convincing performance. Can they also turn out organists who are capable of communicating the joy of playing great music, the sheer *enthusiasm* that made Virgil Fox and E. Power Biggs popular artists? Ed Stout came up with one possible way to choose the right candidates: "The organists' school—they only need one—should line up applicants on either side of a large gymnasium or dance floor, pair them up, and ask them to dance," he joked. "The ones that can dance should be admitted. Those who can't dance should go study something else." Dancing may seem like an irrelevant skill for an organist, but it stands for the liveliness, vivaciousness, and *joie de vivre* that organ recitals seem so often to be missing. The truth is that given any excuse, people will stay home nowadays when organ recitals are offered, and fewer and fewer musicians are training to become organists. In 1985, 728 students were enrolled in music schools as organ majors, but fifteen years later there were only 527, according to a report by the American Guild of Organists, formed in 1896 to set and maintain high performance standards by church musicians (and to protect them from dictatorial clergy).

"As American organists and choir directors reach retirement age, will there be qualified individuals to fill their vacancies?" the Guild worried in an official position statement in January 2002. "There is no shortage of instruments for organists to play," the statement noted, but unless organists actually play them, the pipes will stand silent. Encouraging greater public familiarity with the instrument is one of the Guild's main tasks these days. Anyone interested in the organ, organist or not, can join it (see the Guild's Web site, www. agohq.org). Local chapters hold summer "Pipe Organ Encounters" for young people interested in music but not yet familiar with the organ and offers similar programs for adults and children.

The Organ Historical Society, similarly open to membership (www.organsociety.org), also tries to increase public awareness of the instrument and its music. Its E. Power Biggs Fellowship enables young people to attend its annual conventions and explore dozens of pipe organs of various periods. Some music schools have begun trying to find ways to encourage organ students to interact with other musicians, as the Peabody Conservatory in Baltimore has done by bringing together jazz students and its aspiring organists for improvisation sessions.

Yet how many young organists today do what Virgil Fox said he always did before he started playing the organ? "I think of the many new listeners who may be experiencing its multi-faceted glories for the first time. My aim is to win them over to the music and the instrument," he said. What he and E. Power Biggs had in common—and it was much more than what divided them—was that they were good musicians who were not ashamed of also being entertainers. In their very different ways, they brought magnificent organ music to millions of people who appreciated good music but had thought that organ music belonged only in church.

So it is up to American artists, organists like those quoted in this book and many other talented players, to show that it can be done today as well. "People will take notice of organ music in a place with a good organ," Sir Edward Heath, a former British prime minister and also an organist, told me a few years ago, describing how 2,000 people would show up for Advent choral concerts and organ recitals at Salisbury Cathedral, across the green from his home. "In the hands of a good musician," he said, "people do appreciate organ music."

Organbuilders in America once again command worldwide respect for their work. With inspired playing and bold performance, organists can yet restore "Bach's Royal Instrument" to the prominent place in American musical life that it occupied a century ago.

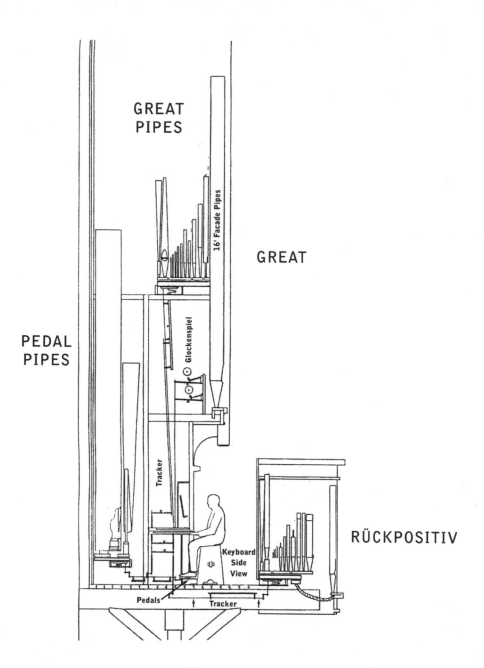

GREAT
PIPES

16' Facade Pipes

GREAT

Glockenspiel

PEDAL
PIPES

Tracker

RÜCKPOSITIV

Keyboard
Side
View

Pedals

Tracker

Cross-section of the organ in Abbey Chapel, Mount Holyoke College,
C.B. Fisk Opus 84

Glossary

This is not a complete glossary of all organ terms. I have tried to avoid most technical terms or to explain them in the text as it goes along. But here are a few that come up throughout the book, grouped logically rather than alphabetically.

For a complete list and an explanation of organ stop names, see Edward L. Stauff's *Encyclopedia of Organ Stops,* available online at www.organstops. org, or Irwin Stevens's *Dictionary of Pipe Organ Stops,* published by Schirmer Books in 1983.

PIPES: There are two common kinds of organ pipes.

Flue pipes are like whistles and produce sound by the vibrations caused when pressurized air passes through the "flue" or mouth of the pipe, which is a horizontal slit near the bottom. The rest of the pipe, above the mouth, is a resonating tube that produces the tone; a pipe as small and thin as a pennywhistle produces a high, shrill note, and a pipe thirty-two feet long with the cross-section of a small elevator shaft produces a deep bass tone that is felt as much as heard. Air passes into the bottom or "foot" of the pipe and exits through its mouth, not the top.

Reeds often imitate trumpets, horns, clarinets, oboes, bassoons, or anachronistic instruments like bombardes, fagotts, and so on. Their sound is produced when a flow of pressurized air makes a metal tongue in the foot of the pipe start vibrating. This metal tongue is a "reed," like the one in the mouthpiece of a clarinet, but made of metal. The tone produced by the vibrations is amplified by the resonating tube (the pipe) above the foot.

One pipe produces only one note, and that note depends on the length of the pipe. Each key on a keyboard controls a separate pipe in each stop; thus an organ with only one stop and a five-octave keyboard with sixty-one notes would have sixty-one pipes.

VOICING: The art of making pipes produce sound by shaping their mouths, resonators, and other parts to give them musical tonal qualities. Voicing also refers to the musical style characteristic of a given organ-builder or school.

SCALING: Scale in organ pipes refers to the relationship between the cross-sectional area of the resonating or "speaking" part of the pipe and its length. Generally, wide-scaled pipes have more fundamental tone and less brightness—perceptibly high overtones—than narrow-scaled pipes.

STOP: Literally, in mechanical-action organs, a knob on a jamb next to the keyboard that pulls or pushes a slat with holes, called a **slider,** in a windchest below a row of pipes. When the stopknob is pulled out, the holes in the slat line up directly under the pipes, and pressurized air can blow into the pipes controlled by that stop when notes are played. When the stopknob is pushed in, the holes do not line up with the pipes, so the slat "stops" pressurized air from blowing through the holes into the pipes when notes are played. Generally speaking, a "stop" is a set of pipes controlled by a knob, usually one for each note on the keyboard or pedalboard, producing a particular tone color described by the stop's name (diapason, oboe, and flute, for example). **"Pulling out all the stops"** brings on "full organ," fortissimo—and, by extension, it means to go all out.

BOMBARDE: A powerful reed stop, originally in French classical organs, at sixteen-foot pitch (q.v.) in manuals, sixteen- and (as contra-bombarde) thirty-two-foot pitch in pedals. It was named after a wind instrument that was a predecessor of the bassoon. Also refers to a division of a large organ with trumpets and other loud solo stops.

DIAPASON: Synonymous with "Principal," the tone unique to the pipe organ. Diapason pipes are usually the biggest ones seen standing in the façade. Speaking display pipes can also be called "Prestant" or "Praestant," meaning "standing in front." The French equivalent is "Montre," meaning "display." Diapasons are a family of stops called **FOUNDATIONS** (or "fonds" in French, or "Prinzipal" in German or Dutch).

STRINGS: Narrow pipes producing a tone keener than diapason stops, with harmonics recalling the tone of cellos or violins.

CÉLESTE: A stop, often of string tones, with two pipes speaking on each note, one tuned slightly sharp, producing a shimmering or undulating effect.

RANK: A row of pipes, sixty-one on organs with sixty-one-note keyboards. Rank would be synonymous with stop if all stops had only one rank, but mixtures and other compound stops can have two or more ranks of pipes.

WINDCHEST: The box full of air under pressure on which the pipes stand, with a valve, or pallet, under each pipe to admit air when the stop controlling that particular pipe is activated and the note is played.

WIND PRESSURE: A measurement of the strength of the air that blows through the mouth or foot of a pipe to produce sound. Organ wind pressure is usually measured in "inches"—the number of inches a column of water in a U-shaped tube would be lifted if a hose full of air at that pressure were attached to one end. Two to three inches is low; twenty to thirty inches is high—about what it takes to blow up a rubber balloon, but of course at much greater volume passing through the mouth of a big organ pipe. Three inches of pressure is equivalent to one-tenth of a pound per square inch.

ACTION: The mechanism by which the keys make organ pipes speak. In mechanical action, "trackers" of wood or metal and other devices link the keys and pedals with the valves underneath the pipes that let air into the pipes from the windchest when notes are played; organs played this way are said to have **tracker action**. In **electropneumatic** action, pressing a key closes an electrical circuit that activates a magnet that works a pneumatic motor under the pipe and allows air into the pipes to make them sound.

The most common electropneumatic mechanism is based on the **pitman chest,** a device perfected by Ernest M. Skinner that uses small discs with flexible leather membranes over the key channel that pop up and down under air pressure instantaneously when a magnet is activated, letting air into the pipes.

PITCH: Described in an organ by the length of the lowest pipe in a rank, since the length of a pipe is the primary determinant of pitch.

An eight-foot rank—"unison" pitch—has a middle-C pipe that sounds at the same pitch as middle C on a piano. It is called an eight-foot rank because the lowest note is produced by a pipe that is about eight feet long if it is not closed or stoppered at the top.

A four-foot rank sounds an octave higher; a sixteen-foot rank sounds an octave lower than unison. A two-foot rank sounds two octaves higher than unison; a thirty-two-foot rank sounds two octaves lower. Some huge organs even have sixty-four-foot pipes for subsonic rumblings; many organs have one-foot stops whose highest notes are almost at the upper limit of human hearing.

HARMONICS: The basic tone produced by a pipe open at one end, like a tubular metal organ pipe, is the "first harmonic."

The "second harmonic" is the first natural overtone—an octave higher. The "third harmonic" is the second natural overtone—an octave plus a fifth, or twelve notes, higher. The "fourth harmonic" is the third overtone, two octaves higher, and so on. The series of overtones in an open pipe speaking at "unison" or normal pitch can be reinforced by "partials" produced by organ pipes in correspondingly different lengths. For example, playing middle C on open stops at various pitches produces sound as follows:

8 foot = unison pitch = middle C
4 foot = second harmonic = C above middle C
$2\,^2/_3$ foot = third harmonic = G above high C
2 foot = fourth harmonic = C two octaves above middle C
$1\,^3/_5$ foot = fifth harmonic = E above that
$1\,^1/_3$ foot = sixth harmonic = G above that
$1\,^1/_7$ foot = seventh harmonic = B-flat above that
1 foot = eighth harmonic = C three octaves above middle C
16 foot = suboctave pitch = C below middle C
32 foot = two Cs below middle C

Pipes higher than four-foot pitch are often referred to collectively as "upperwork."

MUTATIONS: Stops that do not speak at unison pitch but at higher overtones, to reinforce or alter the tone quality of the ensemble. The $2\,^2/_3$-, $1\,^3/_5$-, and $1\,^1/_7$-foot stops are examples of mutations.

MIXTURE: A "compound" stop—one with more than one pipe for each note—to reinforce harmonic overtones in an ensemble, in combination with other stops. A mixture can have two, several, or even more ranks of pipes in pitches as in the list above—its tonal composition may vary with each successive octave on the keyboard.

OPEN: A pipe that is not stopped at the upper end. Open pipes produce tones with both odd and even harmonics or overtones. An eight-foot open diapason pipe's notes speak at the same pitch as a piano, and the lowest note comes from a pipe about eight feet long.

CLOSED OR STOPPED: A pipe with a stopper or cap blocking the upper end. Stopped pipes produce tones that are an octave lower than those of open pipes of the same length, and they resonate with only the odd-numbered harmonics. A stop labeled eight-foot stopped diapason speaks at piano pitch, but all its pipes are only half as long as those of an eight-foot open diapason.

CONSOLE: The "flight deck" of an organ, with the keyboards, pedalboards, stop knobs, pedals, and couplers that play the pipes. Sometimes called a "keydesk" when built into the main mechanism of a tracker-action organ.

MANUAL: An organ keyboard. A small organ may have only one; larger organs have three, four, five, and sometimes more keyboards, each one controlling a separate division of the organ. A standard organ keyboard usually has fifty-six or sixty-one notes; piano keyboards have eighty-eight.

PEDAL: A keyboard played by the feet, usually with thirty or thirty-two notes, mostly for bass notes but also for solo voices at higher pitches. The **pedal organ** is the pipes and stops controlled by the pedalboard alone.

COUPLER: A device, usually controlled by a tabular switch above the keyboards, that makes pipes on different keyboards or in different octaves speak together when the coupler is on; manuals can also be coupled to pedals. In tracker-action organs, couplers actually depress the keys of the keyboards coupled to the one being played.

COMBINATION: A control that allows the organist to bring on several or many stops instantaneously.

PISTON: A button that controls a preset combination of stops and brings them all on at once, so that they do not have to be drawn by hand separately.

Pistons run on electric, electropneumatic, or solid-state devices that can be changed for each performance to bring on whatever combination of stops the organist wants for the occasion.

REGISTRATION: The art of choosing and drawing stops in combination to produce tone color. The term also refers to the stop combinations drawn by a player or suggested by the composer for the various parts of a piece of music.

DIVISION: An individual section of an organ, with its own set of pipes and tonal character. An organ with several divisions is really several separate organs.

GREAT: The main division or foundation of an organ. The term also refers to the keyboard that controls it.

SWELL: A section of an organ with its own keyboard and pipes enclosed in a cabinet or chamber, with louvered shutters or "shades" that the organist can open or close with a foot-operated **SWELL PEDAL**, to make the sound of the pipes seem to "swell" when they are being played.

RÉCIT: A division of a French classic organ with solo voices played against accompaniment on another manual. In French Romantic organs, the equivalent of the English "Swell" section, and often referred to as "Récit expressif."

CHOIR: Originally, the division of a church organ used for accompanying the singers of the choir, usually not as loud and powerful as other sections, and usually enclosed, with a separate keyboard.

POSITIV: The German baroque counterpart to the choir division of an English organ; in French organs, **POSITIF;** in American ones, sometimes **POSITIVE.** The name also applies to, and no doubt originated with, small portable organs of a few stops used to play figured bass in baroque choral music. A positiv organ is always unenclosed and has a bright, clear ensemble rich in upper harmonics.

RÜCKPOSITIV: A positiv organ placed separately from the rest of the instrument, at the player's back.

EXPRESSION: The capability of raising or lowering the volume of organ pipes as they are played by opening and closing shutters in an enclosed pipe chamber.

ENCLOSED: A division or set of pipes set in a chamber with shutters that can be opened and closed to increase or lower volume.

Recordings

Digital technology has captured high-fidelity recordings of pipe organs from all over the world on CDs produced by scores of different recording companies. The classical music recording sections of large book or record stores usually have organ music in the instrumental collection section. Looking under the names of organ composers—Bach, Franck, Daquin, Dupré, Vierne, Messiaen, Duruflé, Mendelssohn, and Widor, for example—can also produce good results. Some stores list recordings under performers' names.

Readers interested in recordings by E. Power Biggs may find some CD reissues of his Columbia Masterworks LPs by Sony Entertainment Corp. Virgil Fox recordings are available on CDs by BMG Classics, EMI Classics, MCA Classics, and others; a listing is available on the Web site of the Virgil Fox Society, at www.virgilfox.com.

For readers with a particular interest in the American organs described in this book, here are some additional sources.

JAV Recordings, Inc., has a documentary series on E. M. Skinner and Aeolian-Skinner organs, including most of those mentioned in these pages. These and JAV's recordings of Cavaillé-Coll, Fisk, and other instruments are available through its Web store at www.pipeorgancds.com.

The Organ Historical Society, Box 26811, Richmond, VA 23261, (804) 353-9226, fax (804) 353-9266, has an extensive online catalog of organ CDs, including a wide "theatre organs" selection, at www.ohscatalog.org.

The Web site for the Public Radio program *Pipedreams* (www. pipedreams.org) offers an online audio archive of several hundred broadcasts, as well as extensive organ-related references and links.

See also:

Pro Organo, PO Box 8338, South Bend, IN 46660-8338, (800) 336-2224, fax (574) 271-9191.

Gothic Records, 10 Harrison Street, Suite 311, Seattle, WA 98109, (800) 735-4720; www.gothicrecords.com.

Dorian Recordings, 8 Brunswick Road, Troy, NY 12180, (518) 274-5474, www.dorian.com.

Loft Recordings, 1122 East Pike Street, PMB 1017, Seattle, WA 98122-3934, (877) 783-5638; www.loftrecordings.com.

Notes

INTRODUCTION

xiv "The king of all instruments": Mozart, letter to his father, October 17, 1777.

xv "Johann Sebastian Bach had access to pipe organs": For the organs Bach played, see Christoph Wolff, *Johann Sebastian Bach: The Learned Musician* (New York: W. W. Norton & Company, 2000), pp. 77–92 and passim.

xv "I've even had people ask me whose arrangement": E. Power Biggs, in "The New Aeolian-Skinner Organ in Symphony Hall, Boston," dedication program, November 14, 1949.

CHAPTER 1

4 "Descriptive Circular": This and similar historical material, and information about Ryder and other early American builders, in the American Organ Archives of the Organ Historical Society in the library of Westminster Choir College in Princeton, N.J., Stephen L. Pinel, archivist.

5 "Poor but disconcerted parents": Skinner, "Some Reminiscences by Ernest M. Skinner," in *Stop, Open and Reed*, published by Skinner Organ Company, Vol. I, No. 4, 1922, republished in facsimile by the Organ Historical Society, Richmond, Virginia, 1997.

5 "Pumping the bellows in the Baptist Church in Taunton": Skinner, "Reminiscences."

6 "I am content to do the best possible work": For this quotation and Ryder's biographical details, see *George H. Ryder, 1838–1922, Organist and Organbuilder,* Harrisville, N.H., Boston Organ Club Chapter of the Organ Historical Society, Inc., 1995.

6 "An illtempered idiot": Skinner, letter to Barbara Owen, April 16, 1957, quoted in Dorothy J. Holden, *The Life and Work of Ernest M. Skinner* (Richmond, Va., The Organ Historical Society, 1985), p. 7; see also "Reminiscences."

8   "An organ going south": Skinner, "Reminiscences."

9   "An aggregation of strident mixtures": Skinner, "Reminiscences."

10   "Lofty in conception": Skinner, "Reminiscences."

11   "No Mr. Pitman connected with it": Article, "Pitman-Chest Action," in the *American Organist,* June 1936.

11   "Kiss No. one": Skinner, letter to "Nedward," (Ned Hastings), July 29, 1957, courtesy of Stan Howe, Bethel, Me.

12   "Please put some butter on it": quoted in Holden, pp. 73–74.

13   "Business in the metropolis": Holden, p. 27.

13   "Hope-Jones claimed that the stop was mine": Holden, p. 32.

15   "Thar she blows": Holden, p. 40.

15   "The most heavenly sound": Holden, p. 42.

16   "Unable to deliver his organs on time": Holden, pp. 40–41.

16   "Usually wound up spending more money": Holden, p. 65.

16   "Arthur H. Marks . . . ": Details on his investment in Skinner's company in "Arthur Hudson Marks: An Autobiography," in *Stop, Open and Reed,* Vol. 2, No. 1, 1924, and Holden, pp. 64–66.

17   "Making thousands of friends for the organ": "Broadcasting the Skinner Organ," in *Stop, Open and Reed,* Vol. 2, No. 1, 1924.

18   "Dogs, chickens, horses, convulsions of nature": Skinner, "Organ Building as a Fine Art," in *Stop, Open and Reed,* Vol. 3, No. 1, 1925.

19   "Resources are as ample as those of the finest symphony orchestra": "The Capitol Theatre Organ, Boston, Mass.," in *Stop, Open and Reed,* Vol. I, No. 4, 1922.

20   "Over a million copies": Interview with Edward Millington Stout III in Hayward, California, February 9, 2002.

20   "Turned out 2,451 instruments": *The Diapason,* as reported in *Austin Organs,* by Orpha Ochse, published by the Organ Historical Society, 2001, p. 263.

20   "If the average American knew": Skinner, "A Trip Abroad at Home," in *Stop, Open and Reed,* 1927.

CHAPTER 2

21   "The big instrument" at the Chicago Exposition: This organ, several times rebuilt and expanded, was moved after the exposition and exists today as the Henry Simmons Frieze Memorial Organ in Hill Auditorium at the University of Michigan in Ann Arbor.

23 "The largest organ in the world . . . musical effects never before heard outside the Grand Orchestra": George Ashdown Audsley, "Description of the Grand Concert Organ to be erected in Festival Music Hall of the Louisiana Purchase Exposition previous to its installation in Convention Hall, Kansas City, Missouri," printed in facsimile, 2002, by Friends of the Wanamaker Organ, Inc.

25 "Few of the 13,000,000 people who paid 50 cents" and details of the St. Louis installation: Frederick R. Webber, "The St. Louis Exposition Organ," quoted in Ray Biswanger, *Music in the Marketplace: The Story of Philadelphia's Historic Wanamaker Organ* (Bryn Mawr, Pa., Friends of the Wanamaker Organ, Inc., 1999), p. 28.

25 "Opened American ears to a new, high standard": Wayne Leupold, ed., *The Organ Music of Alexandre Guilmant*, Wayne Leupold Editions, Inc., sold through E. C. Schirmer, Boston, 1990.

26 "Kindly desist, young man": Interview with Wright in Binghamton, N.Y., May 2000, and later clarified by Carolyn Albaugh.

27 "An insult to American patriotic pride": Ochse.

27 "The only three bars that I know": Lemare, *Organs I Have Met: The Autobiography of Edwin H. Lemare, 1866–1934* (Los Angeles: The Schoolcraft Company, 1956, republished by the Organ Literature Foundation, Braintree, Mass.), p. 67.

28 "Send new tuba from factory": Ochse, pp. 175 and 177.

28 "10,392 people paid a dime apiece": Ochse, p. 178. The San Francisco municipal organ was badly damaged by the earthquake of 1989.

29 "One must even forgive a printer": Lemare, p. 64.

29 "Carnegie Organ Fund matching grants": "Curious Facts from the Organ's History," The Westfield Center, Easthampton, Mass., published on the Westfield Center's Web site, www.westfield.org. Documents on Carnegie grants and gifts for church organs are in the Columbia University Libraries Rare Book and Manuscript Library in New York City.

30 "The eager mob swept all before it": *Stop, Open and Reed,* Vol. I, No. 4, 1922.

31 "They were seen sweeping sidewalks": Louis Vierne, "Music in America," translated by William Hays, in Rollin Smith, *Louis Vierne: Organist of Notre-Dame Cathedral* (Hillsdale, N.Y., Pendragon Press, 1999), pp. 694ff.

32 "The Aeolian": Rollin Smith, *The Aeolian Pipe Organ and Its Music* (Richmond, Va., the Organ Historical Society, 1998), passim. The

book, referred to as "Smith" below, is the definitive history of the Aeolian Company and its works, with complete descriptions of the instruments and player rolls it produced and extensive background material on the artists who played them and the patrons who bought them.

32 "The private dwellings of the wealthier classes": Audsley's phrase.

33 "Unplayable by the fingers and feet": Smith, pp. 171–176.

33 "Charles Schwab . . . Archer Gibson": Smith, pp. 91–96.

33 "John D. Rockefeller Jr." and the Aeolian organ at Kykuit: Contract from the Aeolian Company for the residence of Mr. John D. Rockefeller, Pocantico Hills, New York, and correspondence including letter from Archer Gibson to Robert Gumbel, Office of John D. Rockefeller Jr., dated June 16, 1923, in folder 145–146, box 15, Homes-Pocantico Hills, General, New House and Garden, Office of the Messrs. Rockefeller (OMR), Rockefeller Family Archives, Rockefeller Archive Center (RAC), Pocantico Hills, N.Y.

33 "To his many enjoyments, the very wealthy man of New York and its suburbs now adds what only a prince of affairs could possess": "Rich Men Who Have Organs Built in Their Homes," *The New York Times,* September 17, 1911, p. SM12.

35 "Lorenzo and the other Medicis": Samuel N. Behrman, *Duveen,* published in New York by Harmony Books, in 1982, p. 46, quoted in Smith, p. 131.

35 "Longwood": Smith, pp. 109–115.

36 "After dinner your guests want to hear the organ": "Why You Should Buy a Residence Organ," in *Stop, Open and Reed,* Vol. I, No. 2, 1922. (A 1927 Skinner brochure, "The Skinner Residence Organ," describes the "musician among your guests" differently: "She will find to her surprise that the Skinner Organ is not only a self player," it says.)

37 "The cost of a high-grade automobile": "The Skinner Residence Organ," published by Skinner Organ Co., New York City, 1927.

38 "Rodman Wanamaker acquired . . . the world's largest organ": Biswanger, p. 54.

42 "Charles-Marie Courboin . . . billows of opulent sound": Details on Courbain and Stowkowski in Biswanger, pp. 85–91.

43 "There came out of that little organ so much pleasure": Biswanger, p. 40.

43 "It will annoy people": Biswanger, pp. 196–197.

44 "The organization of these concerts was remarkable": Marcel Dupré, *Recollections,* translated and edited by Ralph Kneeream (Miami, CPP/ Belwin, Inc., undated), p. 85.

45 "Vierne enjoyed equal success on his three-month tour . . . in 1927": Vierne also played the opening concert April 11, 1927, on the four-manual, 108-stop organ, Opus 1177 built by Casavant Frères Ltée of St. Hyacinthe, Québec, for Phillips Academy, Andover, Massachusetts, that was replaced in 1981 by an Andover Organ Company instrument. The Casavant was relocated in 2001 to St. Andrew's Lutheran Church in Mahtomedi, Minnesota.

46 "No limit": Dupré, p. 85.

47 "The organ in the Grand Court survived": Biswanger, pp. 212–221, passim.

48 "There is no exact count": Stephen D. Smith, *Atlantic City's Musical Masterpiece* (Portsmouth, N.H., Peter E. Randall, for the Atlantic City Convention Hall Organ Society, Inc., 2002), p. 464, and passim.

49 "The Atlantic City monster": Stephen D. Smith, *The Atlantic City Convention Hall Organ* (Annapolis, Md., the Atlantic City Convention Hall Organ Society, Inc., 1998), passim. The society publishes regular editions of *The Grand Ophicleide* and maintains a Web site, www. acchos.org.

CHAPTER 3

51 "I lost the damned umbrella": in Holden, p. 107.

52 "That man will never work for us": Holden, p. 108. Details of Skinner's second trip to Europe in *Stop, Open and Reed,* Vol. 3, No. 1, 1925.

53 "Proof against wood lice": Contract between Skinner Organ Company, Inc., and Church in Cuba Society, Havana, dated February 17, 1926, in Skinner archives held by Edward Millington Stout III in Hayward, Ca., courtesy of Joseph A. Vitacco III.

54 "Mademoiselle Boulanger vill play it and I vill conduct": Aaron Copland and Vivian Perlis, *Copland: 1900 Through 1942* (New York, St. Martin's Griffin, 1999), p. 92.

54 "The largest pipe organ of any concert hall in the city": Rollin Smith, p. 15.

54 "Ready to commit murder": Copland, p. 104.

54 "A loud and jarring honk": Copland, pp. 107–108.

55 "The pernicious teachings of Hope-Jones": Henry W. Willis, "My First American Visit," in *Stop, Open and Reed,* Vol. 3, No. 1, 1925, p. 29.

55 "I want you to get all I can give you tonally": Henry Willis III letter to Skinner dated May 25, 1926, in Charles Callahan, *The American Classic Organ: A History in Letters* (Richmond, Va., the Organ Historical Society, 1990), p. 14. Callahan's volume is a fascinating compilation of correspondence by Skinner, G. Donald Harrison, Willis, and various members of their entourages. Callahan's *Aeolian-Skinner Remembered: A History in Letters* (Randall M. Egan, Kenwood Abbey, Minneapolis, Minn., 1996) is another rich source of detail about Harrison's personal life and recollections.

55 "My chap Harrison": Willis letter to Zeuch, May 25, 1926, in Callahan, *American Classic,* p. 15.

56 "An English gentleman, not an American go-getter": Description of Harrison by T. Scott Buhrman in "Clarity and Its Development," in *The American Organist,* February 1937.

56 "There is no money in it": Skinner, "G. Donald Harrison," in *Stop, Open and Reed,* Vol. 5, No. 1, 1929, p. 9.

57 "More and more valuable as time goes on": Catlin to Willis, June 11, 1926, in Callahan, *American Classic,* p. 16.

57 "Harrison will help you guide Skinner's feet": Willis to Zeuch, May 11, 1927, in Callahan, *American Classic,* p. 20.

58 "Influence the Skinner people to build imitations of the Willis organ": Harrison, letter to J. Michael Harrison, July 29, 1946, courtesy of J. M. Harrison.

58 "My confidence in his judgment stands at 100 per cent": Skinner, "G. Donald Harrison," letter written December 21, 1927, published in *The Diapason* in January 1928 and reprinted in *Stop, Open and Reed,* Vol. 5, No. 1, 1929, p. 9.

58 "It . . . need not be so": Harrison, "The Impressions of a British Organ Builder After Two Years' Experience in America," in *Stop, Open and Reed,* Vol. 5, No. 1, 1929, p. 11.

60 "5,000 people came": Holden, pp. 127–128.

60 "My dear Mr. Skinner": Dupré to Skinner, November 20, 1929, collection of Stan Howe, Bethel, Me.

60 "I want to say right here": Skinner to Harrison, November 23, 1929, in

Callahan, *American Classic,* p. 44. "That recent masterpiece of yours, the Princeton organ": Holden, p. 134.

61 "The most unethical set of salesmen on the face of the earth": Skinner letter to John D. Rockefeller Jr., dated January 24, 1927, in box 76, folder 601, Record Group III 2 N, Religious Interests, Riverside Church, Organ—Bids, etc. 1926, Office of the Messrs. Rockefeller (OMR), Rockefeller Family Archives, Rockefeller Archive Center (RAC), Pocantico Hills, N.Y.

62 "Let Mr. Harrison finish the organ": Jonathan Ambrosino, "The Most Unusual Skinner: An Historical Perspective," jacket in JAV Recordings, "Woolsey Hall," "Great Organbuilders of America, A Retrospective," Vol. 14, 2001.

62 "Over my dead body": Skinner to Davison, November 8, 1930, in Callahan, *American Classic,* p. 64.

62 "Cold and unsympathetic," "withheld $3,000": Holden, p. 144.

64 "Richmond, your father cannot afford": Holden, p. 148.

64 "When Marks found this out . . . five years more": Skinner letter to W. K. Kellogg, September 26, 1941, quoted in Holden, p. 148.

64 "He was not forbidden to enter the doors": Holden, pp. 148–149.

64 "In 1931, . . . only twenty-seven new organs": Holden, p. 156.

65 "Skinner Organ Co.'s net earnings after expenses": Moody's Manual of Investments, reports assembled by Joseph A. Vitacco III. "Arthur H. Marks had joked": "Arthur Hudson Marks, An Autobiography," in *Stop, Open and Reed,* Vol. 2, No. 1, 1924.

65 "Not a step in the direction of big business": Holden, p. 157.

67 "They were bad musically": Holden, pp. 161–162.

68 "You persist in the patently erroneous idea": Holden, pp. 162–163.

68 "A stool pigeon, a cat's paw, a figurehead": Holden, pp. 163–164.

68 "We got along perfectly": Holden, p. 167.

68 "We undo everything that has been done": Holden, pp. 169–170.

69 "Filled with tonal charm": Holden, p. 172.

70 "When—but only when—directed": Holden, pp. 173–174.

70 "I have done everything in my power": A. H. Marks to S. W. Williams and W. D. Hardy, July 25, 1933, in Callahan, *Aeolian-Skinner Remembered,* pp. 1–2.

71 "Some damn fool has come along and just ruined it": Holden, p. 179.

71 "I only build 'em pretty good": Holden, p. 181.

72 "Another world of sound and beauty": Glenn Dillard Gunn in the *Washington Herald,* quoted in Holden, pp. 186–187.

72 "My only handicap is insufficient capital": Skinner to W. K. Kellogg, September 26, 1941, quoted in Holden, p. 195.

72 "A steady drain": Aeolian-Skinner Depression financial figures, from Moody's Manual of Investment reports, assembled by Joseph A. Vitacco III.

73 "Sterilize—I mean clarify—the organ": Skinner letter, *The Diapason,* November 1941, quoted in Holden, p. 199.

73 "I feel rather certain that Mr. Skinner is responsible": Joseph S. Whiteford letter to Searle Wright, copy to Virgil Fox, dated February 19, 1951, provided courtesy of the Virgil Fox Society.

74 "Me or the cat": Skinner to Ned Hastings, October 21, 1953, collection of Stan Howe.

74 "I stay mostly at home": Skinner to "Nedward" (Ned Hastings), July 29, 1957, collection of Stan Howe.

74 "I prefer Offenbach": Ernest M. Skinner's voice recorded on JAV recordings promotional CD JAVS 2, 2000.

74 "Any need for a flue voicer?" Skinner letter to Willis, February 28, 1958, in Callahan, *American Classic,* p. 437.

75 "I have devoted the best years of my life": Ernest M. Skinner and Richmond H. Skinner, *The Composition of the Organ,* edited by Leslie A. Olsen (Ann Arbor, Mich., Melvin J. Light, 1981), pp. 12–13 and 292.

75 "Great men all saw their worlds crumble about them": *The Diapason,* January 1961, quoted in Holden, p. 248.

77 "A culture that is second to none in the world": Harrison to J. Michael Harrison, July 29, 1946, letter courtesy of J. M. Harrison.

77 "How fortunate All Saints Worcester was burned down": Willis letter to Harrison, May 30, 1932, in Callahan, *American Classic,* p. 107.

77 "All of us were influenced by French organs": William Self, *For Mine Eyes Have Seen* (the Worcester Chapter of the American Guild of Organists, 1990), pp. 54–56.

78 "Harrison's heavy drinking . . . naturalized as an American citizen": Description of Harrison's life in America by J. Michael Harrison, "Years 1931 to 1948 (1)," in Callahan, *Aeolian-Skinner Remembered,* pp. 3–11.

79 "I was able to work out something": Harrison to Henry Willis, December 19, 1945, in Callahan, *American Classic,* pp. 222–225.

80 "My God it does it": Joseph S. Whiteford to Jack B. Schneider, October 3, 1959, quoting a Harrison letter to Whiteford; in Callahan, *Aeolian-Skinner Remembered*, pp. 162–168.

80 "Something which in a shadowy sort of way": Callahan, *American Classic*, p. 140.

CHAPTER 4

82 "Should do very well in this direction": E. Power Biggs Collection, American Guild of Organists Organ Library, Boston University School of Theology ("Biggs papers"), letter dated March 15, 1922.

82 "A capital start": Biggs papers.

82 "He had settled on E. Power Biggs": Barbara Owen, *E. Power Biggs, Concert Organist* (Bloomington, Indiana University Press, 1987), p. 7.

83 "Many of the organs terrible": Owen, p. 5.

84 "Never properly finished": Owen, p. 10.

84 "Pep, go, zip": Owen, p. 11.

85 "Not quite flawless": Owen, p. 18.

85 "I doubt it": Owen, p. 22.

86 "A selection of crowd-pleasers": Program in Biggs papers.

86 "Mr. Bigs wasnt there": Biggs papers.

86 "Time to develop as a player": Owen, p. 30.

87 "It is certainly good for something": Quoted in Owen, p. 30.

87 "Smashing dissonances": Quoted in Owen, p. 31.

88 "Organ music, well played, can be as engrossing": *Boston Evening Transcript*, November 13, 1935, in Biggs papers.

88 "A bright future for the organ": Quoted in Owen, p. 34.

89 "Our stops are all too loud or too soft": Albert Schweitzer, *J. S. Bach* (Breitkopf & Härtel, Wiesbaden, 1972), p. 257. See also his "Organ Music and Organ Design in Germany and France," translated by Charles Ferguson, in *The Tracker, Journal of the Organ Historical Society*, Vol. 36, No. 1, 1992, pp. 13–27.

89 "Biggs suggested that the University should commission a 'Bach organ'": *The Diapason*, May 1, 1937.

90 "A small organ to be used as a demonstration model": Owen, p. 36, cited from a taped interview with John Fesperman of the Smithsonian Institution.

90 "See how it sounds": Owen, p. 37, citing Fesperman interview.

91 "An attempt has been made to recapture these desirable qualities": Harrison notes in Germanic Museum concert program, in Biggs papers.

92 "The beautiful tone of the instrument": Owen, p. 39.

92 "It was apparent . . . There were times when the voices did not appear to 'blend'": *Boston Evening Transcript*, in Biggs papers.

92 "Music so new, so arresting, so alive": *The American Organist*, March 1938, in Biggs papers.

92 "I revel in all organ literature": Owen, p. 42.

93 "The music's the thing": *The American Organist*, March 1938, in Biggs papers.

94 "I wish we could have an instrument like that": Owen, p. 43.

94 "Bach as Bach should be": Owen, p. 44.

94 "More interested in Mr. Biggs than in the instrument": Owen, p. 57.

95 "Fine, send it up to Tanglewood": Biggs notes, typewritten on his private letterhead, dated January 1977, in Biggs papers.

96 "One of the most successful instruments we have made": Owen, p. 82.

96 "I must have the first performance": Biggs notes, January 1977.

98 "Some generous and interested person": Coolidge correspondence, letter of January 16, 1941, in Biggs papers.

100 "She agreed to give the $500": Coolidge correspondence, in the Biggs papers.

100 "The first of a series of ten organ recitals": Biggs papers.

100 "Best musical offerings": Biggs papers.

101 "Real organ playing": Biggs papers.

101 "We are enjoying your broadcasts so much": Coolidge letter of November 9, 1942, in Biggs papers.

101 "How very generous": Biggs letter of January 16, 1944, in Biggs papers.

102 "Never without female companionship": Owen, p. 62.

102 "Not allowed to accept your services gratis": Owen, p. 68.

103 "The instrument itself . . . cloistered servitude": Newspaper clipped by Biggs, in the Biggs papers.

104 "Maestro: again my thanks": Letter from Daniel R. Pinkham Jr., February 26, 1944, in Biggs papers.

104 "Quincy Porter . . . Roy Harris": Eileen Hunt, "E. Power Biggs: Legacy of the Performing Artist," D.M.A. dissertation, School of Music, Boston University, 1986, in the Biggs papers.

104 "This was bait indeed": *Musical America,* March 25, 1945.

105 "More E. Power Biggs to You": David McCord, *Odds Without Ends,* Boston, Little, Brown & Co., 1954.

106 "Sixteen million attended baseball games": Proposal offered by Hugh Hooks, Hollywood agent for Columbia Artists Management, in 1949, from a 1946 sketch by Biggs, in Biggs papers.

106 "Your pictorial genius": Biggs letter to Disney, December 7, 1945, in Biggs papers.

107 "A pile of music in the barn": Correspondence with Harmony Ives, quoted in Eileen Hunt's dissertation, cited above, in Biggs papers.

107 "They have been extremely kind to me": Callahan, *Aeolian-Skinner Remembered,* pp. 24–25, and letter to the author from J. Michael Harrison, June 10, 2002.

107 "Resonance is the priceless ingredient": Owen, p. 90.

108 "Does he really believe . . . ?" Owen, p. 60.

108 "We know far more today . . . ": Owen, pp. 83–84.

109 "The contract was signed": Callahan, *Aeolian-Skinner Remembered,* pp. 38–39.

110 "It is bad stuff . . . a difficult thing to break": G. Donald Harrison to J. Michael Harrison, December 30, 1946, copy provided by J. M. Harrison.

110 "Nitroglycerin pills": See Callahan, *American Classic,* p. 444.

111 "Raiding the organ literature": Boston Symphony Orchestra program, "The New Aeolian-Skinner Organ in Symphony Hall, Boston," November 14, 1949, in Biggs papers.

112 "A full house": Review clipped, in Biggs papers.

112 "Mechanically, everything is right up to date": Boston Symphony Orchestra program, in Biggs papers.

114 "Smell the hog and hear the grunt": Emerson Richards to William King Covell, April 19, 1955, in Callahan, *American Classic,* p. 397.

114 "An Aeolian-Skinner flavor": Harrison letter, June 25, 1947, in Callahan, *American Classic,* pp. 250–254.

114 "Something had soured their relationship": Emerson Richards's theory, Callahan, *Aeolian-Skinner Remembered,* pp. 88–89.

115 "Compelled to purchase it": Biggs letter about Germanic Museum organ to Dirk Flentrop, September 22, 1956, Owen, p. 129.

116 "We can hardly depend on it": letter in Biggs papers.

116 "Any hard feeling": Callahan, *American Classic,* pp. 357ff.

117 "You can contrive it": Callahan, *American Classic,* p. 368.

118 "Studebaker," Owen, pp. 99–102.

118 "The ghost of Hamlet's father": Owen, p. 103.

118 "Some of their business practices": Biggs, letter of May 7, 1955, in Biggs papers.

119 "Enough space on the jacket": Letter from Laurence Minot Channing to William P. Homans Jr., August 12, 1954, in Biggs papers.

119 "On June 14 . . . a fatal heart attack": Callahan, *Aeolian-Skinner Remembered,* pp. 30, 77, and letter from Helen Harrison to Eric Harrison, June 28, 1956, in Callahan, *American Classic,* p. 433.

120 "Peggy Biggs was present": Letter to the author from Mary Harrison (Mrs. J. Michael Harrison), June 21, 2002.

120 "Nothing in our experience at Symphony Hall": Biggs letter to Ormandy, October 30, 1956, in Biggs papers.

CHAPTER 5

122 "They see you before they hear you": Richard Torrence and Marshall Yaeger, *Virgil Fox (The Dish): Based on a Memoir by Ted Alan Worth* (New York, Circles International, 2001), pp. 254–255.

122 "I can outplay any organist living": Richard Dyer, "Who Is the World's Best Organist? Ask Virgil Fox," *The New York Times,* September 29, 1974.

122 "As Many Hands as He Has Teeth": Harold C. Schonberg, "Music: Fox in Last of 4 Organ Recitals," *The New York Times,* February 25, 1970.

122 "Fox was . . . a throwback": Jonathan Ambrosino, "Present Imperfect: A Perspective on the Past Century of American Organbuilding," in *The Tracker, Journal of the Organ Historical Society,* Vol. 42, No. 3, 1998, p. 33.

123 "His ideas about Bach . . . its Billy Sunday": Schonberg, "Fox Plays Sophisticated New Organ," *The New York Times,* October 3, 1974.

123 "When I got to the loft": Walter Peterson, interview with Virgil Fox, July 18, 1970, courtesy Richard Torrence.

124 "It started out light, delicate, and soft . . . ": *Dish,* pp. 14–15.

125 "Paris is the promised land": Fox, *The American Organist,* March 1933.

126 "Virgil said . . . ": *Dish,* p. 79.

126 "Balked at paying the $50 fee": *Dish,* p. 106.

127 "Wraps its sound around you—and squeezes": Frank H. Taylor, quoted in Biswanger, *Music in the Marketplace,* p. 233.

127 "The cathedral is packed": E. M. Skinner to William King Covell, May 7, 1943, in Callahan, *American Classic*, p. 191.

128 "Fox was able to live at her house": Interview with Jane Boutwell, November 2000.

128 "He was a brand new private": Letter to the author from Colonel Augustin Mitchell Prentiss Jr., January 27, 2001.

129 "People will come to hear you play, dear boy": *Dish*, p. 87.

130 "I feel that he is not only an unusually fine musician": Anne Archbold to John D. Rockefeller Jr. (JDR Jr.), December 9, 1945, in folder 596, box 76, Record Group III 2 N, Religious Interests, Riverside Church, Organ—General, 1946–1951, Office of the Messrs. Rockefeller (OMR), Rockefeller Family Archives, Rockefeller Archive Center (RAC), Pocantico Hills, N.Y.

131 "Everything about it is wrong": Memo to JDR Jr. from "jw", December 15, 1947, in folder 596, box 76, RG III 2 N, Religious Interests, Riverside Church, Organ—General, 1946–1951, OMR, Rockefeller Family Archives, RAC.

131 "No organist should be allowed to impose his pet idiosyncrasies": Willis to Harrison, December 31, 1948, in Callahan, *American Classic*, pp. 268–269.

131 "A loss of $8,000": Correspondence on the organ, in folder 595, box 76, RG III 2 N, Religious Interests, Riverside Church, Organ—General 1951–1959, OMR, Rockefeller Family Archives, RAC.

132 "Perhaps we should make Mr. Fox either a deacon or a trustee": JDR Jr. to Dr. McCracken, August 27, 1948, extract filed in folder 596, box 76, RG III 2 N, Religious Interests, Riverside Church, Organ—General 1951–1959, OMR, Rockefeller Family Archives, RAC.

132 "Very dull and heavy": Memo to Riverside Church trustees from A. LeRoy Chipman, May 6, 1949, in same folder as above, OMR, Rockefeller Family Archives, RAC.

132 "We will never have any peace or quiet": JDR Jr. to Chipman, August 11, 1949, in same folder as above, OMR, Rockefeller Family Archives, RAC.

132 "You know where to check in": Fox letter to Roberta Bailey, July 13, 1949, made available to the author by her son, Marc Johnson in Bailey papers.

132 "She arrived at the church": Bailey—Roberta Bailey Johnson after her

marriage in 1957 to Richard F. Johnson—was Fox's manager at the height of the first part of his career. She made notes for a book to be called *It Led to a Castle* but died in 1997 before she could complete it. Richard Johnson made these notes available to the author before his own death in 2001. The information in her notes and in interviews with Johnson, a friend of the author's for nearly fifty years, form another major part of this chapter. Her notes, in the author's possession, are cited below as "Bailey."

133 "What chord should I play now": *Dish,* pp. 36–37.

133 "You have to help these poor starving artists out": Carlo Curley, *In the Pipeline: Memoirs of an International Concert Organist* (London, Harper-Collins, 1998), p. 46.

134 "Virgil is in Nassau": Bailey.

134 "$10,000 in her will": *Dish,* p. 303.

135 "Biggs really gave VF the worst organ . . . I'll play on 'junk'": Bailey.

136 "A standing ovation": *The Diapason,* July 1, 1950.

137 "Deeply affecting sensitivity": Review, "Internationaler Kongress für Kirchenmusik: Das Orgelkonzert von Virgil Fox," *Der Bund,* September 1952, in Bailey papers.

138 "A new organ": *Dish,* pp. 80–81.

139 "Filled the gas tank": Bailey.

139 "A check for $500 . . . engaged for a flattering fee": JDR Jr. letter to Fox dated July 16, 1951, and Fox reply in folder 471, box 63, RG III 2 H, Friends and Services/Friends and Relations, Virgil Fox, 1950–1953, OMR, Rockefeller Family Archives, RAC.

140 "I must have been a fish"; "Mr. Fox is a delightful young man"; "I've already had one delicious 'dip'": Fox letter to JDR Jr. and Mrs. Rockefeller dated November 27, 1951; JDR Jr. reply to Fox dated November 29, 1951, JDR letter to Hilda Aberg dated November 29; and Fox letter to JDR Jr. dated Dec. 13, 1951, in folder 471, box 63, RG III 2 H, Friends and Services/Friends and Relations, Virgil Fox, 1950–1953, OMR, Rockefeller Family Archives, RAC.

140 "Mr. Whiteford hoped that some system could be worked out": Memo from George J. Heidt to A. LeRoy Chipman, April 15, 1952, copy in folder 595, box 76, RG III 2 N, Religious Interests, Riverside Church, Organ—General 1951–1959, OMR, Rockefeller Family Archives, RAC.

140 "A $104,000 contract . . . pledge from John D. Rockefeller Jr.": Letter

from Chipman to "Junior," May 7, 1952, in folder 597, box 76, RG III 2 N, Religious Interests, Riverside Church, Organ—Pledges for Rebuilding, 1950–1954, OMR, Rockefeller Family Archives, RAC.

140 "Walking on air": Letter from Virgil Fox to "My dear Mr. and Mrs. Rockefeller," undated, in folder 597, box 76, RG III 2 N, Religious Interests, Riverside Church, Organ—Pledges for Rebuilding, 1950–1954, OMR, Rockefeller Family Archives, RAC.

141 "Several more things that I would like to have": Letter from Virgil Fox to T. Raymond St. John, Esq., dated December 5, 1952, copy in folder 597, box 76, RG III 2 N, Religious Interests, Riverside Church, Organ—Pledges for Rebuilding, 1950–1954, OMR, Rockefeller Family Archives, RAC.

141 "Worthy of very careful consideration": Letter from G. Donald Harrison to T. Raymond St. John, Esq., dated December 17, 1952, copy in folder 597, box 76, RG III 2 N, Religious Interests, Riverside Church, Organ—Pledges for Rebuilding, 1950–1954, OMR, Rockefeller Family Archives, RAC.

142 "Eggs as you wanted them": JDR Jr. letter to Virgil Fox dated January 26, 1953, in folder 595, box 76, RG III 2 N, Religious Interests, Riverside Church, Organ—General 1951–1959, OMR, Rockefeller Family Archives, RAC.

142 "Master-servant relationship": Richard Torrence recalls seeing a letter in Fox's files; see *Dish*, pp. 81–82.

142 "Eggs to order . . . beautiful in every respect": Virgil Fox letter to JDR Jr. and Mrs. Rockefeller, and JDR Jr. reply to Fox dated April 6, 1953, in folder 471, box 63, RG III 2 H, Friends and Services/Friends and Relations, Virgil Fox, 1950–1953, OMR, Rockefeller Family Archives, RAC.

144 "A net loss": Letter from Joseph S. Whiteford to George J. Heidt dated July 10, 1956, Heidt memo to Riverside Church Board of Trustees dated January 4, 1957, and Heidt letter to Whiteford dated January 24, 1957, in folder 595, box 76, RG III 2 N, Religious Interests, Riverside Church, Organ—General 1951–1959, OMR, Rockefeller Family Archives, RAC.

146 "To call attention to itself or to entertain": Riverside Church Archives, Church Music, and quoted in the press.

146 "Avoided all those damned Yankees": Curley, p. 46.

147 "In their front row seats . . . I do not feel": JDR Jr. draft letters to Fox dated April 28, 1955; Robert J. McCracken letter to JDR Jr. dated May 4, 1955, and JDR Jr. letter to McCracken dated May 9, 1955, in folder 595, box 76, RG III 2 N, Religious Interests, Riverside Church, Organ—General 1951–1959, OMR, Rockefeller Family Archives, RAC.

148 "Bought for $68,000": *Dish*, p. 311.

148 "There was room in the basement . . . over the years the organ grew": Curley, p. 62.

151 "You crucify me and the music": *Dish*, p. 173.

151 "Not aligned with the tempo of the organ": Letter from Mrs. L. D. Maxwell-Sparrow to the author, March 16, 2001.

151 "Would I agree to take over": *Dish*, p. 227.

152 "A gay lad and lass from Rangoon": *Dish*, p. 96.

152 "Virgil 'groupies:'" *Dish*, p. 108.

152 "He heard about Richard Torrence": *Dish*, pp. 146–147.

152 "Suicide": *Dish*, p. 148.

152 "In a quandary": Fox to Bailey, April 24, 1962, in Bailey papers.

153 "Because you cannot promote me": Ibid.

153 "An occasional organist": Fitch to Roberta Bailey, April 24, 1962, in Bailey papers.

153 "You will like him, I think": Fox to Roberta Bailey, April 24, 1962, in Bailey papers.

154 "His client intended to terminate": James F. Hoge to Roberta Bailey, May 1, 1963, in Bailey papers.

154 "Very difficult not to become quite bitter": Bailey to James Hoge, dated June 20, 1963, in Bailey papers.

154 "I know he is not a forthright person": Bailey to Hoge, July 8, 1963, in Bailey papers.

154 "My new man, Cameo": *Dish*, pp. 146 and 152–153.

155 "You can imagine what a mess it is": Joseph Whiteford letter to E. Power Biggs dated August 28, 1962, quoted in Owen, pp. 150–151.

155 "The Philharmonic will have their hands full": "Organ Debut Due in Lincoln Center," *The New York Times*, December 13, 1962.

155 "It was breathtaking": *Dish*, p. 166.

156 "Every note in place": Mary Monroe, conversation with the author, September 2001.

157 "Virgil was shaken": *Dish*, p. 167.

157 "Half the audience had left": Interview with Richard Torrence, October 2000.

157 "Frenzied standing ovation": *Dish*, p. 168.

158 "Printed on every sheet": Richard Torrence, note to the author, August 2001.

158 "Moods and sonic fireworks": "Virgil Fox Offers 2d Organ Recital at Philharmonic," *The New York Times*, January 22, 1964.

159 "The boy could be his grandson": *Dish*, p. 178. *Dish* does not identify Snyder by his full name.

159 "Beat his back with an umbrella": *Dish*, 227–228.

160 "Too big for Riverside": *Dish*, pp. 228–230.

160 "He will be succeeded": "Dr. Fox Retires Tomorrow as Organist at Riverside," *The New York Times*, May 31, 1965.

CHAPTER 6

161 "Billing Columbia for the excess baggage": Biggs papers, and Owen, p. 112.

162 "One seems never to have heard the music before": Owen, p. 124.

163 "The importance of tracker action": Biggs recollections taped in 1973, quoted in Owen, p. 116.

164 "The older organs take the laurels": "Vicarious Organ Tour on Disks," *The New York Times*, April 17, 1955.

164 "Not last year or this": "Back Aloud," in "The Talk of The Town," the *New Yorker*, June 7, 1958.

165 "The pressure of other work": Biggs papers.

165 "Would you like to consider the idea": Biggs letter, quoted in Owen, p. 129.

165 "THIS IS IT!" Biggs letter, quoted in Owen, p. 130.

166 "I guess our lesson is": Biggs papers, 1957 recording trip.

166 "Robert C. Creel" excerpts: Department of State letter dated Sept. 20, 1956, in Biggs papers.

167 "Now I've missed three": Biggs letter, quoted in Owen, p. 124.

168 "The 'vandalism' . . . inflicted on Handel's organ": See Owen, pp. 124–126.

168 "Biggs sold the Harrison organ": Owen, p. 130.

168 "It took a little while . . . for the lessons . . . to be learned": Owen, p. 45.

170 "The ceremony lacked the solemnity": Owen, p. 131.

170 "These make-believe devices": Biggs, "The Record: An Explanation," in "The Organ," Columbia Records, 1958.

170 "Articulate and beautiful pipe tone . . . a sort of 'chiff'": Biggs, "The Organ," manuscript in Biggs papers.

171 "The organ appears to possess a fatal appeal . . . A return to basic principles": Biggs, "The Record: An Explanation."

171 "Biggs's voice is the voice of a prophet": Owen, p. 127.

172 "Among the many casualties": Biggs papers.

172 "Unfortunately they wouldn't pay even that": Owen, p. 73.

172 "A cruel disease": Owen, p. 210.

173 "These early American organs": Biggs, "The Organ and Music of Early America," essay in "The Organ in America," Columbia Masterworks, 1960.

174 "A nasty letter": Owen, p. 144.

175 "Lacking pipes, they lack the first essential": Biggs letter to George E. Judd Jr., dated October 12, 1957, in Biggs papers.

175 "Almost acceptable": Biggs letter dated June 1, 1963, in Biggs papers.

176 "Just musical drivel": Biggs papers.

176 "Poor old Jimmy!" Fox, quoted by Ted Alan Worth in *Dish*, p. 68.

176 "Even Mr. Biggs is human": Lorene S. Banta, *The American Organist*, November 1960.

177 "A stressful situation": Owen, p. 155.

177 "St. Mark's Cathedral in Seattle . . . whose organist had been smitten": David Dahl, "The Tracker Organ Revival in the Pacific Northwest in the 20th Century," in *The Tracker, Journal of The Organ Historical Society*, Vol. 42, No. 2, 1998, pp. 34–35.

177 "Far better than the previous version": Owen, p. 173.

178 "Proposing to show us the celestial regions": Owen, p. 180.

178 "This is the place, one feels": Biggs, "Impressions of the Thomaskirche," in "E. Power Biggs Plays Bach in the Thomaskirche," Columbia Records/CBS. Inc., 1971.

179 "Alexander Schuke of Potsdam": The Schuke organ was removed in a renovation after the reunification of Germany in 1989 and went to the Cathedral of St. Mary in Fürstenwalde. It was replaced by a new sixty-one-stop organ made by Gerald Woehl of Marburg, "constructed to play the organ works of Bach the way he intended," according to the Web site of St. Thomas Church, www.thomaskirche.org.

179 "Really high drama": Owen, p. 182.

180 "E. Power Biggs is in Rags": Owen, p. 192.

181 "Long and roaring applause": *The Diapason,* January 1975.

181 "Where is the symmetry of organ pipes": Owen, p. 204.

182 "Over his dead body": The pipe organ intended for Carnegie Hall went to the State University of New York in Purchase in 1977.

182 "Think of the Concertgebouw": "Electronic 'Pipe Organs' Distressing to Biggs," *The New York Times,* June 9, 1976.

182 "The way God intended organs to be built": Biggs letter dated March 31, 1975, in Biggs papers.

182 "He may not have the dexterity now": "Music: Soloists Highlight Tully Organ Dedication," *The New York Times,* April 15, 1975.

183 "If the elbow was stiff": Owen, p. 207.

184 "The rollicking forward scout of scholarship": Ibid.

184 "We did try very hard to pull him through": Pierce letter dated April 5, 1977, in Biggs papers.

185 "You're quite a swinger on the harpsichord": George Wright letter, 1977, in Biggs papers.

185 "Biggs created his own memorial": Owen, p. 213.

CHAPTER 7

188 "I always thought you were just a showman": *Dish,* pp. 212–213.

189 "The sound was dreadful and unmusical": *Dish,* p. 216.

191 "Divisions in the sun-porch, the attic, and also the basement": Curley, p. 61.

191 "The hole in the wall": "Virgil Fox Turning His House into a Case for a Pipe Organ," *The New York Times,* February 25, 1968.

192 "In Fox's opinion, this is a backward move": "Fox, Virgil (Keel)," *Current Biography,* January 1964.

192 "Dried owl shit": Marshall Yaeger in *Dish,* p. 278.

193 "Fine if you intend to wallow around": "Who Is the World's Best Organist? Ask Virgil Fox," by Richard Dyer, *The New York Times,* September 29, 1974.

193 Listening to Virgil Fox's organ recital": "2d of Four Recitals Given by Virgil Fox," *The New York Times,* Nov. 26, 1969.

193 "Organ aficionados turn out en masse": "Music: Fox in Last of 4 Organ Recitals," *The New York Times,* February 25, 1970.

194 "I'll call the album 'Heavy Organ'": *Dish,* pp. 273–274.

195 "I understand that he actually did speak": *Dish,* p. 270.

195 "Dry ice": Curley, p. 77.

195 "We arrive, and there are hippies and non-hippies": William F. Buckley Jr., *Cruising Speed: A Documentary* (New York, G. P. Putnam's Sons, 1971), p. 51.

196 "So plucky-wucky the portamentos," etc.: Buckley, pp. 51–52.

196 "Homoerotic fantasies": Quoted in Richard Dyer, *The New York Times,* September 29, 1974.

196 "Homey-eccentric spoken remarks": "A Virgil Fox Program," *The New York Times,* January 16, 1976.

197 "What I think about the purists": "Virgil Fox, The Legendary 1973 Concert: Heavy Organ at Carnegie Hall," BMG Classics, BMG Music, 09026-688162.

198 "Hell's Angels": Marc Johnson, conversation with the author, November 2001.

198 "That person is, of course, yourself, Mr. Fox": Letter from Harry Sterling III to Virgil Fox, July 24, 1974, Bailey papers.

198 "I thoroughly enjoyed," "I hope this time we will have something new": Letters from Dorothy Mortorff, June 21, 1974, and Paul H. Alex, June 19, 1974, Bailey papers.

199 "Mr. Fox is indeed unique": "Fox Plays Sophisticated New Organ," *The New York Times,* October 3, 1974.

199 "Royal V": *Dish,* pp. 327–328.

200 "We could hear shots being fired": Tape of meeting at Hammond Museum, Gloucester, Massachusetts, summer 1974, with Bailey papers.

201 "Pleaded for the $250,000": *Dish,* pp. 310–312.

202 "His intentions did not meet with Mr. Hammond's plan": Form letter from Gloucester Committee for the Hammond Museum, Inc. dated August 31, 1974, in Biggs papers.

202 "Mr. Virgil Fox is totally disqualified": Biggs to Medeiros, October 9, 1974, in Biggs papers.

203 "I, the Fox": Fox quote from tape of meeting, summer of 1974; notes of meeting with committee members in Gloucester, Mass., on October 2, 1974, by Richard Johnson, both in Bailey papers.

203 "Mrs. Shouse provided something": Letter from Mrs. Jouett Shouse to

The Most Reverend Humberto Medeiros, dated April 15, 1974, Bailey papers.

204 "It's a hell of an agenda": "Music Notes: Virgil Fox's Big Plans," *The New York Times,* June 15, 1975.

204 "Judith Martin": "Virgil Fox: This Musician's Castle Is His Home," by Judith Martin, *Washington Post,* May 12, 1975.

204 "One disaster after another": *Dish,* pp. 311–312.

205 "Lost all privacy": Interview with Torrence, October 2000, and *Dish,* 310–313.

205 "More than the museum could afford": "Museum directors resign from jobs," *Gloucester Daily Times,* July 15, 1975.

205 "Dick and I, believe it or not, worked very hard for you": Roberta Bailey Johnson letter to Virgil Fox, President, Board of Trustees, Hammond Museum, Inc., July 11, 1975, Bailey papers.

206 "Five months later, Fox was out too": "Castle trustees, organist clash— Virgil Fox Out," *Gloucester Daily Times,* December 4, 1975, Bailey papers.

206 "Losses and legal fees": Virgil Fox letter to Roberta Bailey, undated, postmarked December 11, 1978, Bailey papers.

206 "He kept the Harvard organ": Fox sold the Harvard organ to the First Baptist Church of Bakersfield, California, in 1976. Fisk's firm shipped it from the warehouse where it had been stored in Manchester, Massachusetts, but the church had no use for the wooden carvings and pipes of the façade, which became part of a Fisk organ in the First Presbyterian Church of Charleston, West Virginia. Interview with Steven Dieck, March 2002.

206 "Casa Lagomar": *Dish,* pp. 310–313.

206 "No mistaking the bump I felt": *Dish,* pp. 344–345.

207 "This was not Fox's first cancer scare": Bailey notes.

207 "Ending it all": *Dish,* p. 345.

207 "Honeydew time": *Dish,* p. 354.

209 "Only palliative therapy (but no cure) was possible": *Dish,* p. 358.

209 "I've always preferred my organs upright": *Dish,* p. 364.

209 "Scraping the bottom of the barrel": "A Little Bach by Fox," *The New York Times,* January 19, 1978.

210 "Named as his heir": "Last Will and Testament of Virgil Fox," dated June 24, 1978, filed with Circuit Court of Palm Beach County, Florida, copy courtesy of Steven Frank of the Virgil Fox Society. Fox

also willed $20,000 to his brother, Warren, and stipulated that his mother, Bird Fox, should receive Snyder's inheritance if he should not survive Fox. This will replaced one dated June 24, 1958, that provided that Fox's mother and Weagly should share his estate equally.

210 "Fox and Snyder went through with the process": *Dish,* p. 371.

210 "I'm going to roll General Grant around in his tomb": "Virgil Fox Returning to Scene of His Chimes," *The New York Times,* May 3, 1979.

212 "I am determined that this shall not be a stuffy occasion. . . . Silence was observed in the great nave": "Virgil Fox, 1912–1980, Soli Deo Gloria," BCD 8005, c 1990 by Bainbridge Entertainment Co., Inc. Available through the Virgil Fox Society, www.virgilfox.com.

212 "He's dying of cancer": *Dish,* p. 375.

213 "So weak and sore from bone cancer": *Dish,* pp. 388–389.

213 "It is finished": Interview with Robert Hebble, November 2000.

214 "Snyder yearned impossibly to share in Fox's brilliance": Marc Johnson, conversation with the author, March 2002.

214 "Members of the Virgil Fox Society recovered the organ console": *Dish,* pp. 401–403, and conversation with Steven Frank of the Virgil Fox Society, April 2002.

214 "Dazzled by a genius": *Dish,* pp. 403–404.

CHAPTER 8

216 "He violently opposed Bach's desire": Holden, p. 199.

217 "Not a copy of any organ Gottfried Silbermann built": C. B. Fisk, Inc. Web site, www.cbfisk.com/organs, and interview with Steven A. Dieck, President, at C. B. Fisk, Inc. in Gloucester, Massachusetts, March 21, 2002.

218 "Asked that the Harrison nameplate be removed": Callahan, *Aeolian-Skinner Remembered,* pp. 305, 319, and 355, and Self, *For Mine Eyes Have Seen,* pp. 205–209.

219 "Why not ours": Callahan, *Aeolian-Skinner Remembered,* p. 363.

219 "Organists found many of these instruments anemic": Jonathan Ambrosino, "Present Imperfect," *The Tracker,* Vol. 42, No. 3, 1998, p. 31.

219 "The only two all-mechanical-action organs": Callahan, *Aeolian-Skinner Remembered,* p. 528.

220 "Austin backed out of the talks": Ochse, *Austin Organs,* pp. 475–476.

220 "The firm closes down": Michael Harrison's thoughts about organ-

building companies: Callahan, *Aeolian-Skinner Remembered*, p. 32, undated letter (1947) from J. M. Harrison to G. D. Harrison.

220 "166 of them": Tracker-action organs ordered from abroad, Ochse, pp. 444–445.

220 "A moderate viewpoint": Ochse, p. 445.

221 "A musician will not expect to change stops electrically": Fenner Douglass, "A Historical Perspective," on Duke University Chapel Web site: www.chapel.duke.edu/organs/Flentrop/memorial/douglass.htm.

222 "A limited constellation of keys": John Brombaugh, "The Brombaugh Organ in Duke University Chapel," on Duke University Chapel Web site: www.chapel.duke.edu/organs/Brombaugh/FromBuilder.htm.

223 "An attractive novelty": Jack M. Bethards, *The American Organist*, April 2000.

224 "One loves each one and hates each one . . . the way one loves and hates one's children": *Charles Brenton Fisk: A Retrospective*, videotape produced by SFM Productions, Stephen F. Malionek, 1996.

225 "Not wanting to be a part of it if that was the case": comments by Virginia Lee Fisk on an early version of this manuscript, June 2002.

225 "American organs were totally unsuited": Video, *Charles Brenton Fisk: A Retrospective*.

225 "The most avant-garde American organ builder": *Charles B. Fisk, Organ Builder*, Vol. 2, *His Work*, compiled and edited by Barbara Owen (Easthampton, Mass., Westfield Center for Early Keyboard Studies, 1986), p. 1.

226 "I can safely say": Owen, *Charles B. Fisk*, p. 8.

226 "The weakness in his liver": Dieck interview, March 21, 2002.

227 "An animate object": Video, *Charles Brenton Fisk: A Retrospective*.

228 "High-strung organ": Essay written by Charles Fisk in December 1982 for a recording by Christa Rakich, C. B. Fisk Web site, www.cbfisk.com/organs/op046.

229 "Brainstorming": Dieck interview.

229 "Andreas Silbermann organ that Melville Smith loved": Owen, "Charles B. Fisk," p. 29.

230 "The 'unattainable' ideal": Owen, *Charles B. Fisk*, p. 57.

230 "I think he had an inkling": Video, *Charles Brenton Fisk: A Retrospective*.

232 "The necessary additional funds": Ibid., and Dieck interview.

232 "With all possible authority": Owen, *Charles B. Fisk*, p. 74.

233 "Make sure the team stays together": Dieck interview.

233 "It would just sit there": Ibid.

234 "Take one of your standard organs": Ibid.

234 "The full panoply of distinctive organ sounds": Owen, *Biggs,* pp. 86–87.

236 "A brain-mechanism": Jean Guillou, *L'Orgue, souvenir et avenir* (Paris, Buchet/Chastel-Pierre Zech, 1996), pp. 152–153.

237 "A multi-purpose organ": notes made in 1980, cited in Owen, *Charles B. Fisk,* pp. 149–151.

238 "The beefy, decibel-rich sound was now coming from the 'stick' organs": Ambrosino, "Present Imperfect," *The Tracker,* Vol. 42, No. 3, p. 33.

239 "The flavor of hamburger": *24 Heures,* Lausanne, January 18, 1999, "L'orgue bostonien de la Cathédrale s'annonce divin. Mais certains doutent."

CHAPTER 9

241 "Tinkerers": Fisk notes cited in Owen, *Charles B. Fisk,* pp. 149–151.

243 "A renowned master": Charles Krigbaum essay in the record jacket of Joseph A. Vitacco III's two-CD set, "Woolsey Hall," JAV Recordings, 2001.

243 "Still playing reliably": Interview with Joseph F. Dzeda, March 24, 2002.

243 "The builder himself would recognize": Jonathan Ambrosino, "Skinner Organ Opus 820," JAV Recordings, Vol. 20.

244 "No one would have given the time of day": Scott Cantrell, "Getting Winded," *Symphony,* May–June 2001.

245 "Cincinnati Museum Center organ": press release on the E. M. Skinner Concert Organ, April 3, 2002, from the museum, and conversations with Harley Piltingsrud, curator, spring 2002. Piltingsrud also rediscovered how proper tanning can keep leather used in pipe organs from deteriorating.

246 "New or restored concert hall organs being planned": See Cantrell, "Getting Winded."

246 "The lack of an organ": James R. Oestreich, "A Bittersweet Goodbye with Might Have Beens," *The New York Times,* Arts & Leisure, May 12, 2002.

247 "A true pipe organ": John Rockwell, "Why Do They Bar the Pipe Organ?" *The New York Times,* June 2, 1985.

248 "Tears in their eyes": Interview with Dr. John Weaver, June 15, 2002.

249 "People I'd never expect to be interested": Telephone conversation with James W. Haas, March 14, 2002. Information about the organ pavilion project is available on its Web site at www.sfpavilion.org.

249 "Restoration, and not rebuilding": Jonathan Ambrosino, in "Saint Peter's Episcopal Church," Skinner Organ Company Opus 836, 1930, JAV Recordings, Great Organbuilders of America: A Retrospective, Vol. 2, 1998.

249 "Our opinions": John Bishop in *The American Organist,* June 2002.

249 "Leave it as it is": "A conversation with Margaret Mueller," in Skinner Organ Company, Opus 712–1929, JAV Recordings, Great Organbuilders of America: A Retrospective, Vol. 10, 2000.

251 "Hog heaven": "Orchestrating a Pipe Organ, Piece by Piece," *The New York Times,* April 27, 1993.

254 "Cuckoo clock": *Dish,* p. 202.

255 "Better eclectic organs": Fisk lecture at McGill University, May 26–28, 1981, reprinted on the Fisk Web site (www.cbfisk.com).

256 "Musicianship and quality": Jack M. Bethards, "A Brief for the Symphonic Organ," essay dated January 14, 2002, for the British Institute of Organ Studies.

256 "It's quite simple": Bethards, letter to the author, June 3, 2002.

256 "Organists' attitudes": Leonard Raver, quoted in "Is It the King of Instruments?" by Allan Kozinn, *The New York Times,* March 15, 1981.

257 "A peculiar admixture": Haig Mardirosian, in *The American Organist,* March 2002.

257 "I was so furious": Gaylord Carter, *The Million Dollar Life of Gaylord Carter* (Oakland, California, Paramount Theatre of the Arts, Inc., 1995), p. 145.

258 "I improvise, instead of doing pieces from the organ literature": Interview with Dorothy Papadakos, May 2002.

259 "What am I saying that no one else has said": Interview with Kent Tritle, July 2002.

259 "Sets all over the state of Vermont": Interview with John Weaver, June 2002.

259 "How can any human being sustain interest . . . ": Interview with Ken Cowan, July 2002.

259 "In the same league as the organ's own repertoire": Bethards, "A Brief for the Symphonic Organ."

260 "The artistry of touch": Interview with James David Christie, June 2002.

261 "It is simplistic to think that there is only ONE kind of organ . . . Quality can create an audience": Owen, e-mail to the author, June 2002.

261 "It's important to hear the person playing . . . no more distracting than libretto subtitles at the opera": Interview with Peter Stoltzfus, June 2002.

263 "Win them over to the music and the instrument": Fox, "Statement by Virgil Fox for *Music Journal*," undated, in Bailey papers. See also "My Credo," *Music Journal*, February 1967.

Bibliography

Audsley, George Ashdown. *Organ Stops and Their Artistic Registration.* New York, H. W. Gray, 1921.

Barnes, William H., and Edward B. Gammons. *Two Centuries of American Organ Building.* New York, Belwin-Mills, 1970.

Biswanger, Ray. *Music in the Marketplace: The Story of Philadelphia's Historic Wanamaker Organ.* Bryn Mawr, Pa., Friends of the Wanamaker Organ, 1999.

Boyd, Malcolm. *The Master Musicians: Bach.* London, J. M. Dent & Sons, 1990.

Callahan, Charles. *Aeolian-Skinner Remembered: A History in Letters.* Minneapolis, Minn., Randall M. Egan, 1996.

Callahan, Charles. *The American Classic Organ: A History in Letters.* Richmond, Va., Organ Historical Society, 1990.

Cantagrel, Gilles. *Bach en son temps.* Paris, Librairie Arthème Fayard, 1997.

Cantagrel, Gilles. *Guide de la musique d'orgue.* Paris, Librairie Arthème Fayard, 1991.

Carter, Gaylord. *The Million Dollar Life of Gaylord Carter.* Oakland, Calif., Paramount Theatre of the Arts, 1995.

Curley, Carlo. *In the Pipeline: Memoirs of an International Concert Organist.* London, HarperCollins, 1998.

Dumoulin, Pierre, director. *Orgues de l'Île-de-France,* Vol. 4. Paris, Aux Amateurs de Livres, 1992.

Dupré, Marcel. *Recollections.* Miami, CPP/Belwin, undated.

Fauquet, Joel-Marie. *César Franck.* Paris, Librairie Arthème Fayard, 1999.

Fock, Dr. Gustav, et al. *Die Arp-Schnitger Orgel der Hauptkirche St. Jacobi Hamburg.* Hamburg, Festschrift, 1961.

Foort, Reginald. *The Cinema Organ.* Vestal, N.Y., Vestal Press, 1970.

Forkel, J. N. *Über Johann Sebastian Bachs Leben, Kunst und Kunstwerke,* facsimile edition. Berlin, Henschelverlag, 1974.

Grace, Harvey. *French Organ Music Past and Present.* New York, H. W. Gray, 1919.

Guillou, Jean. *L'Orgue, souvenir et avenir.* Paris, Buchet/Castel-Pierre Zech, 1996.

Hill, Peter, ed. *The Messiaen Companion.* London and Boston, Faber and Faber, 1995.

Holden, Dorothy J. *The Life and Work of Ernest M. Skinner.* Richmond, Va., Organ Historical Society, 1985.

Jaquet-Langlais, Marie-Louise. *Ombre et lumière: Jean Langlais, 1907–1991.* Paris, Éditions Combre, 1995.

Kinzey, Allen, and Sand Lawn. *E. M. Skinner/Aeolian-Skinner Opus List,* new revised edition. Richmond, Va., Organ Historical Society, 1997.

Lemare, Edwin H. *Organs I Have Met.* Los Angeles, Schoolcraft, 1956; republished by the Organ Literature Foundation, Braintree, Mass.

Lukas, Victor. *A Guide to Organ Music.* Portland, Ore., Amadeus Press, 1989.

Murray, Michael. *Marcel Dupré: The Work of a Master Organist.* Boston, Northeastern University Press, 1985.

Neumann, Werner. *Das kleine Bachbuch.* Salzburg, Residenz Verlag, 1971.

Ochse, Orpha. *Austin Organs.* Richmond, Va., Organ Historical Society, 2001.

Ochse, Orpha. *The History of the Organ in the United States.* Bloomington, Indiana University Press, 1975.

Owen, Barbara. *E. Power Biggs, Concert Organist.* Bloomington, Indiana University Press, 1987.

Owen, Barbara. *The Mormon Tabernacle Organ: An American Classic.* Salt Lake City, Church of Jesus Christ of the Latter-Day Saints, 1990.

Owen, Barbara, ed. *Charles B. Fisk, Organ Builder,* Vol. 2, *His Work.* Easthampton, Mass., Westfield Center for Early Keyboard Studies, 1986.

Rossiter, Frank R. *Charles Ives and His America.* New York, Liveright, 1975.

Schweitzer, Albert. *J. S. Bach.* Wiesbaden, Breitkopf & Härtel, 1972.

Self, William. *For Mine Eyes Have Seen.* Worcester, Mass., Worcester Chapter of the American Guild of Organists, 1990.

Skinner, Ernest M., and Richmond H. Skinner. *The Composition of the Organ,* edited by Leslie A. Olsen. Ann Arbor, Mich., Melvin J. Light, 1981.

Smith, Rollin. *The Aeolian Pipe Organ and Its Music.* Richmond, Va., Organ Historical Society, 1998.

Smith, Rollin. *Louis Vierne: Organist of Notre-Dame Cathedral.* Hillsdale, N.Y., Pendragon Press, 1999.

Smith, Stephen D. *The Atlantic City Convention Hall Organ: A Pictorial Essay About the World's Largest Pipe Organ.* Portsmouth, N.H., Peter E. Randall, for the Atlantic City Convention Hall Organ Society, 2001.

Smith, Stephen D. *Atlantic City's Musical Masterpiece: The Story of the World's Largest Pipe Organ.* Portsmouth, N.H., Peter E. Randall, for the Atlantic City Convention Hall Organ Society, 2002.

Sumner, William Leslie. *The Organ: Its Evolution, Principles of Construction, and Use.* London, Macdonald & Co., 1962.

Swafford, Jan. *Charles Ives: A Life with Music.* New York, W. W. Norton, 1996.

Torrence, Richard, and Marshall Yaeger. *Virgil Fox (The Dish): Based on a Memoir by Ted Alan Worth.* New York, Circles International, 2001.

Williams, Peter, and Barbara Owen. *The New Grove Organ.* New York, W. W. Norton, and London, Macmillan Press, 1988.

Willis, Arthur. *Organ.* Yehudi Menuhin Music Guides. New York, Schirmer Books, 1984.

Wolff, Christoph. *Johann Sebastian Bach: The Learned Musician.* New York, W. W. Norton, 2000.

Photo Credits

Index

PUBLICAFFAIRS is a publishing house founded in 1997. It is a tribute to the standards, values, and flair of three persons who have served as mentors to countless reporters, writers, editors, and book people of all kinds, including me.

I. F. STONE, proprietor of *I. F. Stone's Weekly,* combined a commitment to the First Amendment with entrepreneurial zeal and reporting skill and became one of the great independent journalists in American history. At the age of eighty, Izzy published *The Trial of Socrates,* which was a national bestseller. He wrote the book after he taught himself ancient Greek.

BENJAMIN C. BRADLEE was for nearly thirty years the charismatic editorial leader of *The Washington Post.* It was Ben who gave the *Post* the range and courage to pursue such historic issues as Watergate. He supported his reporters with a tenacity that made them fearless, and it is no accident that so many became authors of influential, best-selling books.

ROBERT L. BERNSTEIN, the chief executive of Random House for more than a quarter century, guided one of the nation's premier publishing houses. Bob was personally responsible for many books of political dissent and argument that challenged tyranny around the globe. He is also the founder and was the longtime chair of Human Rights Watch, one of the most respected human rights organizations in the world.

❦

For fifty years, the banner of Public Affairs Press was carried by its owner, Morris B. Schnapper, who published Gandhi, Nasser, Toynbee, Truman, and about 1,500 other authors. In 1983 Schnapper was described by *The Washington Post* as "a redoubtable gadfly." His legacy will endure in the books to come.

Peter Osnos, *Publisher*